SUMMER BEFORE GRADE 4

MATH plus READING

AMERICAN EDUCATION PUBLISHING™
Columbus, Ohio

Copyright © 2004 School Specialty Publishing. Published by American Education Publishing™, an imprint of School Specialty Publishing, a member of the School Specialty Family.

Printed in the United States of America. All rights reserved. Except as permitted under the United States Copyright Act, no part of this publication may be reproduced or distributed in any form or by any means, or stored in a database or retrieval system, without prior written permission from the publisher, unless otherwise indicated.

Send all inquiries to:
School Specialty Publishing
8720 Orion Place
Columbus, OH 43240-2111

ISBN 0-7696-3333-1

8 9 10 COU 12 11 10 09

Table of Contents
by Section

Summer Link Math 7
Summer Link Reading 99
Summer Link Test Practice 191

Summer Link Math
Table of Contents

Patterns 8–9

Place Value 10

Rounding and Estimating 11–12

Addition 13–19

Subtraction 20–25

Review: Addition and Subtraction 26–28

Multiplication 29–36

Division 37–43

Number Puzzles 44–45

Review: Addition, Subtraction, Multiplication, and Division 46–47

Percents, Fractions, and Decimals 48–60

Time 61–62

Money 63–69

Measurement 70–75

Geometry 76–81

Graphs 82–85

Roman Numerals 86–87

Glossary 88

Answer Key 89–97

Developmental Skills for Fourth Grade Success 98

Summer Link Reading
Table of Contents

Summer Before Grade 4 Recommended Reading 100

Capital Letters, Punctuation, and Articles 101–104

Homophones 105–108

Parts of Speech 109–144

Word Choice 145–146

Synonyms and Antonyms 147–152

Alliteration 153

Sentence Structure 154–172

Reading Passages 173–174

Poetry 175–176

Reading a Schedule 177–179

Glossary of Reading and Language Arts Terms 180

Answer Key 181–189

Developmental Skills for Fourth Grade Success 190

This page intentionally left blank.

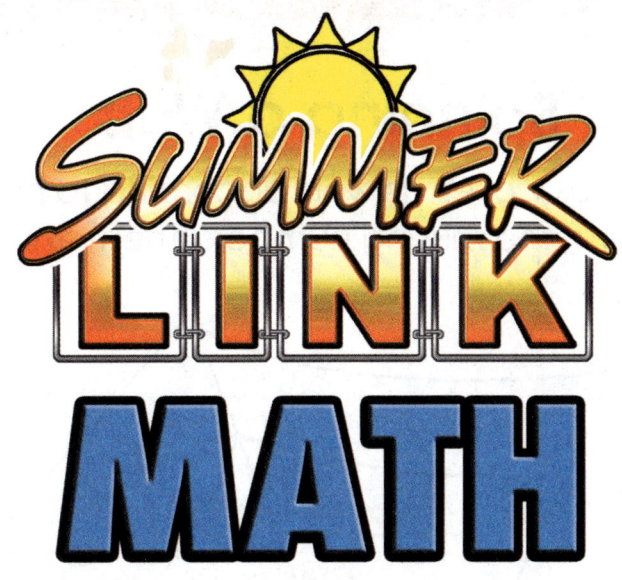

Name _____

Spinning a Web

Directions: The spider has woven its web according to number patterns. Can you discover them? Fill in the missing numbers. Then, explain the pattern on the lines below.

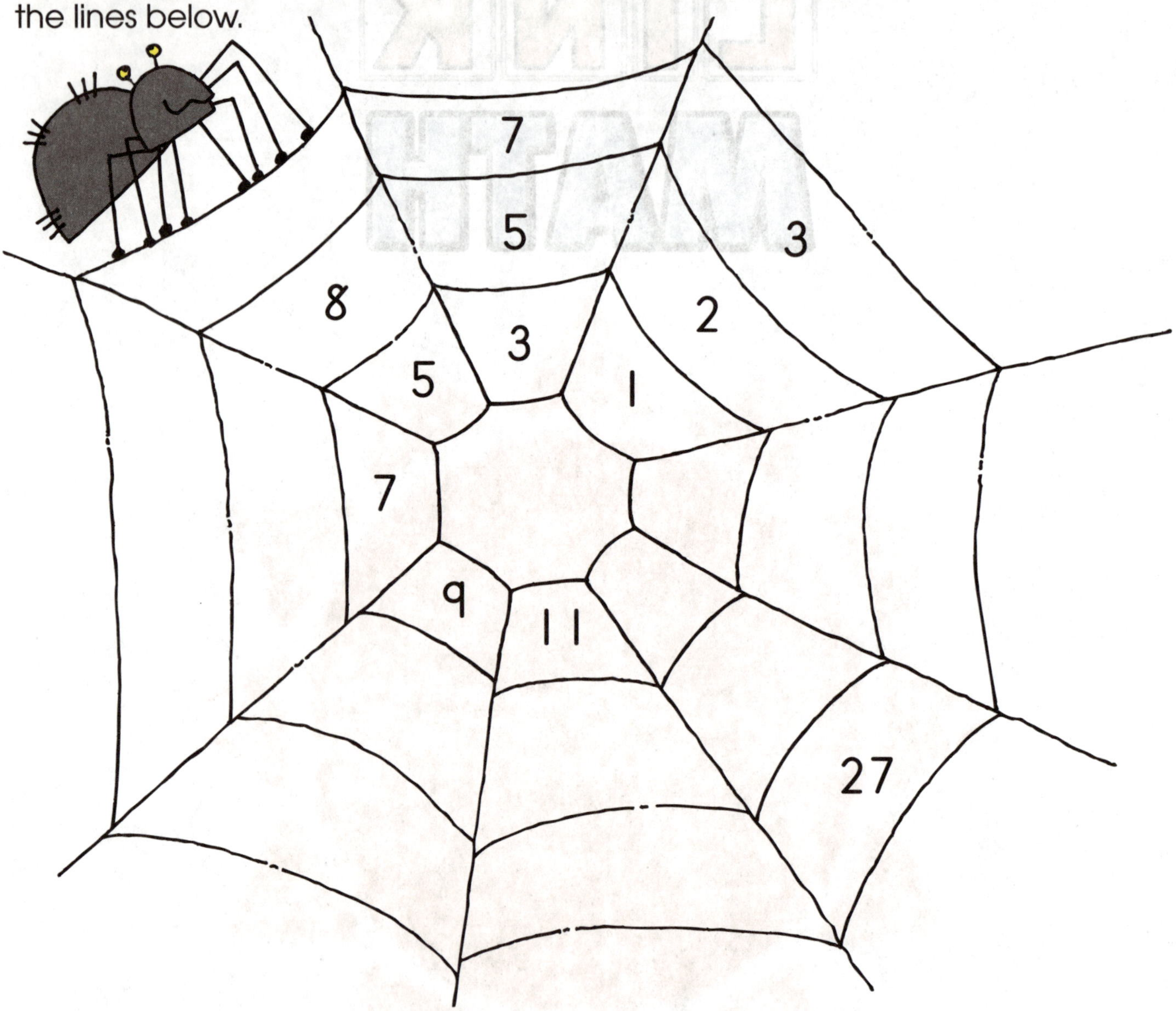

_____

_____

_____

Summer Link Super Edition Grade 4

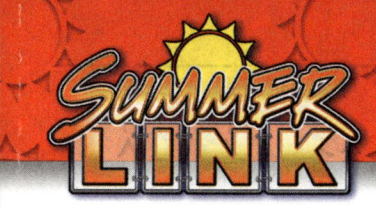

Name _____

Extra!!!

Directions: Use these clues to figure out this logic puzzle. Write a ● in the correct boxes and draw an **X** in all the rest.

Clues:
1. Harry gave a party for Jim yesterday.
2. Jim opened a gift from Bob, the pitcher.
3. Harry is not the catcher.

Who plays each position?
Catcher _____
Pitcher _____
Shortstop _____

	Catcher	Pitcher	Shortstop
Harry			
Jim			
Bob			

Place Value Riddles

Directions: Using the clues below, choose the number each riddle describes. As you read, draw an **X** on all the numbers that do not fit the clue. After you have read all the clues for each riddle, there should be only one number left.

305   3005   35   3050   3500   769   6,379   973   3,796   3,691

1. I am greater than 300.
2. I have a 5 in the ones place.
3. I have a zero in the hundreds place.
4. Circle the number.

1. I have a number greater than 6 in the tens place.
2. I am between 3,000 and 4,000.
3. I have a 6 in the hundreds place.
4. Circle the number.

423   4023   324   3,412   2,143   4058   584   845   5048   8540

1. I have a 2 in the tens place.
2. I am less than 1,000.
3. I have a 4 in the ones place.
4. Circle the number.

1. I have a 4 in the tens place.
2. I am greater than 5,000.
3. I have a 0 in the hundreds place.
4. Circle the number.

Now, fold a blank sheet of paper in half three times to create eight boxes. Create eight of these place value riddles. You may want to use words like these when writing your clues:

ones, tens, hundreds, thousands place
greater than
less than
have a ___ somewhere

Summer Link Super Edition Grade 4

Rounding: Hundreds and Thousands

When rounding to the nearest hundred, the key number is in the tens place. If the tens digit is 5 or larger, round up to nearest hundred. If the tens digit is 4 or less, round down to the nearest hundred.

Examples:
Round 871 to the nearest hundred.
7 is the key digit.
If it is more than 5, round up.
Answer: 900

Round 421 to the nearest hundred.
2 is the key digit.
If it is less than 4, round down.
Answer: 400

Directions: Round these numbers to the nearest hundred.

255 _____   368 _____   443 _____   578 _____
562 _____   698 _____   99 _____   775 _____
812 _____   592 _____   124 _____   10,235 _____

When rounding to the nearest thousand, the key number is in the hundreds place. If the hundreds digit is 5 or larger, round up to the nearest thousand. If the hundreds digit is 4 or less, round down to the nearest thousand.

Examples:
Round 7,932 to the nearest thousand.
9 is the key digit.
If it is more than 5, round up.
Answer: 8,000

Round 1,368 to the nearest thousand.
3 is the key digit.
If it is less than 4, round down.
Answer: 1,000

Directions: Round these numbers to the nearest thousand.

8,631 _____   1,248 _____   798 _____
999 _____   6,229 _____   8,461 _____
9,654 _____   4,963 _____   99,923 _____

Estimating

To **estimate** means to give an approximate, rather than an exact, answer. To find an estimated sum or difference, round the numbers of the problem, then add or subtract. If the number has 5 ones or more, round up to the nearest ten. If the number has 4 ones or less, round down to the nearest ten.

Directions: Round the numbers to the nearest ten, hundred, or thousand. Then add or subtract.

Examples:

Ten

```
  74 →   70
+ 39 → + 40
            110
```

```
  64 →   60
- 25 → - 30
             30
```

Hundred

```
  352 →   400
- 164 → - 200
             200
```

Thousand

```
  7,681 →   8,000
+ 4,321 → + 4,000
             12,000
```

Round these numbers to the nearest ten.

```
  18 →          49 →          67 →
+ 24 →        - 33 →        - 56 →
```

Round these numbers to the nearest hundred.

```
  255 →         526 →         102 →
-  99 →       + 145 →        - 75 →
```

Round these numbers to the nearest thousand.

```
  8,361 →        9,926 →
+   889 →      + 3,645 →
```

Summer Link Super Edition Grade 4

Addition

Directions: Add.
Example:

Add the ones.

26
+21

7

Add the tens.

26
+21

47

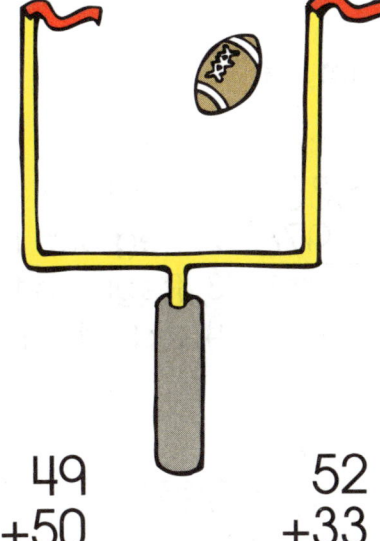

18
+11

24
+35

38
+21

49
+50

52
+33

75
+12

83
+16

67
+32

44
+25

28
+41

68 + 20 = ___   54 + 25 = ___   71 + 17 = ___

The Lions scored 42 points. The Clippers scored 21 points.
How many points were scored in all? _____

Name _____

Addition: Regrouping

Directions: Study the example. Add using regrouping.

Example:

```
   5,356    Steps:
  +3,976    1. Add the ones.
   9,332    2. Regroup the tens. Add the tens.
            3. Regroup the hundreds. Add the hundreds.
            4. Add the thousands.
```

```
   6,849         1,846         9,221
  +3,276        +8,384        +6,769
```

```
   2,758         5,299         7,932
  +3,663        +8,764        +6,879
```

A plane flew 1,838 miles on the first day. It flew 2,347 miles on the second day. How many miles did it fly in all? _____

Summer Link Super Edition Grade 4

Name _____

Hitting the Addition Target

Directions: Find the sums.

1. 24
   91
   +66

2. 37
   52
   +90

3. 72
   58
   +89

4. 19
   46
   + 7

5. 68
   33
   +84

6. 97
   50
   +22

7. 59
   75
   +41

8. 85
   8
   +99

9. 44
   63
   +29

10. 36
    55
    +74

11. 98
    86
    +27

12. 88
    17
    +62

13. 57
    39
    +80

14. 79
    53
    +81

15. 48
    25
    +19

16. 18
    95
    +54

17. 78
    64
    +83

18. 82
    9
    +67

19. 43 + 98 + 16 = _____

20. 86 + 45 + 26 = _____

Directions: Solve the problems.

21. Tim scored 51 points. Leonard scored 92 points. Paul scored 70 points. How many points did their team score in all? _____

22. Allison scored 65 points. Lauren scored 34 points. Sara scored 73 points. How many points did their team score in all? _____

Grand Prix Addition

Directions: Solve each problem. Beginning at 7,000, run through this racetrack to find the path the race car took. When you reach 7,023, you're ready to exit and gas up for the next race.

3,536 +3,482	1,792 +5,225	3,838 +3,178	3,767 +3,248	1,874 +5,140	4,809 +2,204
3,561 +3,458	4,162 +2,858	3,771 +4,213	4,123 +2,887	5,879 +1,132	1,725 +5,287
3,544 +3,478	1,273 +5,748	2,435 +5,214	4,853 +2,156	3,589 +3,419	5,218 +1,789
5,997 +1,026	5,289 +1,713	3,698 +3,305	4,756 +2,248	4,248 +2,757	4,658 +2,348
4,853 +2,147	2,216 +4,785	1,157 +6,412	3,720 +3,698	3,612 +3,552	1,687 +5,662

Summer Link Super Edition Grade 4

Dial-a-Word

Directions: Use the phone pad to calculate the "value" of the words.

Example: PHONE = 74663
PHONE = 7 + 4 + 6 + 6 + 3 = 26

(your name) = _____ = _____

CALCULATOR = _____ = _____

DICTIONARY = _____ = _____

PET TRICKS = _____ = _____

BASEBALL GAME = _____ = _____

COMPUTERS = _____ = _____

TENNIS SHOES = _____ = _____

ADDITION = _____ = _____

MENTAL MATH = _____ = _____

Magic Squares

Directions: Some of the number squares below are "magic" and some are not. Squares that add up to the same number horizontally, vertically, and diagonally are "magic." Add the numbers horizontally and vertically in each square to discover which ones are "magic."

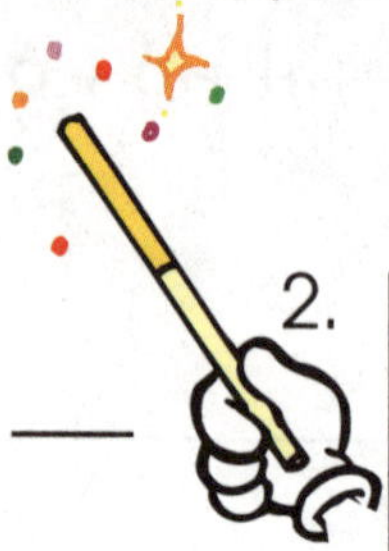

Example:

4	9	2	15
3	5	7	15
8	1	6	15
15	15	15	15

Magic? __yes__

1.

7	2	1
3	4	8
5	9	6

Magic? _____

2.

6	11	4
5	7	9
10	3	8

Magic? _____

3.

3	8	1
2	4	6
7	0	5

Magic? _____

4.

2	7	0
1	3	5
6	9	4

Magic? _____

5.

5	10	3
4	6	8
9	2	7

Magic? _____

6.

7	12	5
6	8	10
11	4	9

Magic? _____

7.

1	2	3
4	5	6
7	8	9

Magic? _____

8.

6	7	4
1	5	9
8	3	2

Magic? _____

Challenge: Can you discover a pattern for number placement in the magic squares? Try to make a magic square of your own.

"Bee" Ware

Directions: Help Papa Bear find the shortest route in and out of this honeycomb without going through or next to any cell where a bee is. Add the numbers in each cell that your path goes through. The path with the lowest sum is the shortest.

Name _____

Subtraction

Subtraction means "taking away" or subtracting one number from another to find the difference. For example, 10 - 3 = 7.

Directions: Subtract.

Example:

Subtract the ones.

```
  39
 -24
   5
```

Subtract the tens.

```
  39
 -24
  15
```

```
  48        95        87        55
 -35       -22       -16       -43
```

```
  37        69        44        99
 -14       -57       -23       -78
```

66 - 44 = ____   57 - 33 = ____

The yellow car traveled 87 miles per hour. The orange car traveled 66 miles per hour. How much faster was the yellow car traveling?

_____

Subtraction: Regrouping

Directions: Subtract using regrouping.

Examples:

23	1̶2̶³
−18	−18
	5

243	¹13 2̶4̶³
−96	−96
	147

```
   81        76        94       156       341       726
 − 53      − 49      − 38      − 77      − 83      − 29


  568       806       743       903       647       254
 −173      −738      −550      −336      −289      − 69


  730       961       573       604       265       372
 −518      −846      − 76      − 55      − 19      − 59


  111       358       147
 − 82      − 99      − 49


  180       325       873
 −106      − 68      − 35
```

21 Summer Link Super Edition Grade 4

Dino-Might

Directions:
Whenever you use "kid transportation," what is the best thing to do? To find out, solve each problem. Then, write the matching letter above the answer.

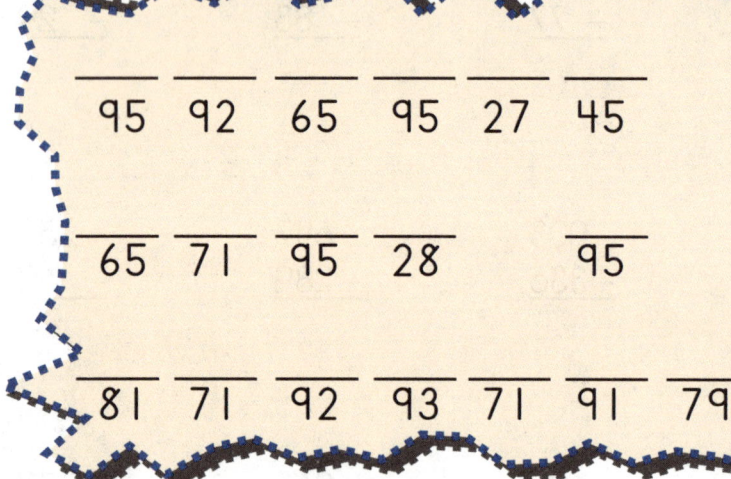

```
___ ___ ___ ___ ___ ___
 95  92  65  95  27  45

___ ___ ___ ___     ___
 65  71  95  28      95

___ ___ ___ ___ ___ ___ ___
 81  71  92  93  71  91  79
```

Remember to regroup when the bottom number is greater than the top number in a column.

A = 148   L = 165   S = 127   M = 168
  − 53   − 73   − 82   − 75

T = 137   H = 178   Y = 90   W = 148
  − 46   − 97   − 63   − 83

E = 124   R = 84   ! = 102
  − 53   − 56   − 23

Mountaintop Getaway

Directions: Solve the problems. Find a path to the cabin by shading in all answers that have a 3 in them.

		98 −52	46 −12	68 −17
79 −53	65 −23	63 −31	86 −32	
59 −45	75 −64	67 −24	87 −54	55 −43
87 −65	44 −32	57 −24	88 −25	75 −61	48 −26
69 −25	95 −24	48 −13	58 −16	35 −13	39 −17

SECRET PATHS

Name _____

Paint by Number

Directions: Solve each problem. Color each shape according to the key below.

664 −482

484 −364

548 −283

614 −453

926 −564

904 −392

629 −583

563 −382

732 −561

642 −462

705 −493

529 −364

635 −573

439 −275

529 −373

853 −522

513 −321

328 −182

626 −394

896 −145

843 −392

If the difference in the tens column is:

1 — blue
2 — blue
3 — orange
4 — yellow
5 — orange
6 — red
7 — yellow
8 — blue
9 — orange

Summer Link Super Edition Grade 4   24

Name _____

Subtraction Search

Directions: Solve each problem. Find the answer in the chart and circle it. The answers may go in any direction.

6,003 −2,737	5,040 −3,338	9,000 −5,725	2	1	6	3	2	7	5
			6	3	3	2	1	0	8
			2	2	1	6	3	3	4
7,200 −4,356	3,406 −1,298	5,602 −3,138	0	2	2	6	5	0	6
			8	5	4	2	0	8	7
			8	9	0	6	1	5	6
7,006 −5,429	3,006 −2,798	3,605 −2,718	3	2	8	4	4	2	1
			8	3	4	8	8	5	0
			8	1	9	8	7	2	9
5,904 −3,917	5,039 −1,954	8,704 −2,496	3	4	5	8	5	6	7
			8	1	3	7	0	4	2
			9	3	2	1	7	0	2

4,081 −3,594	6,508 − 399	5,039 −2,467	9,006 − 575	5,001 −2,351
8,002 −5,686	6,058 −2,175	9,504 −7,368	7,290 −1,801	

25

Summer Link Super Edition Grade 4

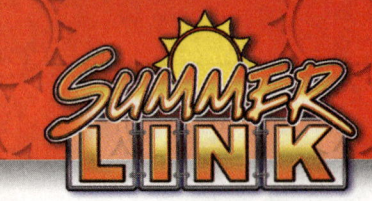

Review

Directions: Add or subtract using regrouping.

```
   28        82        33        67
   56        49        75        94
  +93       +51      +128      +248
```

```
  683       756       818       956
 -495      +139      -387      +267
```

```
 1,588     4,675     8,732     2,938
 - 989    -2,976    -5,664    +3,459
```

To drive from New York City to Los Angeles is 2,832 miles. To drive from New York City to Miami is 1,327 miles. How much farther is it to drive from New York City to Los Angeles than from New York City to Miami?

_____

Summer Link Super Edition Grade 4

Problem-Solving: Addition, Subtraction

Directions: Read and solve each problem. The first one is done for you.

1. The clown started the day with 200 balloons. He gave away 128 of them. Some broke. At the end of the day he had 18 balloons left. How many of the balloons broke?   54

2. On Monday, there were 925 tickets sold to adults and 1,412 tickets sold to children. How many more children attended the fair than adults?   _____

3. At one game booth, prizes were given out for scoring 500 points in three attempts. Sally scored 178 points on her first attempt, 149 points on her second attempt, and 233 points on her third attempt. Did Sally win a prize?   _____

4. The prize-winning steer weighed 2,348 pounds. The runner-up steer weighed 2,179 pounds. How much more did the prize steer weigh?   _____

5. There were 3,418 people at the fair on Tuesday, and 2,294 people on Wednesday. What was the total number of people there for the two days?   _____

Name _____

One for the Record Books

Directions: Solve these problems to learn the amazing records held by these all-time major league players.

Most Hits Pete Rose	Most Stolen Bases Rickey Henderson	Most Games Won (pitcher) Cy Young	Most Strikeouts Nolan Ryan	Most RBIs Hank Aaron
1,582 1,017 + 1,657	456 542 + 299	1,380 − 869	8,203 − 2,489	632 733 + 932

Most Home Runs Hank Aaron	Most Walks Babe Ruth	Most Games Pete Rose	Most Runs Ty Cobb
1,496 − 741	8,579 − 6,523	8,181 − 4,619	5,465 − 3,219

Multiplication: Zero and One

Directions: Any number multiplied by zero equals zero. One multiplied by any number equals that number. Study the example. Multiply.

Example:

How many full sails are there in all?

2 boats x **1** sail on each boat = **2** sails

How many full sails are there now?

2 boats x **0** sails = **0** sails

Directions: Multiply.

1	2	3	4	0	7
x5	x1	x0	x1	x6	x0

9	8	3	4	7	6
x1	x0	x1	x0	x1	x1

Name _____

Soccer Skills

How are soccer players like good students?

Directions: To find out, solve each problem below. Then, write the matching letter above the answer at the bottom of the page.

H	O	E	T	S
3	4	1	1	2
x5	x6	x0	x7	x5

U	T	H	H	D
3	4	3	4	4
x7	x4	x3	x8	x5

Y	E	E	B	A
2	2	3	3	4
x6	x7	x6	x2	x9

T	I	R	H	E
3	4	1	1	1
x9	x7	x3	x1	x2

Summer Link Super Edition Grade 4

Name _____

Multiplication Marathon

Directions: Have someone time you to see how fast you can "run through" these problems.

2	3	5	4	7	9	7	9
x8	x7	x6	x5	x4	x8	x7	x6

5	6	9	3	9	6	8	5
x5	x6	x9	x8	x4	x1	x8	x9

8	4	8	4	3	5	7	4
x3	x7	x9	x8	x9	x7	x8	x9

5	6	9	8	6	7	7	8
x3	x9	x5	x7	x8	x9	x6	x2

  0
x 9
———

Number correct: _____   Time: ____ : ____

Multiplication Table

Directions: Complete the multiplication table. Use it to practice your multiplication facts.

X	0	1	2	3	4	5	6	7	8	9	10
0	0										
1		1									
2			4								
3				9							
4					16						
5						25					
6							36				
7								49			
8									64		
9										81	
10											100

Summer Link Super Edition Grade 4

Name _____

Fact Factory

Factors are the numbers multiplied together in a multiplication problem. The **product** is the answer.

Directions: Write the missing factors or products.

x	5
1	5
5	
4	20
6	
3	
2	10
7	
9	45

x	9
8	72
3	
4	
9	
6	54
7	
2	
1	9

x	7
2	14
5	
	42
8	
7	
4	
	21
0	

x	3
7	
4	
6	
1	
3	
2	
5	
8	

x	1
1	
12	
10	
3	3
5	
7	
6	
4	

x	8
9	
8	
4	
5	
6	
7	
3	
2	

x	2
	24
2	
22	
4	
20	
6	
18	
8	

x	4
2	
4	
6	
8	
	4
	12
	20
	28

x	6
7	
6	
5	
4	
3	
2	
1	
0	

x	10
	20
3	
	40
5	
	60
7	
	80
9	

x	11
4	
7	
9	
10	
3	
5	
6	
8	

x	12
1	
2	24
3	
4	48
5	
6	
7	
8	

Multiplying by a Two-Digit Number

With Regrouping

Directions: Multiply.

1. Multiply by the ones.
   8 × 7 = 56 (Carry the 5.)

$$\begin{array}{r} \overset{5}{6}7 \\ \times 3\,8 \\ \hline 6 \end{array}$$

$$\begin{array}{r} 37 \\ \times 24 \\ \hline \end{array}$$

$$\begin{array}{r} 77 \\ \times 21 \\ \hline \end{array}$$

2. Multiply by the ones.
   8 × 6 = 48 + 5 = 53
   (When they are completed, cross out all carried digits.)

$$\begin{array}{r} \cancel{5} \\ 67 \\ \times 38 \\ \hline 536 \end{array}$$

$$\begin{array}{r} 23 \\ \times 45 \\ \hline \end{array}$$

$$\begin{array}{r} 54 \\ \times 38 \\ \hline \end{array}$$

3. Multiply by the tens. Place a zero in the ones column.
   3 × 7 = 21 (Carry the 2.)

$$\begin{array}{r} \overset{2}{\cancel{5}} \\ 67 \\ \times 38 \\ \hline 536 \\ 10 \end{array}$$

$$\begin{array}{r} 48 \\ \times 62 \\ \hline \end{array}$$

$$\begin{array}{r} 67 \\ \times 29 \\ \hline \end{array}$$

4. Multiply by the tens.
   3 × 6 = 18 + 2 = 20

$$\begin{array}{r} \cancel{2}\,\cancel{5} \\ 67 \\ \times 38 \\ \hline 536 \\ 2010 \end{array}$$

5. Add.
   536 + 2010 = 2,546

$$\begin{array}{r} \cancel{2}\,\cancel{5} \\ 67 \\ \times 38 \\ \hline 536 \\ +2010 \\ \hline 2,546 \end{array}$$

Now, check your answers with a calculator.

Amazing Arms

Directions: What will happen to a starfish that loses an arm? To find out, solve the following problems and write the matching letter above the answer at the bottom of the page.

O. 2,893 × 4

W. 1,763 × 3

W. 7,665 × 5

A. 1,935 × 6

W. 3,097 × 3

E. 2,929 × 4

G. 6,366 × 5

T. 7,821 × 8

L. 6,283 × 7

I. 5,257 × 3

R. 3,019 × 6

N. 2,908 × 7

I. 6,507 × 8

N. 5,527 × 2

L. 6,626 × 3

O. 7,219 × 9

E. 3,406 × 6

___ ___
52,056 62,568

___ ___ ___ ___ ___ ___ ___ ___
5,289 15,771 43,981 19,878 31,830 18,114 64,971 9,291

___ ___ ___ ___ ___ ___ ___ !
11,610 20,356 20,436 38,325 11,572 11,054 11,716

Factor Trees

Directions: Factors are the smaller numbers multiplied together to make a larger number. Factor trees are one way to find all the factors of a number.

Example:

24
6 × 4
2 × 3 × 2 × 2

36
6 × ___
3 × ___ × ___ × ___

40
8 × ___
4 × ___ × ___
___ × ___ × ___

12
___ × 4
___ × ___ × ___

81
___ × ___
___ × ___ × ___

Division: Zero and One

Directions: Study the rules of division and the examples. Divide, then write the number of the rule you used to solve each problem.

Examples:

Rule 1: $1\overline{)5} = 5$ Any number divided by 1 is that number.

Rule 2: $5\overline{)5} = 1$ Any number except 0 divided by itself is 1.

Rule 3: $7\overline{)0} = 0$ Zero divided by any number is zero.

Rule 4: $0\overline{)7}$ You cannot divide by zero.

$1\overline{)6}$ Rule ___ $4 \div 1 =$ ___   Rule ___

$7\overline{)7}$ Rule ___ $9 \div 9 =$ ___   Rule ___

$9\overline{)0}$ Rule ___ $7 \div 1 =$ ___   Rule ___

$1\overline{)4}$ Rule ___ $6 \div 0 =$ ___   Rule ___

Name _____

Division

Division is a way to find out how many times one number is contained in another number. The ÷ sign means "divided by." Another way to divide is to use ⌐ . The dividend is the larger number that is divided by the smaller number, or divisor. The answer of a division problem is called the quotient.

Directions: Study the example. Divide.

Example:

20 ÷ 4 = 5
dividend divisor quotient

quotient
5
4)20
divisor dividend

35 ÷ 7 = ____   7)35   42 ÷ 6 = ____   6)42

2)12   3)18   4)36   5)50

6)24   7)21   8)32   9)27

36 ÷ 6 = ____   28 ÷ 4 = ____   15 ÷ 5 = ____   12 ÷ 2 = ____

A tree farm has 36 trees. There are 4 rows of trees.
How many trees are there in each row? _____

Summer Link Super Edition Grade 4   38

Catch-Up With Division

Directions: Complete each division problem below.

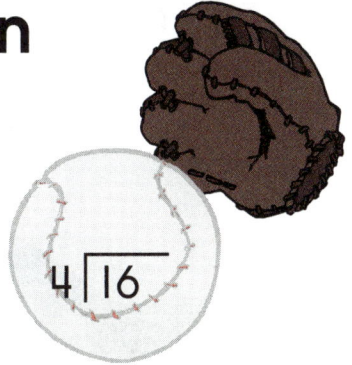

$6\overline{)12}$ $4\overline{)16}$

$4\overline{)32}$ $2\overline{)10}$

$3\overline{)15}$ $6\overline{)6}$

$7\overline{)42}$ $5\overline{)45}$

9 ÷ 3 =   8 ÷ 2 =

48 ÷ 8 =   20 ÷ 4 =

30 ÷ 5 =   21 ÷ 7 =

81 ÷ 9 =   35 ÷ 5 =

15 ÷ 3 =   4 ÷ 2 =

16 ÷ 4 =   40 ÷ 5 =

54 ÷ 6 =   28 ÷ 7 =

28 ÷ 4 =   81 ÷ 9 =

Name _____

Round and Round She Goes . . .

Directions: Take a ride around this wheel. Solve the subtraction problems.

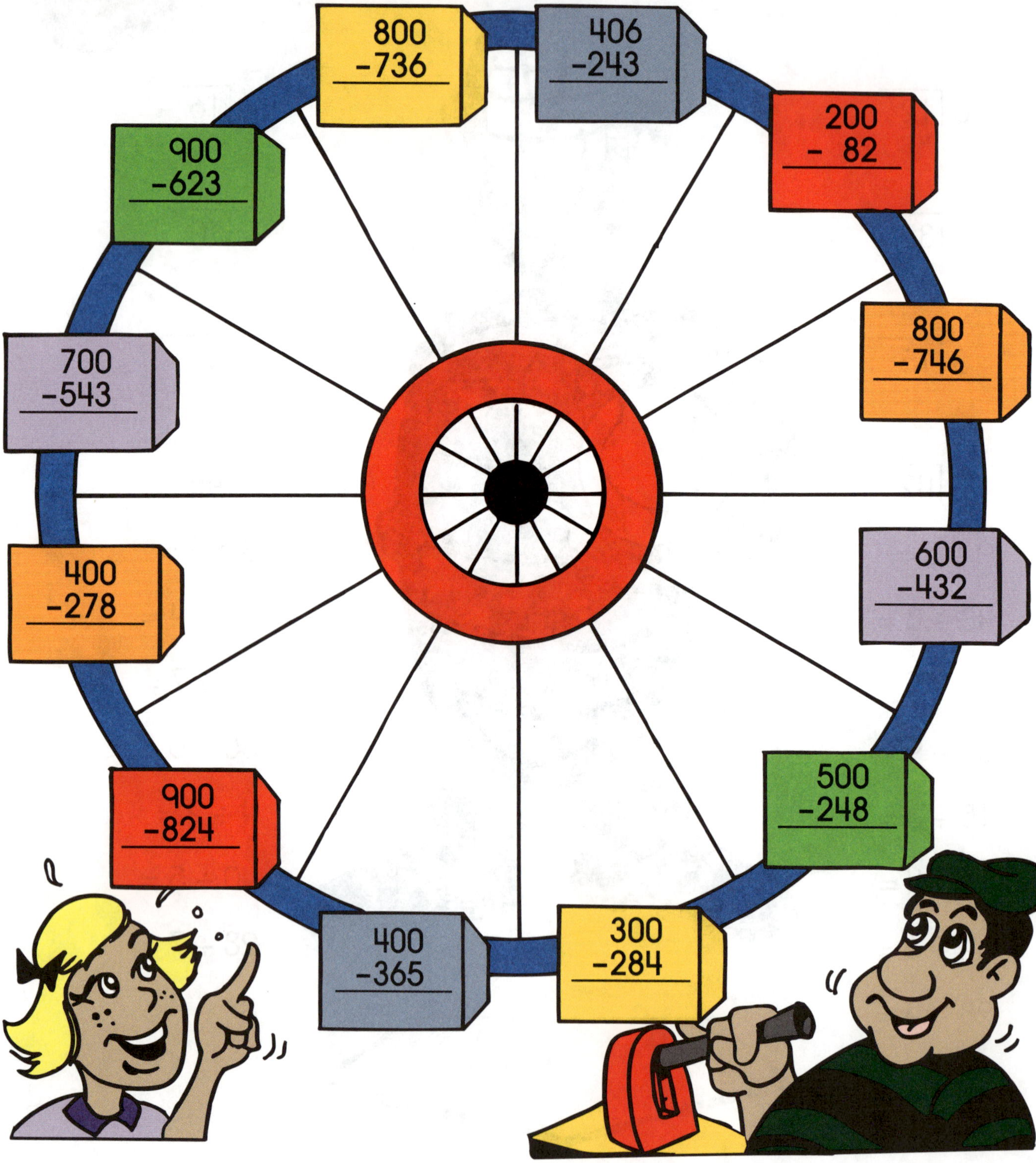

800 − 736

406 − 243

200 − 82

900 − 623

800 − 746

700 − 543

600 − 432

400 − 278

500 − 248

900 − 824

400 − 365

300 − 284

Summer Link Super Edition Grade 4   40

Make It Fair

Directions: While your cookies are baking, practice fair sharing by completing these problems. Circle the objects and write two division problems to go with each picture.

There are six children. Circle the number of cookies each child will get if the cookies are divided equally.

_____ ÷ _____

_____ ÷ _____

There are four dogs. Circle the dog bones each dog will get if the dog bones are divided equally.

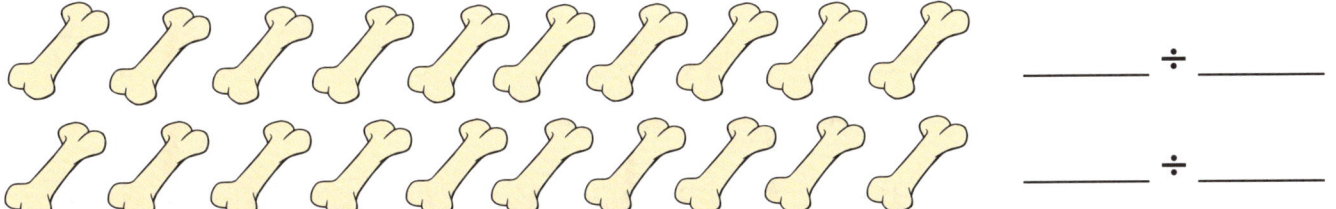

_____ ÷ _____

_____ ÷ _____

Divide the pepperoni so that five pizzas will have the same amount.

_____ ÷ _____

_____ ÷ _____

Divide the books so that there will be the same number of books on three shelves.

_____ ÷ _____

_____ ÷ _____

Division Tic-Tac-Toe

Directions: Solve the problems. Draw an **X** on the odd (9, 7, 5, 3) answers. Draw an **O** on the even (8, 6, 4, 2) answers.

4)36	4)24	10 ÷ 5
5)40	32 ÷ 4	25 ÷ 5
35 ÷ 5	20 ÷ 4	12 ÷ 4

4)32	12 ÷ 4	5)30
4)28	4)20	20 ÷ 4
20 ÷ 5	10 ÷ 5	15 ÷ 5

24 ÷ 4	5)45	28 ÷ 4
5)45	5)20	8 ÷ 4
4)16	5)15	30 ÷ 5

25 ÷ 5	4)8	16 ÷ 4
32 ÷ 4	5)20	5)35
40 ÷ 5	4)12	15 ÷ 5

5)10	4)8	24 ÷ 4
4)36	5)35	4)32
45 ÷ 5	5)30	4)12

8 ÷ 4	45 ÷ 5	4)16
5)25	36 ÷ 4	4)24
5)10	25 ÷ 5	4)36

4)12	5)10	5)45
30 ÷ 5	5)25	35 ÷ 5
4)32	8 ÷ 4	5)20

36 ÷ 4	4)28	16 ÷ 4
24 ÷ 4	5)35	5)40
5)25	8 ÷ 4	36 ÷ 4

28 ÷ 4	5)30	45 ÷ 5
16 ÷ 4	32 ÷ 4	15 ÷ 5
4)20	4)12	4)8

Summer Link Super Edition Grade 4

Division: Checking the Answers

Directions: Divide, then check your answers.

Example:

```
    1 8 2 R 1
4 ) 7 2 9
   -4
    3 2
   -3 2
        9
       -8
        1
```

Check:

```
  1 8 2
x     4
  7 2 8
+     1
  7 2 9
```

Divide	Check	Divide	Check
35) 468	☐ x 35	77) 819	☐ x 77
29) 568	☐ x 29	53) 2,795	☐ x 53

The bookstore puts 53 books on a shelf. How many shelves will it need for 1,590 books? _____

43
Summer Link Super Edition Grade 4

Name _____

Number Puzzles

Directions: Solve these number puzzles.

1

Write your age. _____

Multiply it by 3. _____

Add 18. _____

Multiply by 2. _____

Subtract 36. _____

Divide by 6. (your age) _____

2

Write any number. _____

Double that number. _____

Add 15. _____

Double again. _____

Subtract 30. _____

Divide by 2. _____

Divide by 2 again. _____

3

Write any 2-digit number. _____

Double that number. _____

Add 43. _____

Subtract 18. _____

Add 11. _____

Divide by 2. _____

Subtract 18. _____

4

Write the number of children in your neighborhood. _____

Double that number. _____

Add 15. _____

Double it again. _____

Subtract 30. _____

Divide by 4. _____

Summer Link Super Edition Grade 4   44

Work Your Way to the Top

Directions: In order to be number 1, a team must start at the bottom and win each game to work their way to the top. Start at the bottom and work your way to the top.

3)78

2)91

2)29

2)59

4)58

2)33

3)42

Name _____

Hmm, What Should I Do?

Example: 52 (+) 9 = 61

8 (x) 4 = 32

Directions: Write the correct symbols in the circles.

7 ○ 8 = 56   81 ○ 6 = 75   55 ○ 3 = 52

54 ○ 9 = 6   2 ○ 1 = 2   40 ○ 2 = 38

36 ○ 5 = 31   0 ○ 2 = 2   8 ○ 8 = 64

12 ○ 6 = 18   9 ○ 8 = 72   18 ○ 5 = 23

72 ○ 7 = 65   32 ○ 5 = 37

0 ○ 1 = 0   48 ○ 6 = 8

9 ○ 1 = 9   32 ○ 4 = 8

45 ○ 9 = 5   6 ○ 7 = 42

Summer Link Super Edition Grade 4

Order of Operations

When you solve a problem that involves more than one operation, this is the order to follow:

Parentheses first, then do multiplication and division in order from left to right. Finally, do all addition and subtraction steps, in order from left to right. These rules are called Order of Operations.

Example:

$$2 + (3 \times 5) - 2 = 15$$
$$2 + 15 - 2 = 15$$
$$17 - 2 = 15$$

Directions: Solve the problems using the correct order of operations.

$(5 - 3) + 4 \times 7 =$ _____ $1 + 2 \times 3 + 4 =$ _____

$6 \times 3 - 1 =$ _____ $(8 \div 2) \times 4 =$ _____

$9 \div 3 \times 3 + 0 =$ _____ $5 - 2 \times 1 + 2 =$ _____

Percentages

A **percentage** is the amount of a number out of 100. This is the percent sign: %.

Directions: Fill in the blanks.

Example: 70% = 70/100   40 % = 40/100

30% = ___/100   10% = ___/100

90% = ___/100   40% = ___/100

70% = ___/100   80% = ___/100

___ % = 20/100   ___ % = 60/100

___ % = 30/100   ___ % = 10/100

___ % = 50/100   ___ % = 90/100

Summer Link Super Edition Grade 4

Name _____

Fractions: Division

A **fraction** is a number that names part of an object. It can also name part of a group.

Directions: Study the example. Divide by the bottom number of the fraction to find the answers.

Example:
There are 6 cheerleaders.
$\frac{1}{2}$ of the cheerleaders are boys.
How many cheerleaders are boys?

6 cheerleaders ÷ 2 groups = 3 boys

$\frac{1}{2}$ of 6 = 3 $\frac{1}{2}$ of 8 = __4__

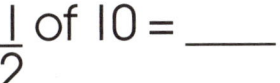

$\frac{1}{2}$ of 10 = ____ $\frac{1}{3}$ of 9 = ____ $\frac{1}{5}$ of 10 = ____

$\frac{1}{4}$ of 12 = ____ $\frac{1}{8}$ of 32 = ____ $\frac{1}{3}$ of 27 = ____

$\frac{1}{5}$ of 30 = ____ $\frac{1}{2}$ of 14 = ____ $\frac{1}{9}$ of 18 = ____

$\frac{1}{6}$ of 24 = ____ $\frac{1}{3}$ of 18 = ____ $\frac{1}{10}$ of 50 = ____

Star Gazing

Directions: To find $\frac{1}{2}$ of the stars, divide by 2.

Example:

$\frac{1}{2}$ of 10 = 5

$\frac{1}{2}$ of 6 = ____

$\frac{1}{2}$ of 8 = ____

$\frac{1}{3}$ of 9 = ____

$\frac{1}{5}$ of 10 = ____

$\frac{1}{4}$ of 8 = ____

$\frac{1}{6}$ of 12 = ____

$\frac{1}{3}$ of 15 = ____

$\frac{1}{2}$ of 16 = ____

$\frac{1}{3}$ of 24 = ____

$\frac{1}{6}$ of 18 = ____

$\frac{1}{4}$ of 12 = ____

$\frac{1}{3}$ of 27 = ____

$\frac{1}{5}$ of 20 = ____

$\frac{1}{6}$ of 18 = ____

$\frac{1}{4}$ of 24 = ____

Fractions: Comparing

Directions: Circle the fraction in each pair that is larger.

Example:

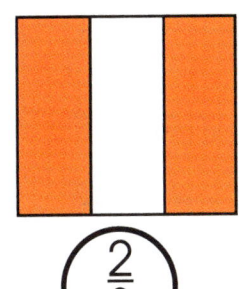

$\underline{\frac{2}{3}}$ (circled)

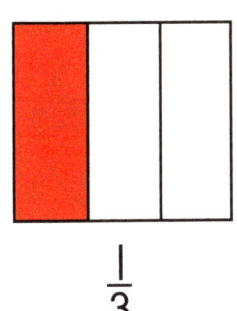

$\frac{1}{3}$

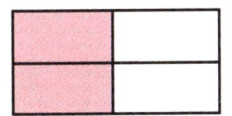

$\frac{2}{4}$

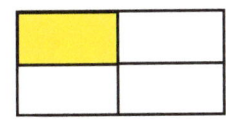

$\frac{1}{4}$

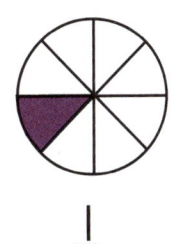

$\frac{1}{8}$

$\frac{2}{8}$

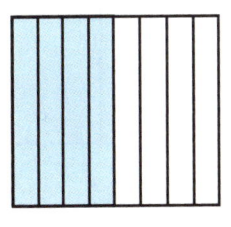

$\frac{1}{2}$

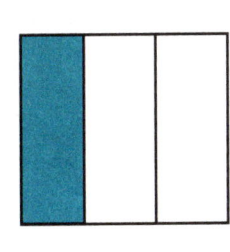

$\frac{1}{3}$

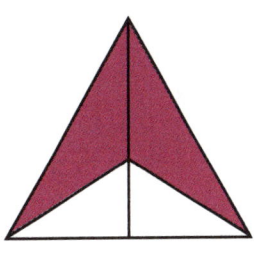

$\frac{2}{3}$

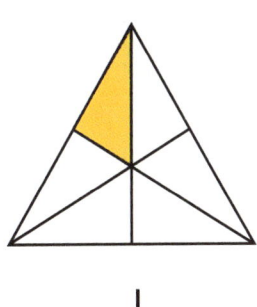

$\frac{1}{6}$

$\frac{1}{4}$ or $\frac{1}{6}$ $\qquad$ $\frac{1}{5}$ or $\frac{1}{7}$ $\qquad$ $\frac{1}{8}$ or $\frac{1}{4}$

More Fractions

Directions: Compare the fractions below. Write < or > in each box.

Examples:

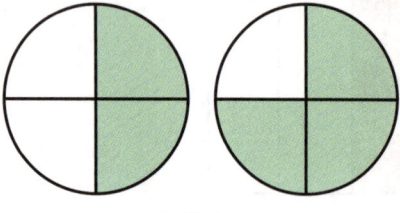
less than

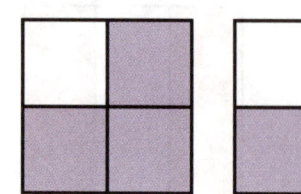
greater than

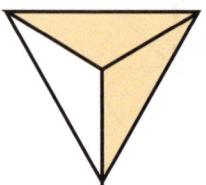

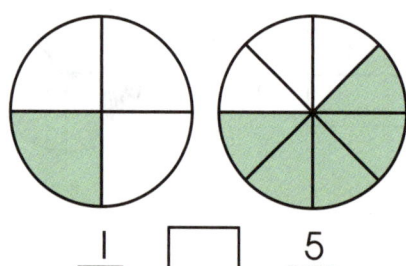

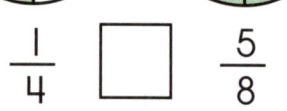

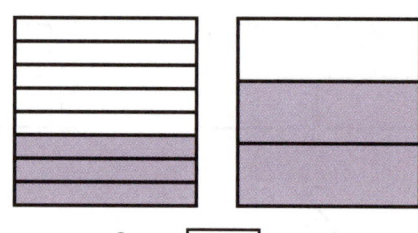

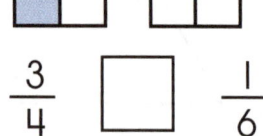

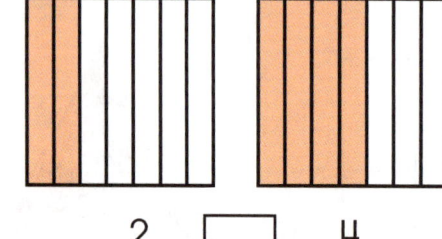

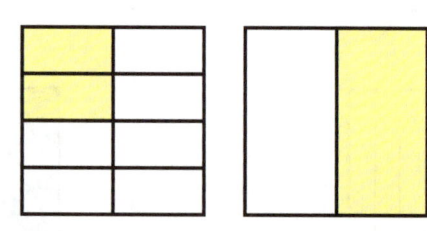

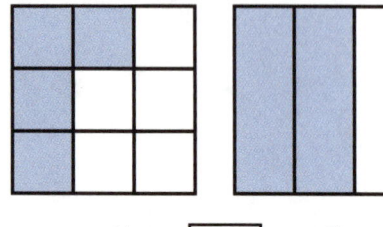

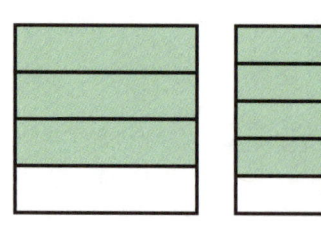

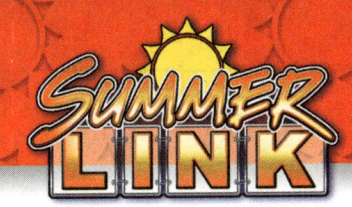

Name _____

Fraction Patterns

Each row contains equivalent fractions except for one. Find which three fractions are equivalent for each row.

Directions: Draw an **X** on the fraction that is not equivalent. On the line, write a fraction that could be in the set. If necessary, draw a picture to help.

Example: | $\frac{1}{2}$ | $\frac{2}{4}$ | $\cancel{\frac{3}{5}}$ | $\frac{4}{8}$ | $\frac{\text{Numerator (N) x 2}}{\text{Denominator (D) x 2}}$ New Fraction $\frac{8}{16}$

New Fraction

1. | $\frac{1}{8}$ | $\frac{2}{16}$ | $\frac{2}{24}$ | $\frac{4}{32}$ | _____

2. | $\frac{3}{4}$ | $\frac{6}{8}$ | $\frac{12}{16}$ | $\frac{20}{30}$ | _____

3. | $\frac{3}{10}$ | $\frac{9}{30}$ | $\frac{27}{90}$ | $\frac{36}{180}$ | _____

4. | $\frac{1}{5}$ | $\frac{3}{10}$ | $\frac{3}{15}$ | $\frac{4}{20}$ | _____

5. | $\frac{3}{7}$ | $\frac{6}{14}$ | $\frac{8}{21}$ | $\frac{12}{28}$ | _____

6. | $\frac{1}{2}$ | $\frac{4}{8}$ | $\frac{16}{32}$ | $\frac{62}{128}$ | _____

7. | $\frac{5}{8}$ | $\frac{9}{16}$ | $\frac{15}{24}$ | $\frac{20}{32}$ | _____

Write a rule to find equivalent fractions.

_____

The Mouse Family

Directions: The Mouse family found a feast of pies. Color the pies to illustrate the problem and answer the question on the line. Write the fraction addition problem in the space.

Example: If Mindy Mouse ate one-third of a pie and her sister Martha ate another one-third of the pie, how much total pie did they eat?

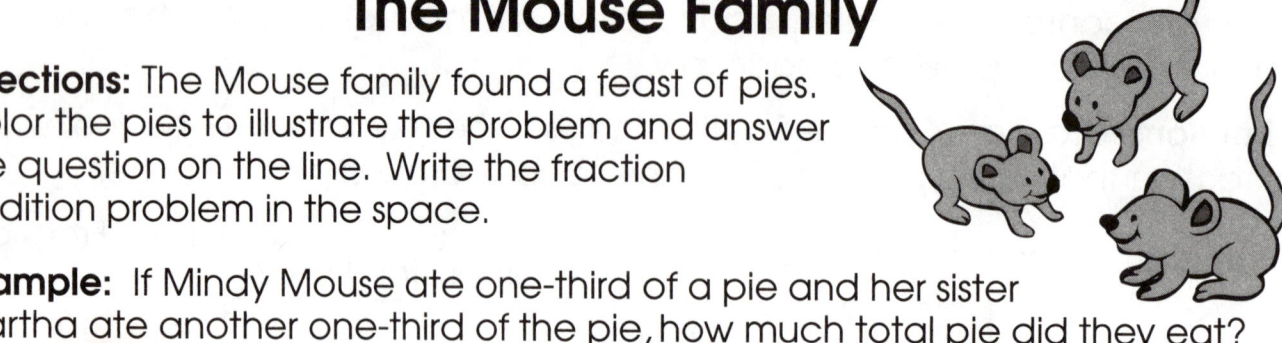

1. Max Mouse found a whole pie and ate one-fifth of it. When he was hungry later, he ate another two-fifths. How much of the pie did he eat?

   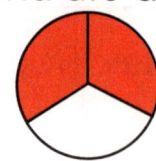

   _____

2. If Mindy gave three-eighths of a pie to her uncle and two-eighths to her cousin, how much did she give away?

   _____

3. Mr. Mouse demanded, "No more pie before bedtime!" Mindy handed her father one-fifth of a pie and Max handed his father another one-fifth. What part of a whole pie was Mr. Mouse holding?

   _____

4. If Max ate three-fifths of a pie and Mindy ate two-fifths of a pie, who ate more pie?

   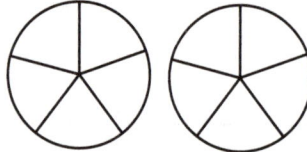

   _____

Summer Link Super Edition Grade 4

Name _____

Sea Math

Directions: Reduce each sum to a whole number or a mixed number in the lowest terms.

$\dfrac{6}{9}$ $\quad$ $\dfrac{4}{5}$ $\quad$ $\dfrac{3}{4}$ $\quad$ $\dfrac{8}{11}$ $\quad$ $\dfrac{2}{5}$
$+\dfrac{6}{9}$ $\quad$ $+\dfrac{6}{5}$ $\quad$ $+\dfrac{2}{4}$ $\quad$ $+\dfrac{8}{11}$ $\quad$ $+\dfrac{3}{5}$

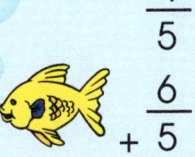 

$\dfrac{8}{9}$ $\quad$ $\dfrac{4}{8}$ $\quad$ $\dfrac{5}{4}$ $\quad$ $\dfrac{4}{3}$ $\quad$ $\dfrac{5}{7}$
$+\dfrac{3}{9}$ $\quad$ $+\dfrac{6}{8}$ $\quad$ $+\dfrac{2}{4}$ $\quad$ $+\dfrac{2}{3}$ $\quad$ $+\dfrac{6}{7}$

$\dfrac{8}{11}$ $\quad$ $\dfrac{3}{12}$ $\quad$ $\dfrac{3}{6}$ $\quad$ $\dfrac{6}{12}$ $\quad$ $\dfrac{4}{8}$ $\quad$ $\dfrac{5}{12}$
$+\dfrac{3}{11}$ $\quad$ $+\dfrac{10}{12}$ $\quad$ $+\dfrac{3}{6}$ $\quad$ $+\dfrac{8}{12}$ $\quad$ $+\dfrac{4}{8}$ $\quad$ $+\dfrac{8}{12}$

$\dfrac{5}{12}$ $\quad$ $\dfrac{7}{13}$ $\quad$ $\dfrac{8}{15}$ $\quad$ $\dfrac{5}{7}$
$+\dfrac{10}{12}$ $\quad$ $+\dfrac{6}{13}$ $\quad$ $+\dfrac{14}{15}$ $\quad$ $+\dfrac{6}{7}$

55 $\qquad$ Summer Link Super Edition Grade 4

Name _____

Fractions to Decimals

When a figure is divided into 10 equal parts, the parts are called **tenths**. Tenths can be written two ways—as a fraction or a decimal. A **decimal** is a number with one or more places to the right of a decimal point, such as 6.5 or 2.25. A decimal point is the dot between the ones place and the tenths place.

Examples:

   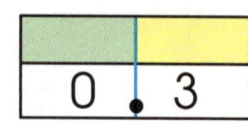

$\frac{3}{10}$ or 0.3 of the square is shaded.

Directions: Write the decimal and fraction for the shaded parts of the following figures. The first one is done for you.

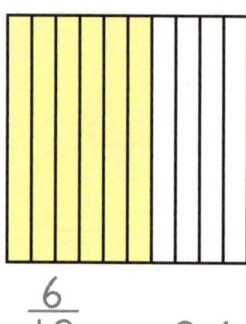

$\frac{6}{10}$ 0.6

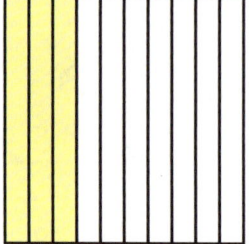   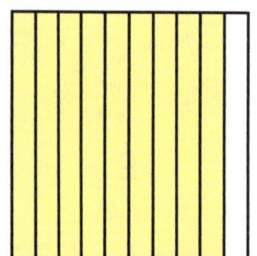   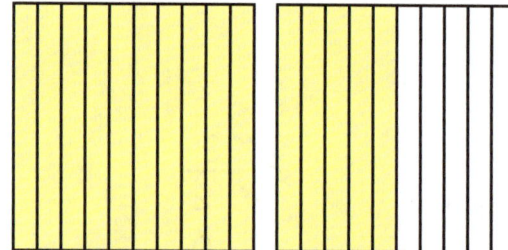

_____   _____   _____   _____

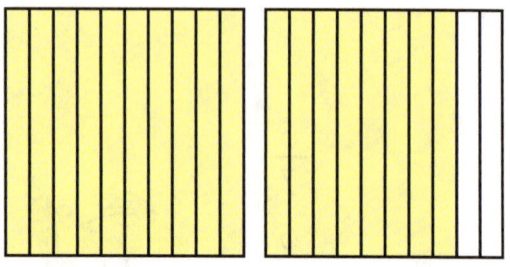   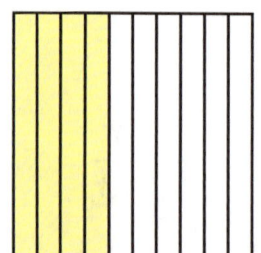   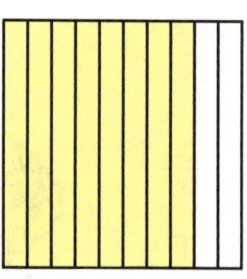

_____   _____   _____   _____

Decimals

A decimal is a number with one or more numbers to the right of a decimal point, such as 6.5 or 2.25. Equivalent means numbers that are equal.

Directions: Draw a line between the equivalent numbers.

.8 $\frac{5}{10}$

five-tenths $\frac{8}{10}$

.7 $\frac{6}{10}$

.4   .3

six-tenths $\frac{2}{10}$

three-tenths $\frac{7}{10}$

.2 $\frac{9}{10}$

nine-tenths $\frac{4}{10}$

Decimals: Addition and Subtraction

Decimals are added and subtracted in the same way as other numbers. Simply carry down the decimal point to your answer.

Directions: Add or subtract.

Examples:

```
  1
  1.3          4.5
+ 2.8        - 2.2
-----        -----
  4.1          2.3
```

```
  1.3      4.6      5.1      6.7
+ 2.2    - 3.4    + 8.8    - 4.3
-----    -----    -----    -----
```

```
  7.9      6.4     11.4      0.5
- 3.7    + 8.7    - 9.5    + 3.6
-----    -----    -----    -----
```

9.3 + 1.2 = ____   2.5 − 0.7 = ____   1.2 + 5.0 = ____

Bob jogs around the school every day. The distance for one time around is .7 of a mile. If he jogs around the school two times, how many miles does he jog each day? _____

Summer Link Super Edition Grade 4

Fractions and Decimals

Directions: Compare the fraction to the decimal in each box. Circle the larger number.

Example:

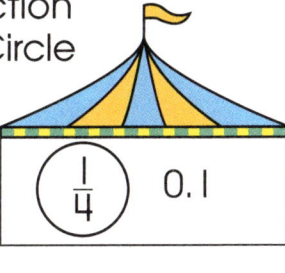

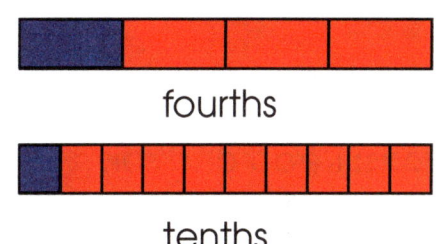

fourths

tenths

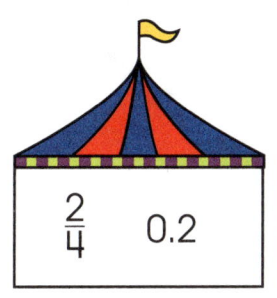 $\frac{2}{4}$ 0.2

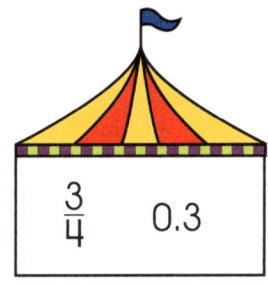 $\frac{3}{4}$ 0.3

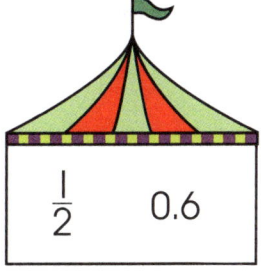 $\frac{1}{2}$ 0.6

 $\frac{1}{4}$ 0.4

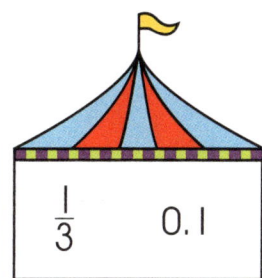 $\frac{1}{3}$ 0.1

 $\frac{1}{4}$ 0.7

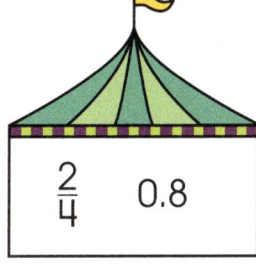 $\frac{2}{4}$ 0.8

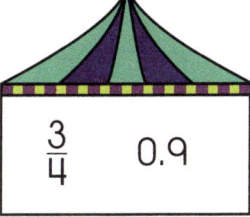 $\frac{3}{4}$ 0.9

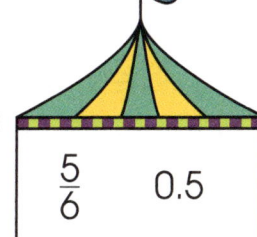 $\frac{5}{6}$ 0.5

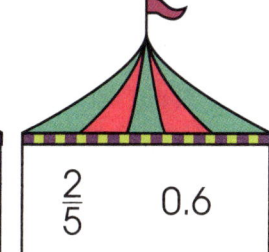 $\frac{2}{5}$ 0.6

 $\frac{3}{12}$ 0.9

 $\frac{1}{6}$ 0.2

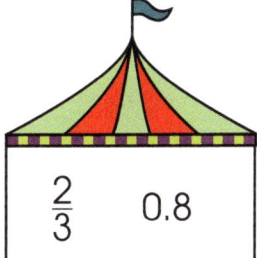 $\frac{2}{3}$ 0.8

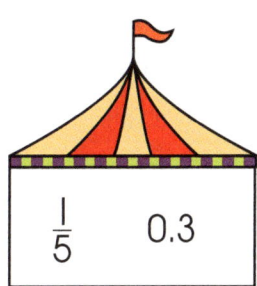 $\frac{1}{5}$ 0.3

 $\frac{2}{5}$ 0.7

 $\frac{3}{10}$ 0.5

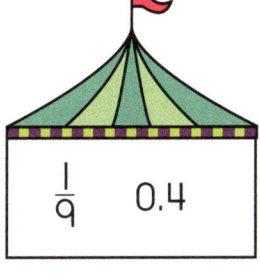 $\frac{1}{9}$ 0.4

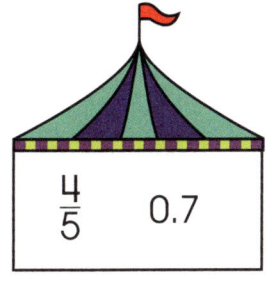 $\frac{4}{5}$ 0.7

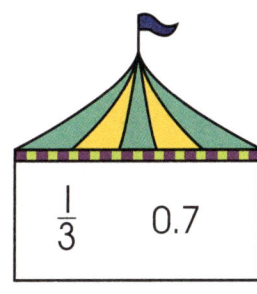 $\frac{1}{3}$ 0.7

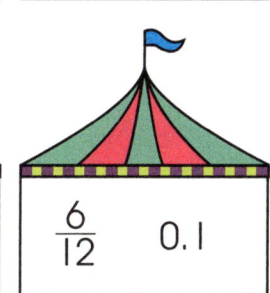 $\frac{6}{12}$ 0.1

Problem-Solving: Fractions, Decimals

A fraction is a number that names part of a whole, such as $\frac{1}{2}$ or $\frac{1}{3}$.

Directions: Read and solve each problem.

1. There are 20 large animals on the Browns' farm. Two-fifths are horses, two-fifths are cows, and the rest are pigs. Are there more pigs or cows on the farm? _____

2. Farmer Brown had 40 eggs to sell. He sold half of them in the morning. In the afternoon, he sold half of what was left. How many eggs did Farmer Brown have at the end of the day? _____

3. There is a fence running around seven-tenths of the farm. How much of the farm does not have a fence around it? Write the amount as a decimal. _____

4. The Browns have 10 chickens. Two are roosters and the rest are hens. Write a decimal for the number that are roosters and for the number that are hens.

   ____ roosters
   ____ hens

5. Mrs. Brown spends three-fourths of her day working outside and the rest working inside. Does she spend more time inside or outside? _____

Summer Link Super Edition Grade 4

Time: Hour, Half-Hour, Quarter-Hour, 5 Min. Intervals

Directions: Write the time shown on each clock.

Example:

7:15   7:00

_____ _____ _____

_____ _____ _____

_____ _____ _____

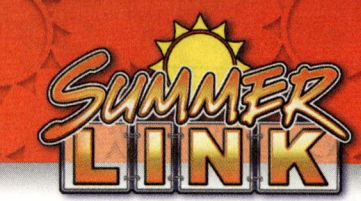

Time: Minutes

A minute is a measurement of time. There are sixty seconds in a minute and sixty minutes in an hour.

Directions: Write the time shown on each clock.

Example:

Each mark is one minute.
The hand is at mark number 6.

Write: 5:06
Read: six minutes after five.

_____ _____ _____ _____

_____ _____ _____ _____

  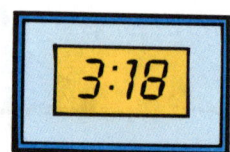 

_____ _____ _____ _____

Money: Counting Change

Directions: Subtract the money using decimals to show how much change a person would receive in each of the following.

Example:
Bill had 3 dollars.
He bought a baseball for $2.83.
How much change did he receive?

$3.00
−$2.83
$ .17

Paid 2 dollars.

Paid 1 dollar.

_____ _____

Paid 5 dollars.

Paid 10 dollars.

_____ _____

Paid 4 dollars.

Paid 7 dollars.

_____ _____

Money: Comparing

Directions: Compare the amount of money in the left column with the price of the object in the right column. Is the amount of money in the left column enough to purchase the object in the right column? Circle yes or no.

Example:

Alice has 2 dollars. She wants to buy a jump rope for $1.75. Does she have enough money?

(Yes)   No

Yes   No

Yes   No

Yes   No

Name _____

Monetary Message

Directions: What's the smartest thing to do with your money? To find out, solve the following problems and write the matching letter above the answer.

$$\overline{}\ \overline{}\ \overline{}\ \overline{}\quad \overline{}\ \overline{},$$
$42.71 $33.94 $50.42 $100.73 $45.70 $2.39

$$\overline{}\ \overline{}\ \overline{}\quad\overline{}\ \overline{}\quad\overline{}\ \overline{}\ \overline{}\ \overline{}$$
$33.94 $26.13 $88.02 $45.70 $2.39 $51.12 $45.70 $11.01 $11.01

$$\overline{}\ \overline{}\ \overline{}\quad\overline{}\ \overline{}\ !$$
$33.94 $88.02 $88.02 $55.76 $42.79

V = $42.13 + 8.29   A = $4.56 + 29.38   N = $4.65 + 21.48   S = $23.46 + 19.25

P = $9.31 + 33.48   L = $6.73 + 4.28   E = $81.49 + 19.24   T = $.42 + 1.94 + .03

U = $50.84 + 4.92   I = $7.49 + 38.21

D = $3.04 + 84.98   W = $1.89 + 49.23

Name _____

Easy Street

Directions: What is each house worth? Count the money in each house on Easy Street. Write the amount on the line below it.

Example:

$2.40   _____   _____   _____   _____

_____   _____   _____   _____   _____

Summer Link Super Edition Grade 4   66

Building a House

Directions: Read about Jonathan's summer job and write the answer to each problem on the line.

1. Over the summer, Jonathan worked 126 hours. His uncle worked 625 hours. How many more hours did Uncle Jake work than Jonathan? _____ more hours

2. It took 630 bricks to build the front wall of the house. The back wall took 725. How many more bricks were needed in the back of the house than in the front of the house? _____ more bricks

3. The side walls of the house contained a total of 934 bricks. If the garage took 168 fewer bricks, how many bricks did it take to build the garage? _____ bricks

4. They used 245 bricks to build a pillar in the front of the house. If Jonathan laid 150 of those bricks and his uncle did the rest, how many bricks did his uncle lay? _____ bricks

5. The bricks in the large pillar cost $282. If the mortar between the bricks cost $218 less, how much did the mortar cost? _____ dollars

6. Jonathan earned $360 helping his uncle this summer. Last summer he made $285. How much more did he make this summer than last? _____ dollars

Problem-Solving

Directions: Read and solve each problem.

1. Ralph has $8.75. He buys a teddy bear and a puzzle. How much money does he have left? _____

2. Kelly wants to buy a teddy bear and a ball. She has $7.25. How much more money does she need? _____

3. Kim paid a five-dollar bill, two one-dollar bills, two quarters, one dime, and eight pennies for a book. How much did it cost? _____

4. Michelle leaves for school at 7:45 a.m. It takes her 20 minutes to get there. On the clock, draw the time that she arrives at school.

5. Frank takes piano lessons every Saturday morning at 11:30. The lesson lasts for an hour and 15 minutes. On the clock, draw the time his piano lesson ends. Is it a.m. or p.m.? Circle the correct answer.

Piggy-Bank Countdown

Tomorrow is Mitzi's mom's birthday, so Mitzi empties her piggy bank and finds that she has just enough to buy a special locket that costs $7.43.

She has one 5-dollar bill, one 1-dollar bill, and 15 coins. There is at least one quarter, one dime, one nickel, and one penny.

Directions: There are at least two combinations of coins that Mitzi might have. Use these charts to show them.

	Quarter(s)	Dime(s)	Nickel(s)	Penny(ies)	Total
Number of Coins					
Amount					

	Quarter(s)	Dime(s)	Nickel(s)	Penny(ies)	Total
Number of Coins					
Amount					

Name _____

Inch

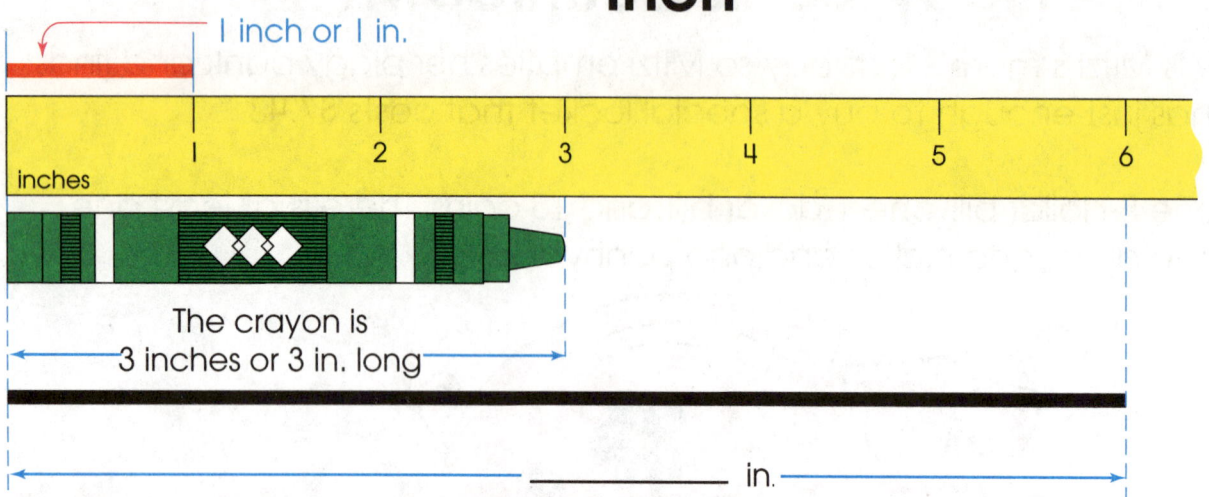

1 inch or 1 in.

inches

The crayon is 3 inches or 3 in. long

_____ in.

Directions: Find the length of each object to the nearest inch.

1. _____ in.

2. _____ in.

3. _____ in.

4. _____ in.

5. _____ in.

Directions: Complete the table.

	From	Length
6.	A to B	_____ in.
7.	A to C	_____ in.
8.	B to D	_____ in.
9.	B to E	_____ in.
10.	A to D	_____ in.

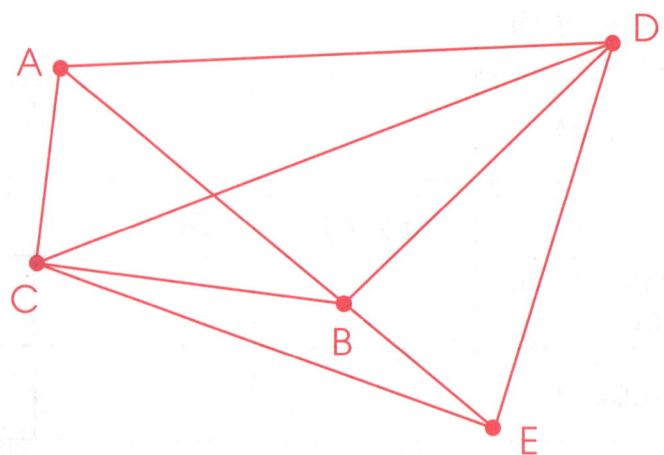

Name ______________________________

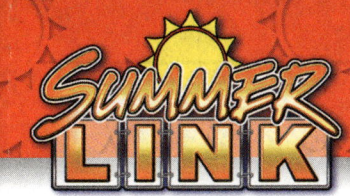

Measurement: Foot, Yard, Mile

Directions: Choose the measure of distance you would use for each object.

1 foot = 12 inches
1 yard = 3 feet
1 mile = 1,760 yards or 5,280 feet

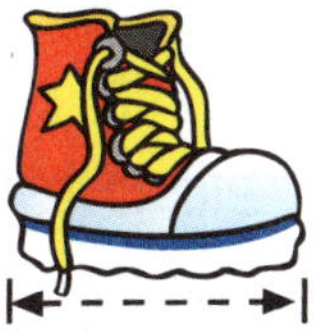

inches

____

____

____

____

____

____

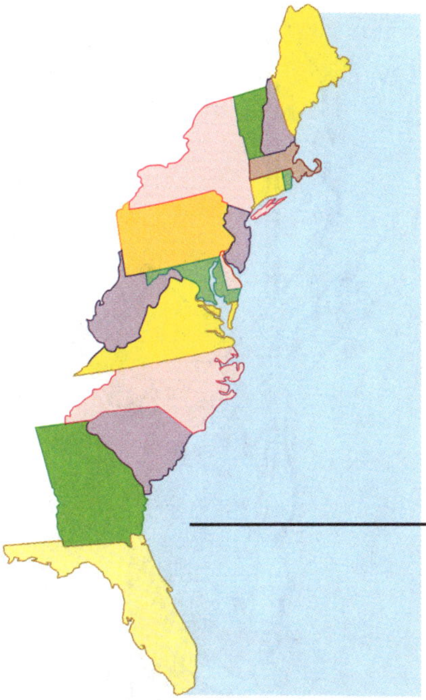

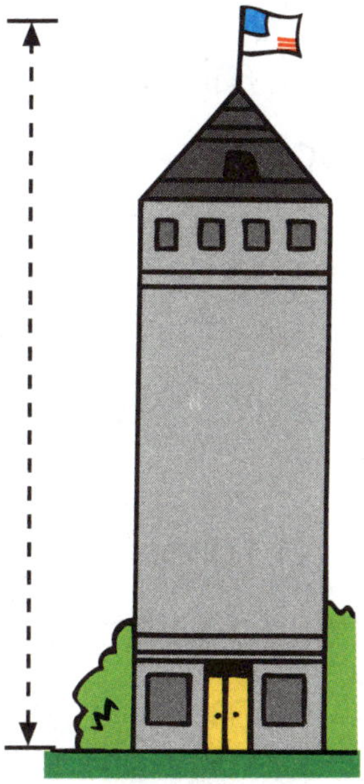

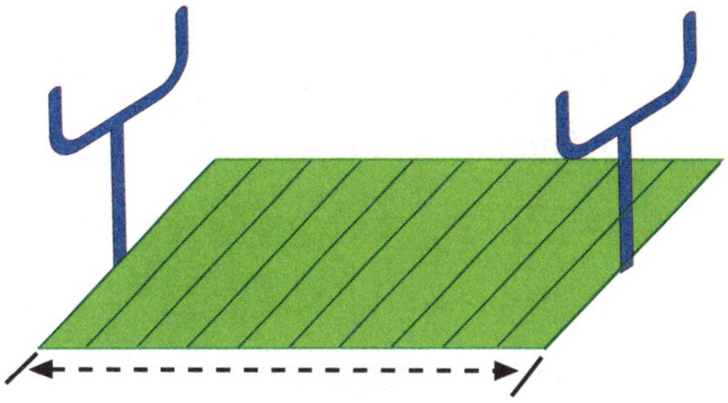

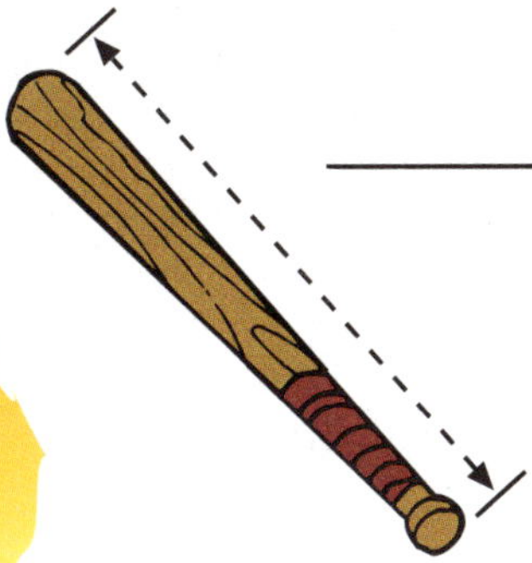

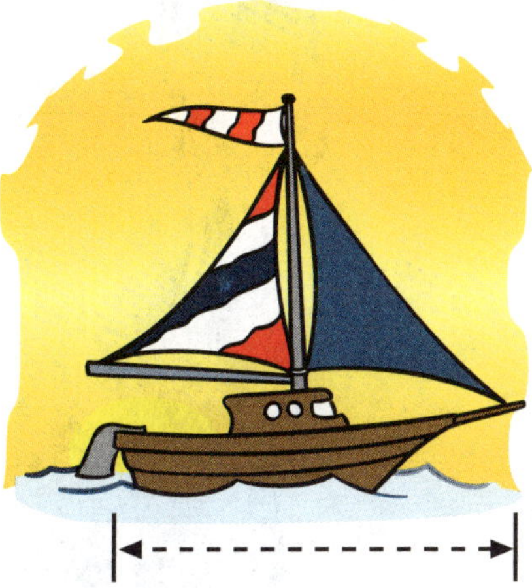

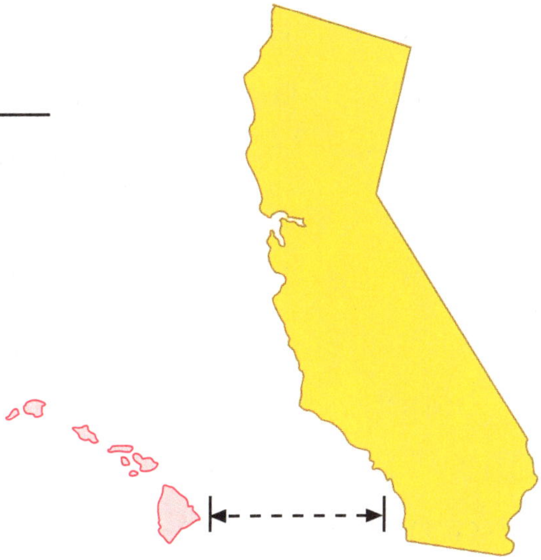

Going the Distance

Directions: Circle the best units of measurement to use for each word problem.

1. The New York Knicks are traveling to Boston to play the Celtics.
   a. inches   b. feet   c. yards   d. miles
2. Barry Sanders runs the length of the field for a touchdown.
   a. inches   b. feet   c. yards   d. miles
3. Karl Malone hits a jump shot for 3 points.
   a. inches   b. feet   c. yards   d. miles
4. The length of a tennis racket.
   a. inches   b. feet   c. yards   d. miles
5. One lap of a pool.
   a. inches   b. feet   c. yards   d. miles
6. The distance from the pitcher's mound to home plate.
   a. inches   b. feet   c. yards   d. miles
7. The width of a hockey puck.
   a. inches   b. feet   c. yards   d. miles
8. The height of a pole vaulter's vault.
   a. inches   b. feet   c. yards   d. miles
9. The distance of the Boston Marathon.
   a. inches   b. feet   c. yards   d. miles
10. The length of a diving board.
    a. inches   b. feet   c. yards   d. miles
11. The width of a trampoline.
    a. inches   b. feet   c. yards   d. miles
12. The distance of a hot air balloon race.
    a. inches   b. feet   c. yards   d. miles

Summer Link Super Edition Grade 4

Name _____

Measurement: Ounce and Pound

Ounces and pounds are measurements of weight in the standard measurement system. The ounce is used to measure the weight of very light objects. The pound is used to measure the weight of heavier objects. 16 ounces = 1 pound.

Example:

8 ounces    15 pounds

Directions: Decide if you would use ounces or pounds to measure the weight of each object. Circle your answer.

ounce   pound

ounce   pound

ounce   pound

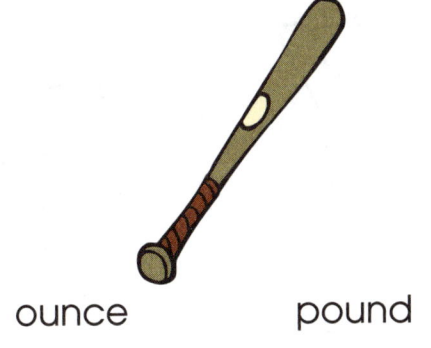

ounce   pound

a chair: ounce   pound   **a table:**   ounce   pound

a shoe: ounce   pound   **a shirt:**   ounce   pound

Metric Measurement: Centimeter, Meter, Kilometer

In the metric system, there are three units of linear measurement: centimeter (cm), meter (m), and kilometer (km).

Centimeters (cm) are used to measure the lengths of small to medium-sized objects. **Meters (m)** measure the lengths of longer objects, such as the width of a swimming pool or height of a tree (100 cm = 1 meter). **Kilometers (km)** measure long distances, such as the distance from Cleveland to Cincinnati or the width of the Atlantic Ocean (1,000 m = 1 km).

Directions: Write whether you would use cm, m, or km to measure each object.

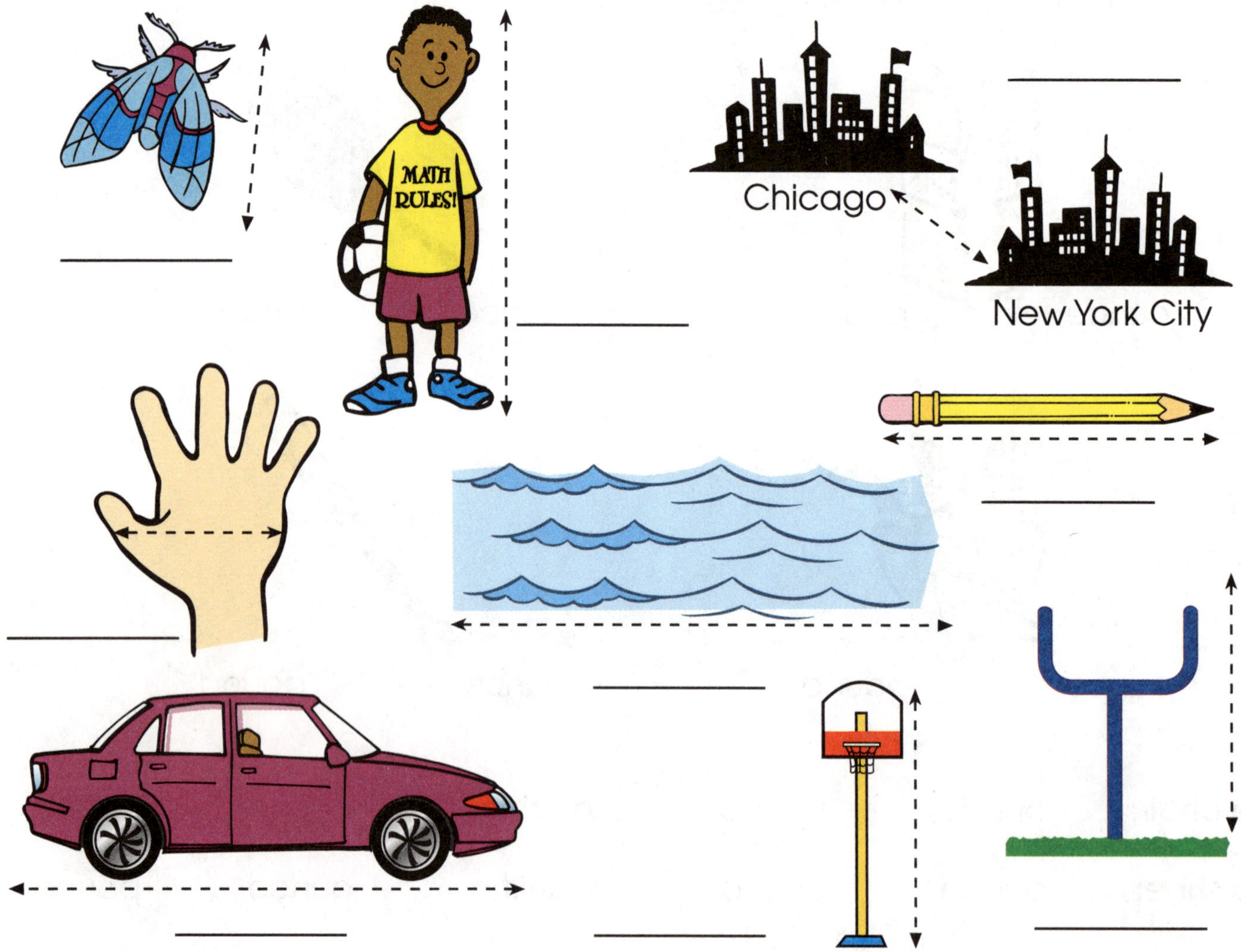

Summer Link Super Edition Grade 4

Name _____

Problem-Solving: Measurement

Directions: Read and solve each problem.

1. This year, hundreds of people ran in the Capital City Marathon. The race is 4.2 kilometers long. When the first person crossed the finish line, the last person was at the 3.7 kilometer point. How far ahead was the winner? _____

2. Dennis crossed the finish line 10 meters ahead of Lucy. Lucy was 5 meters ahead of Sam. How far ahead of Sam was Dennis? _____

3. Tony ran 320 yards from school to his home. Then he ran 290 yards to Jay's house. Together Tony and Jay ran 545 yards to the store. How many yards in all did Tony run? _____

4. The teacher measured the heights of three children in her class. Marsha was 51 inches tall, Jimmy was 48 inches tall, and Ted was $52\frac{1}{2}$ inches tall. How much taller is Ted than Marsha? _____

How much taller is he than Jimmy? _____

Name _____

Geometry: Line, Ray, Segment

A **line segment** has two end points.

Write: AB

A **line** has no end points and goes on in both directions.

Write: CD

A **ray** is part of a line and goes on in one direction. It has one end point.

Write: EF

Directions: Identify each of the following as a line, line segment or ray.

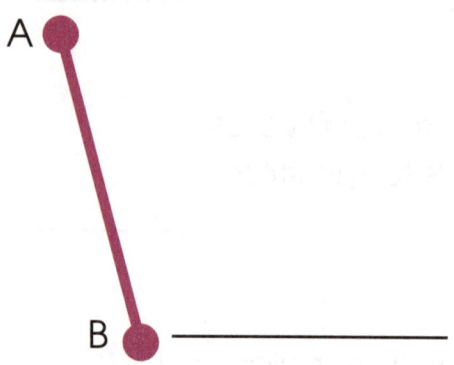

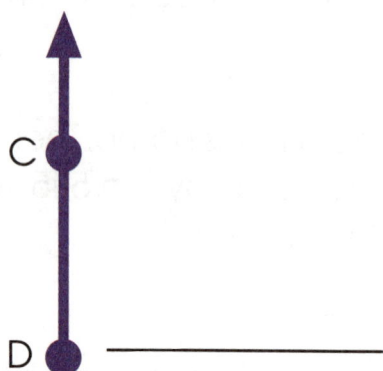

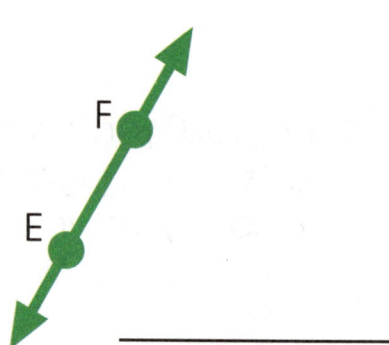

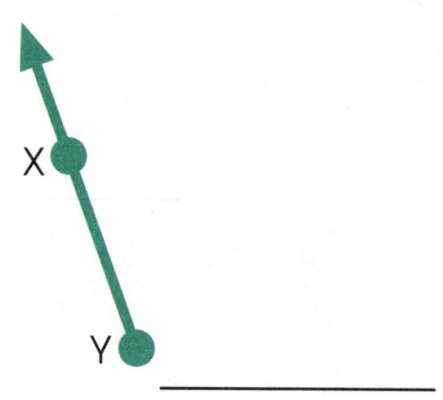

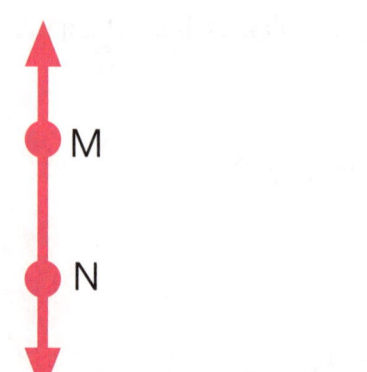

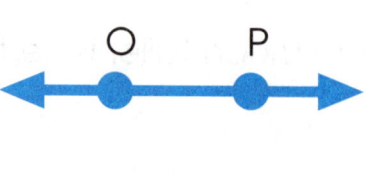

Lines of Symmetry

Directions: A **line of symmetry** divides a figure into two half-figures which are exactly alike. Not all figures have a line of symmetry. Decide if each of the broken lines in the figures below is a line of symmetry. Write *yes* or *no* below each figure.

1. _____   2. _____   3. _____

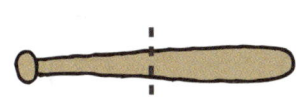 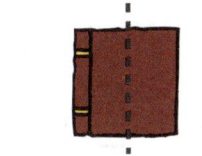 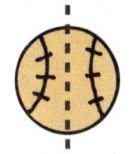

4. _____   5. _____   6. _____

Now, use what you know about symmetry to complete the figures started below. In each partial figure, the broken line is a line symmetry.

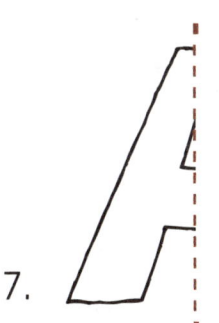   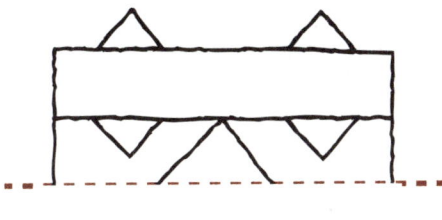   

7.   8.   9.

   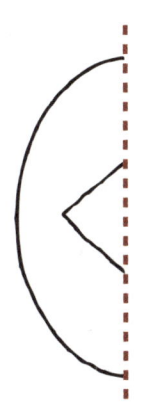   

10.   11.   12.

77   Summer Link Super Edition Grade 4

Name _____

Perimeter Problems

Directions: Perimeter is the distance around a figure. Find the perimeter for the figures below.

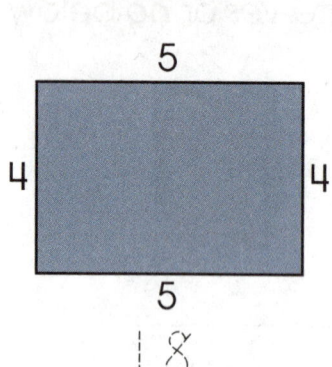
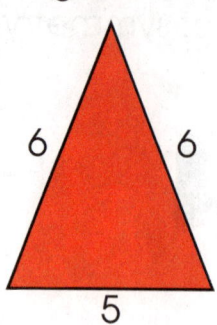
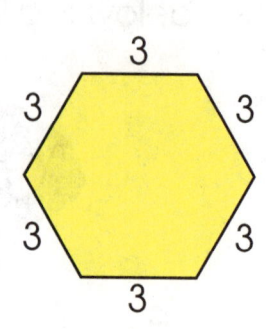
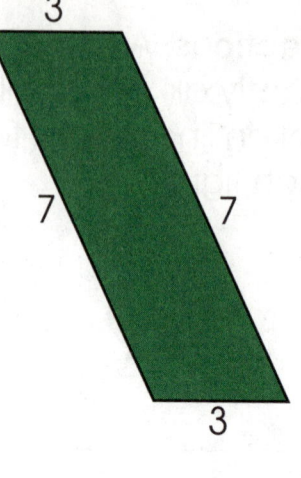

18   _____   _____   _____

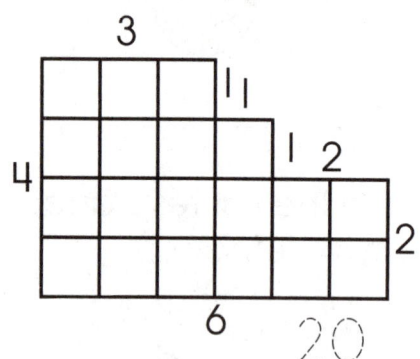

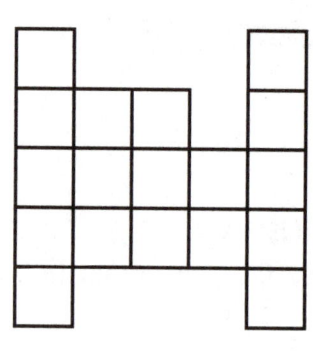

20   _____   _____

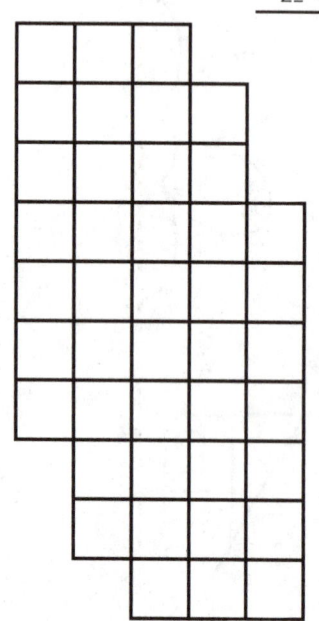
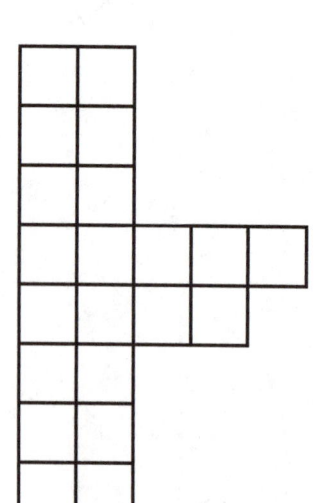

_____   _____   _____

Summer Link Super Edition Grade 4

Name _____

A Square Activity

Directions: The **area** is the number of square units covering a flat surface. Find the area by counting the square units.

Example: 2 squares x 5 squares = 10 squares

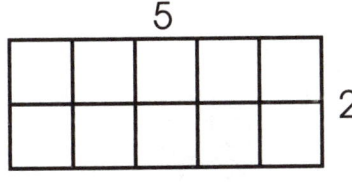

10

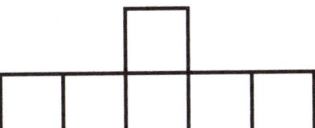

_____

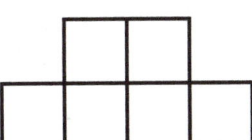

_____

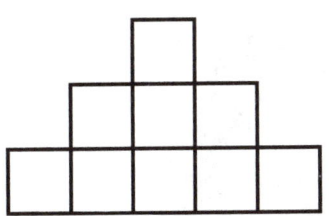

_____

_____

_____

_____

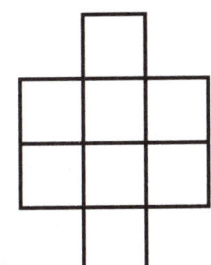

_____

_____

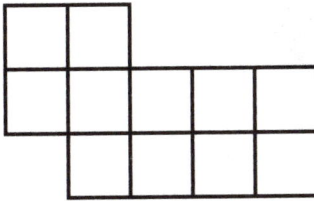

_____

_____

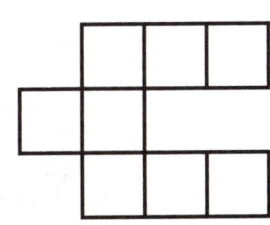

_____

Cover the Area

The Local Area Construction Company has been hired by the city to build a recreation center. They will construct a baseball diamond, a basketball court, and a tennis court. How many square feet of land do they need in order to complete each structure?

Directions: Find the area of each figure below. (Area = L x W) Area = square feet

78 ft.

Area = _____ sq. ft.

36 ft.

50 ft.

94 ft.

90 ft.

90 ft.

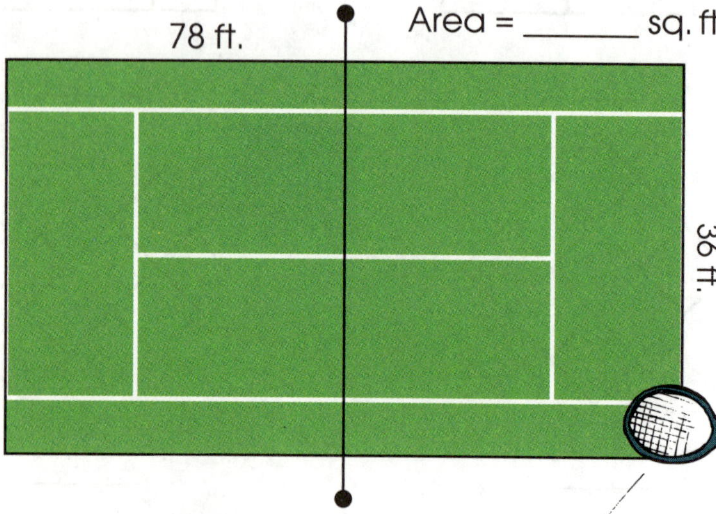

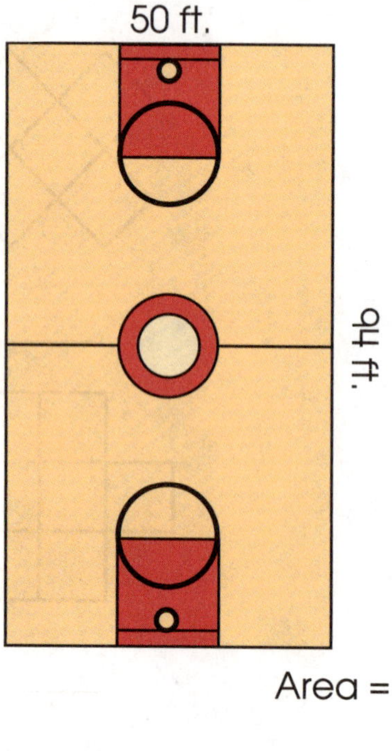

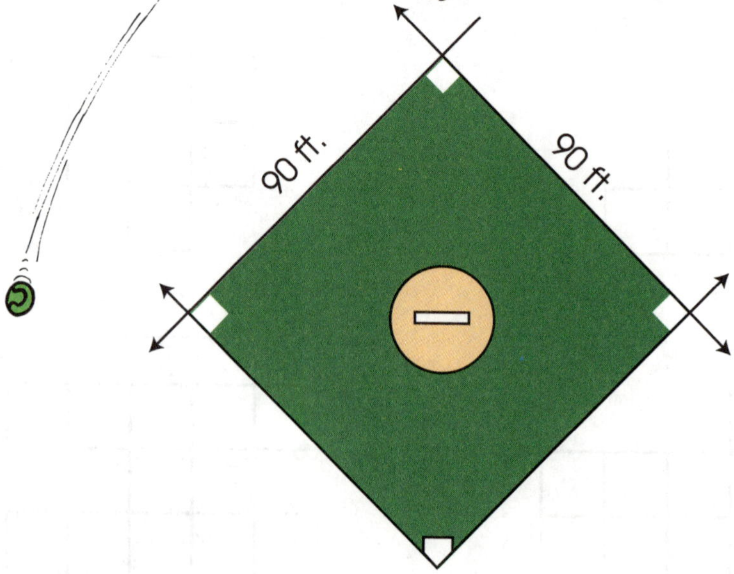

Area = _____ sq. ft.

Area = _____ sq. ft.

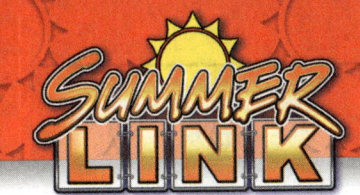

Name _____

Turn Up the Volume

Directions: The **volume** is the measure of the inside of a shape. Find the volume of these shapes by counting the boxes. You might not be able to see all the boxes, but you can tell that they are there.

Example:

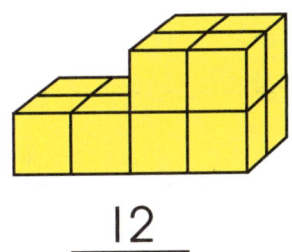

12

_____   _____

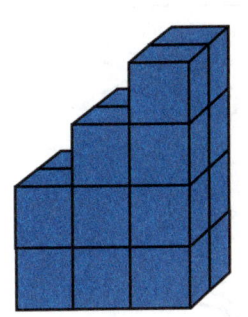

_____

_____

_____

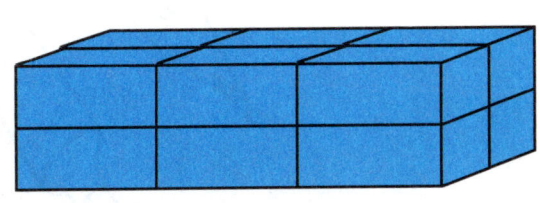

_____   _____   _____

81   Summer Link Super Edition Grade 4

Name _____

Graphs

A **graph** is a drawing that shows information about numbers.

Directions: Color the picture. Then tell how many there are of each object by completing the graph.

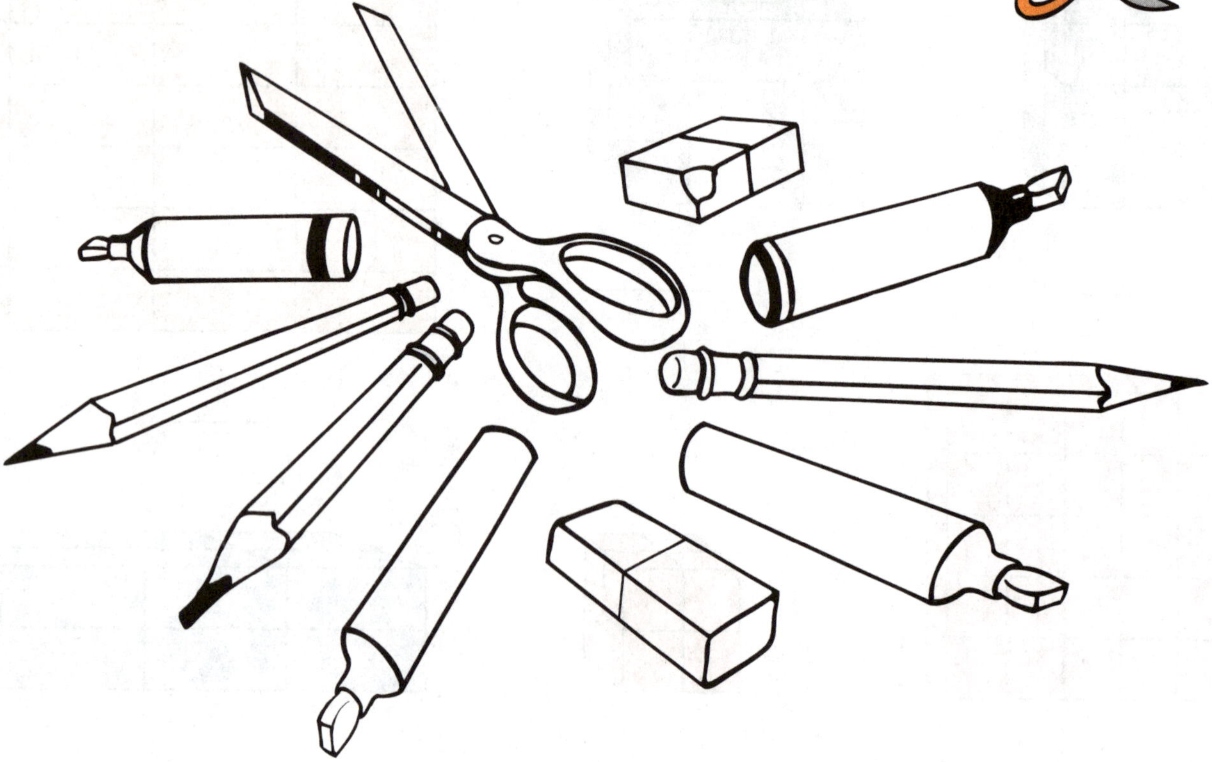

Hot Lunch Favorites

The cooks in the cafeteria asked each third- and fourth-grade class to rate the hot lunches. They wanted to know which food the children liked the best.

The table shows how the students rated the lunches.
Key: Each 👤 equals 2 students.

Food	Number of students who liked it best
hamburgers	👤 👤 👤 👤 👤 👤
hot dogs	👤 👤 👤 👤 👤 👤 👤 👤
tacos	👤 👤 👤 👤 👤
chili	
soup and sandwiches	👤
spaghetti	👤 👤
fried chicken	👤 👤 👤 👤
fish sticks	👤 👤 👤

Directions: Color the bar graph to show the information on the table. Remember that each 👤 equals 2 people. The first one is done for you.

Write the food in order starting with the one that students liked most.

1. _____
2. _____
3. _____
4. _____
5. _____
6. _____
7. _____
8. _____

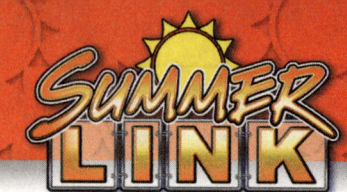

American League West

Directions: Graph the number of games won by each team in the 2002 season.

Team	Won
Anaheim Angels	99
Oakland Athletics	103
Seattle Mariners	93
Texas Rangers	72

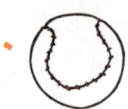

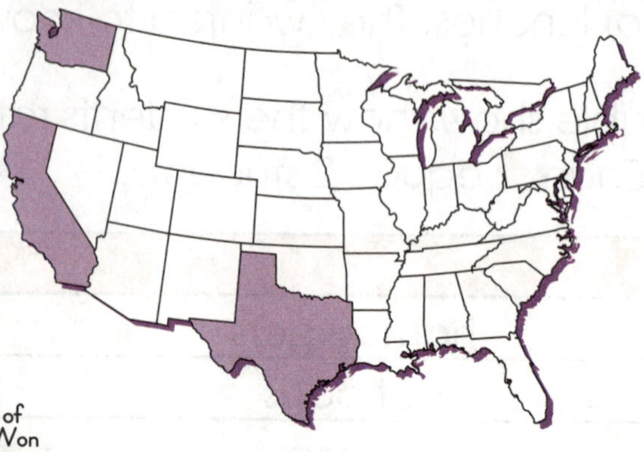

Number of Games Won

	Angels	Athletics	Mariners	Rangers
115				
110				
105				
100				
95				
90				
85				
80				
75				
70				
65				
60				
55				
50				
45				
40				
35				
30				
25				
20				
15				
10				
5				
Teams	Angels	Athletics	Mariners	Rangers

American League East

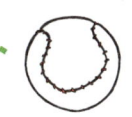

Directions: Graph the number of games won by each team in the 2002 season.

WON
- Baltimore Orioles — 67
- Boston Red Sox — 93
- New York Yankees — 103
- Tampa Bay Devil Rays — 55
- Toronto Blue Jays — 78

Number of Games Won: 115, 110, 105, 100, 95, 90, 85, 80, 75, 70, 65, 60, 55, 50, 45, 40, 35, 30, 25, 20, 15, 10, 5

Teams: Orioles, Red Sox, Yankees, Devil Rays, Blue Jays

Name _____

Roman Numerals

I	1	VII	7
II	2	VIII	8
III	3	IX	9
IV	4	X	10
V	5	XI	11
VI	6	XII	12

Directions: Write the number.

V ____   VII ____
X ____   IX ____
II ____   XII ____

Directions: Write the Roman numeral.

4 ____   5 ____
10 ____   8 ____
6 ____   3 ____

Roman Numerals

I means 1.   V means 5.   X means 10.

II   means 1 + 1 or 2.   III means 1+1+1 or 3.
VI   means 5 + 1 or 6.   IV means 5 – 1 or 4.
XXV means 10 + 10 + 5 or 25.   IX means 10 – 1 or 9.

VII   means 5 + 1 + ____ or ____.   XXI   means 10 + ____ + 1 or ____.

XIV   means ____ + 4 or ____.   XIX   means ____ + 9 or ____.

Complete the following as shown.

	a	b	c	d
1.	XXIV = 24	XX = ____	XII = ____	VIII = ____
2.	IV = ____	XXVI = ____	XVII = ____	XXXI = ____
3.	XXXVI = ____	XXIX = ____	XI = ____	XXXIII = ____
4.	XVIII = ____	IX = ____	XXXIV = ____	XIII = ____
5.	V = ____	XXV = ____	VI = ____	XXI = ____
6.	XXXVIII = ____	XXXV = ____	XXVII = ____	XVI = ____
7.	XXIII = ____	XXXVII = ____	XIV = ____	XXXII = ____

Write a Roman numeral for each of the following.

	a	b	c
8.	3 = ____	7 = ____	15 = ____
9.	19 = ____	22 = ____	28 = ____
10.	30 = ____	20 = ____	39 = ____

Glossary

addition: the operation that combines numbers to create a sum.

area: the amount of surface in a given boundary, found by multiplying length by width.

bar graph: displays information by lengths of parallel rectangular bars.

commutative: a property that allows you to add or multiply two numbers in any order and still get the same answer, such as 2 x 3 = 3 x 2.

congruent: figures that are the same shape and the same size.

coordinates: points located on the same graph.

customary measurement: the standard system for measuring, such as cup, pint, quart, gallon, ounce, pound, inch, foot, yard, mile.

decimal: a number with one or more numbers to the right of a decimal point.

decimal point: a dot placed between the ones place and the tenths place of a number.

denominator: the bottom number in a fraction telling the number of parts in the whole.

difference: the number received when one number is subtracted from another.

digit: a numeral.

dividend: a number that is to be divided by another number.

division: shows how many times one number contains another.

divisor: a number by which another number is to be divided.

fraction: a number that stands for a part of a whole.

geometry: the branch of mathematics that has to do with points, lines, and shapes.

mass: the amount or quantity of matter contained in an object.

metric measurement: a system of measurement based on counting by tens, such as liter, milliliter, gram, kilogram, centimeter, meter, kilometer.

multiplication: taking a number and adding to itself a certain number of times.

numerator: the top number in a fraction showing the number of parts out of the whole.

operations: addition, subtraction, multiplication, division.

ordered pair: lists the horizontal and vertical location of the point, such as (3, 4).

perimeter: the distance around an object found by adding the lengths and widths.

place value: shows by where the numeral is in the number.

polygon: a closed figure that has three or more sides.

probability: the likelihood or chance that something will happen.

quotient: the number received when a number is divided.

regrouping: borrowing numbers from another column to complete the operation.

remainder: the number left over when a number cannot be divided evenly.

rounding: expressing a number to the nearest ten, hundred, thousand, and so on.

subtraction: "taking away" one number from another to find the difference.

sum: the number received when two numbers are added together.

symmetry: when both sides of an object are exactly the same.

Page 8

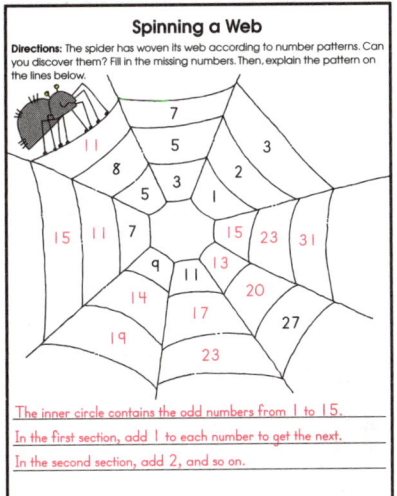

Page 9

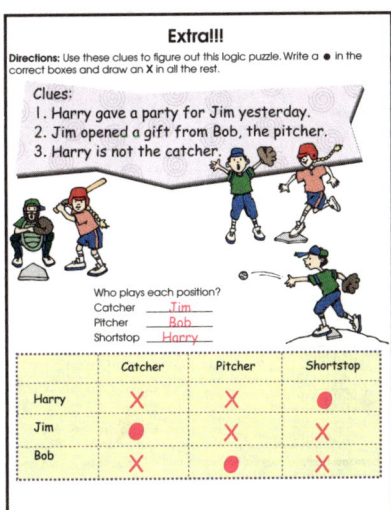

Page 10

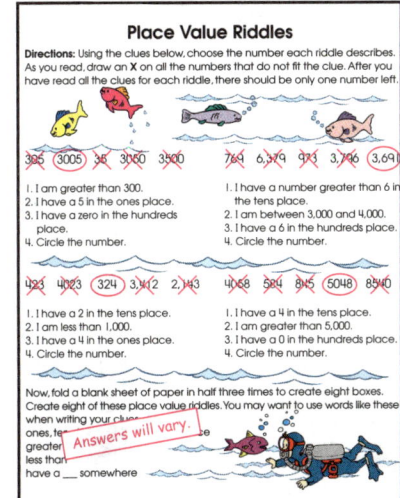

Page 11

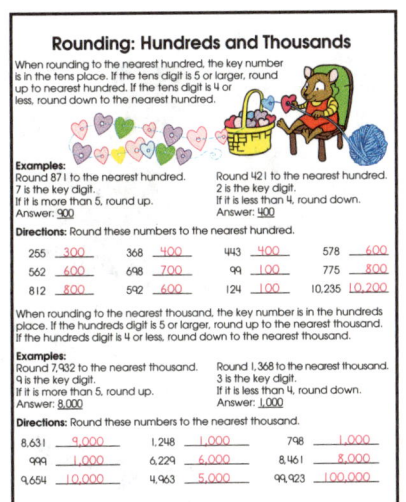

Page 12

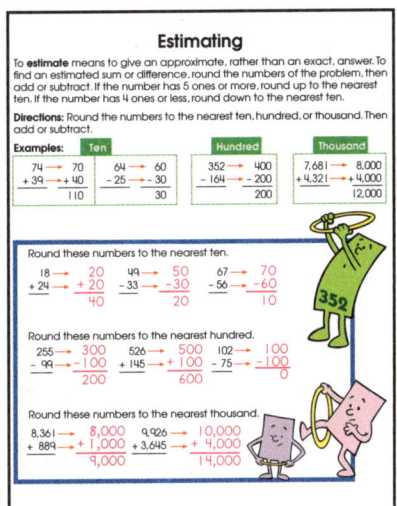

Page 13

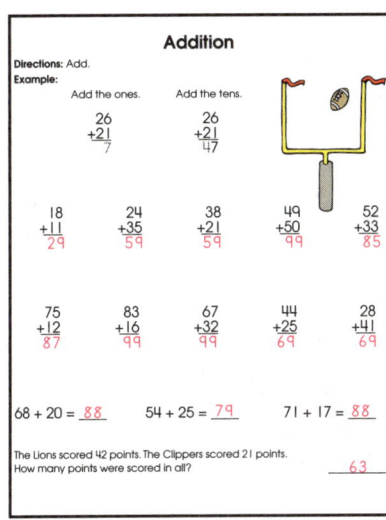

Page 14

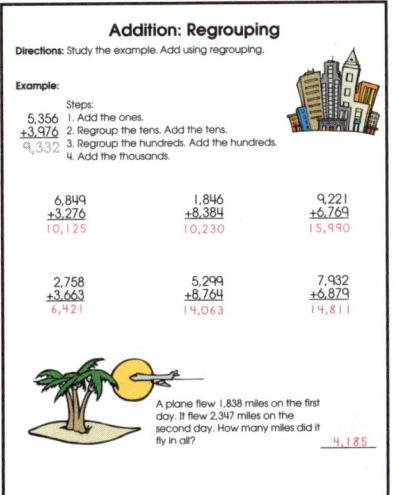

Page 15

Page 16

Page 17
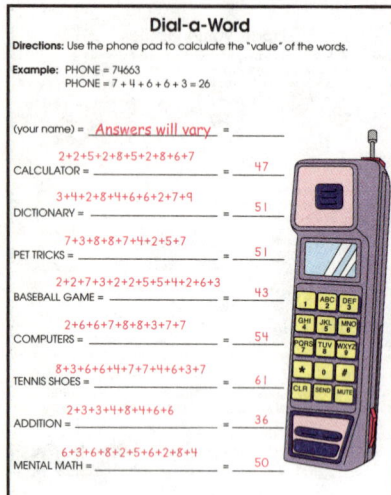

Page 18

Page 19
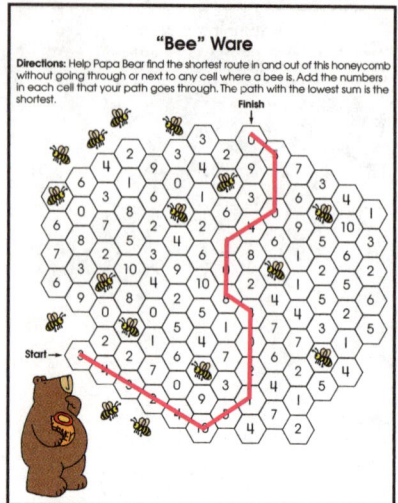

Page 20
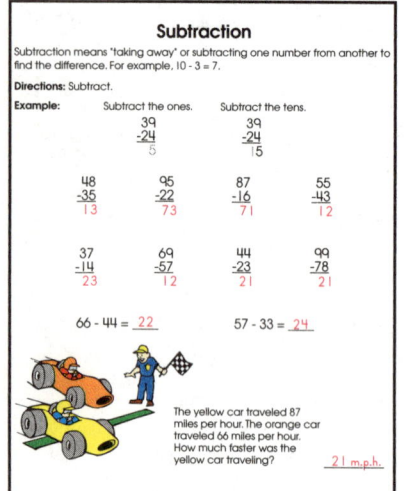

Page 21

Page 22

Page 23

Page 24
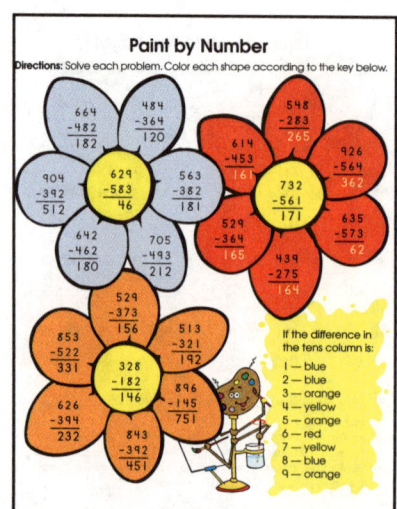

Page 25

Summer Link Super Edition Grade 4

Page 26
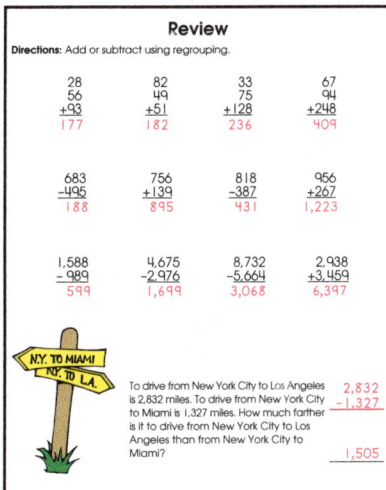

Page 27
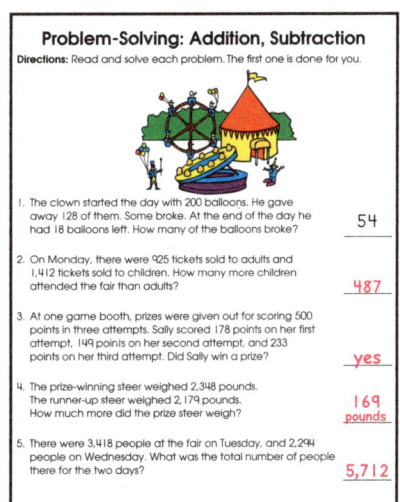

Page 28

Page 29
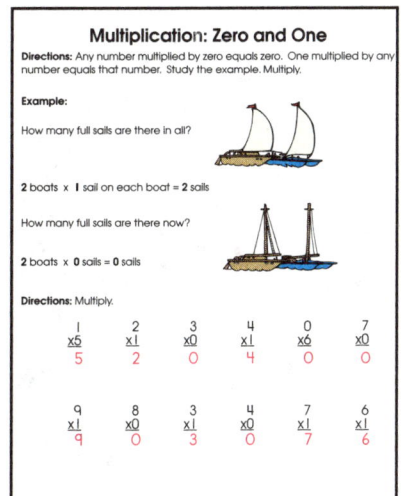

Page 30
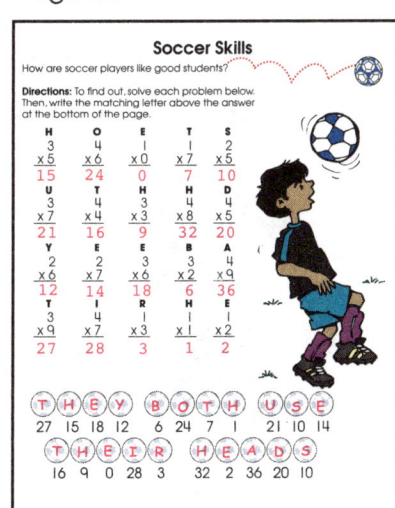

Page 31

Page 32
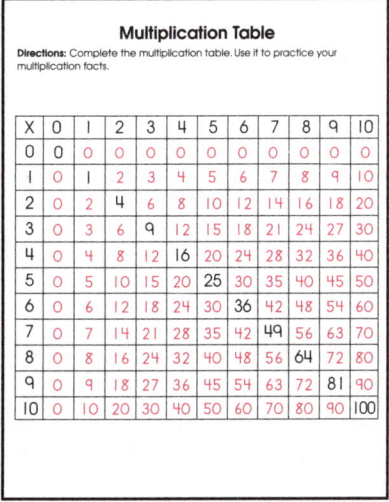

Page 33
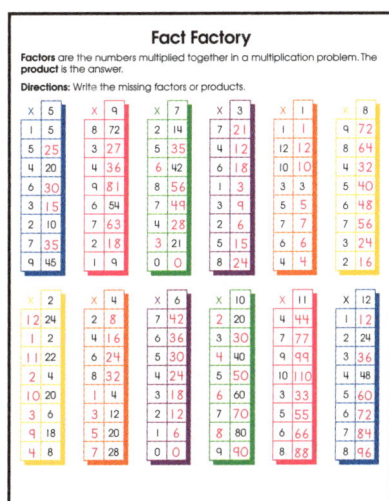

Page 34
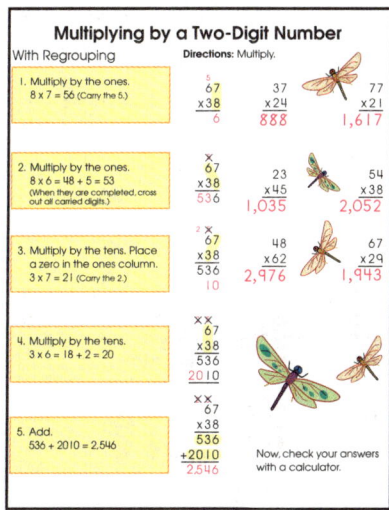

Page 35
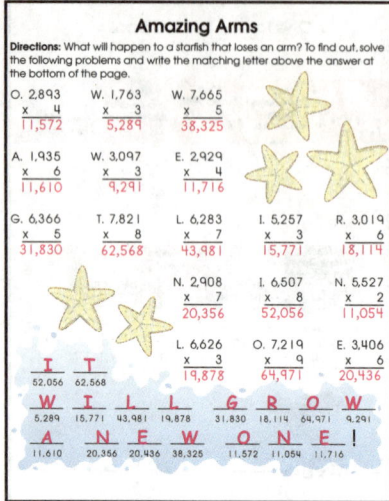

Page 36
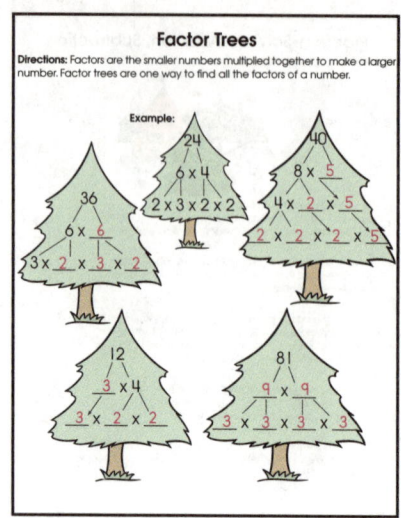

Page 37
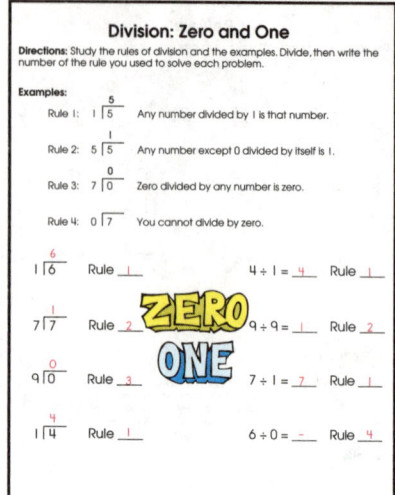

Page 38
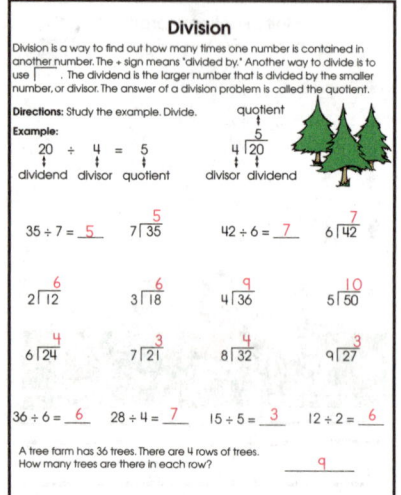

Page 39
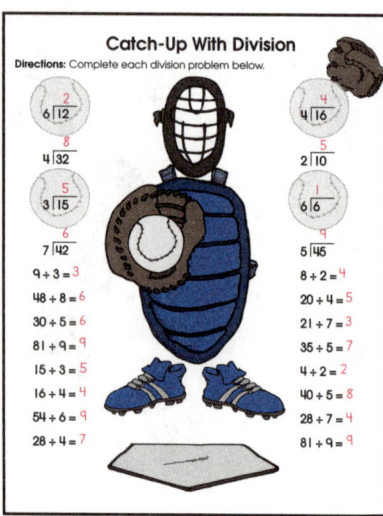

Page 40
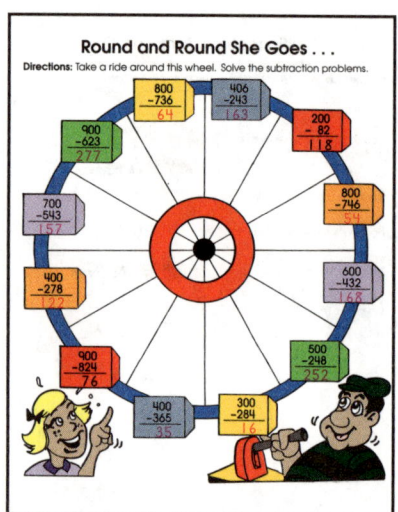

Page 41
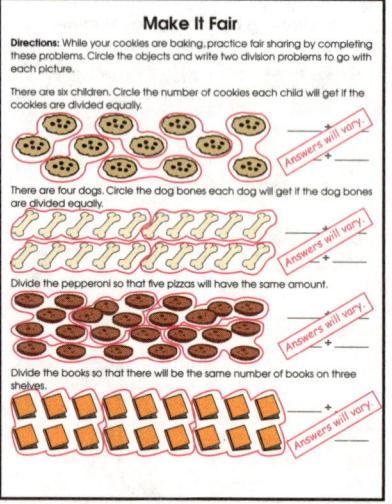

Page 42

Page 43
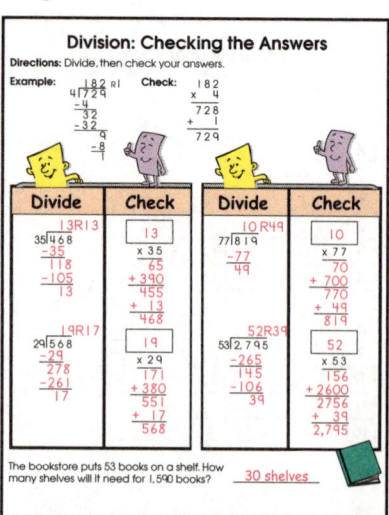

Summer Link Super Edition Grade 4

Page 44
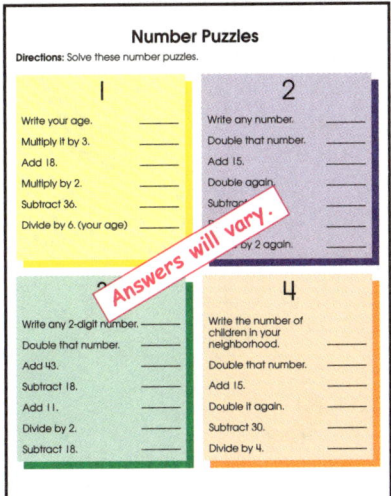

Page 45

Page 46

Page 47
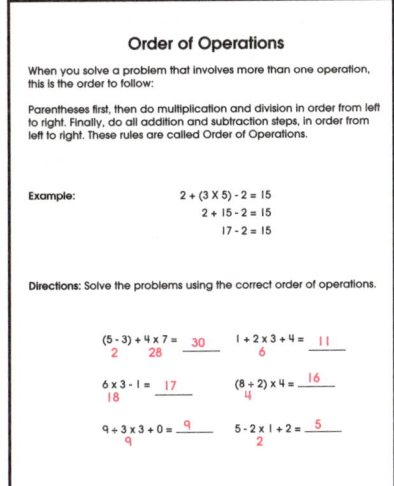

Page 48
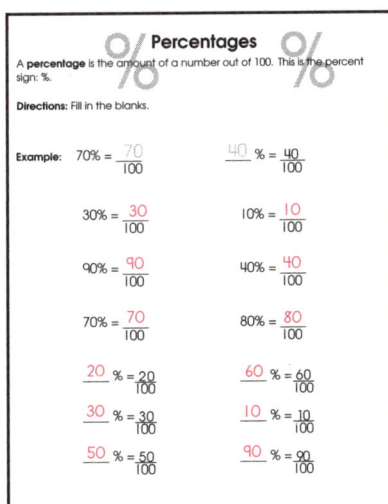

Page 49
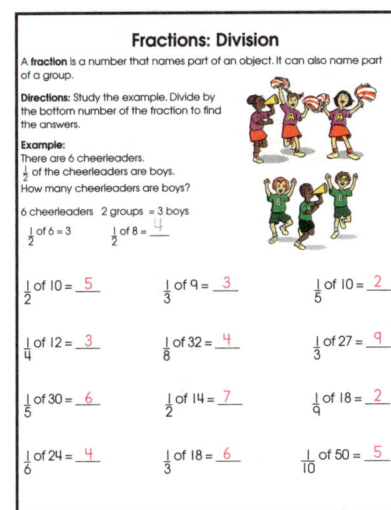

Page 50
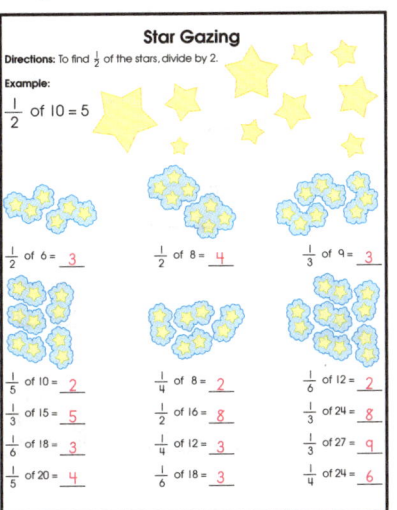

Page 51
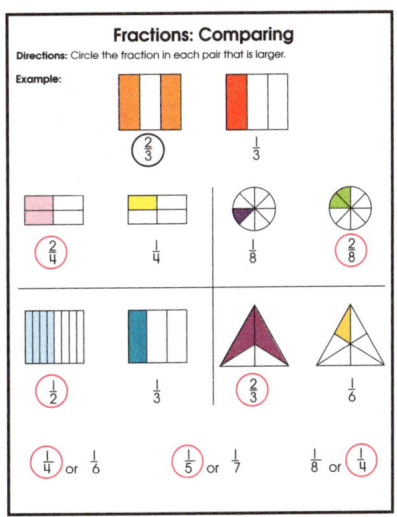

Page 52
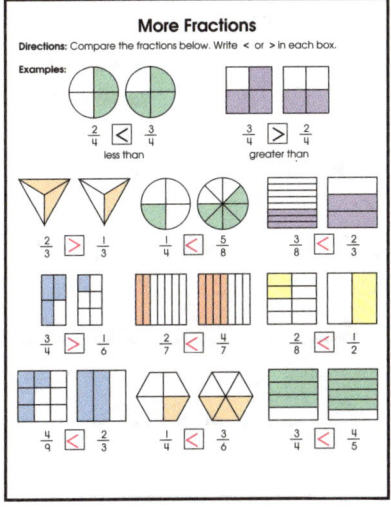

Page 53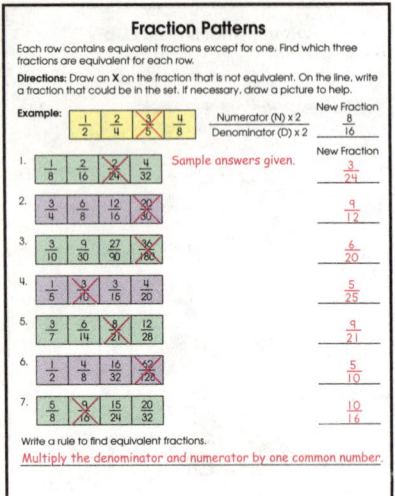

Page 54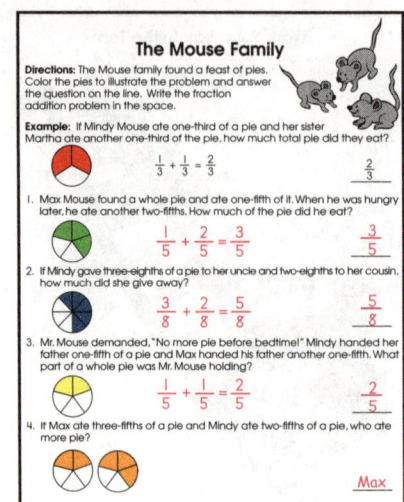

Page 55

Page 56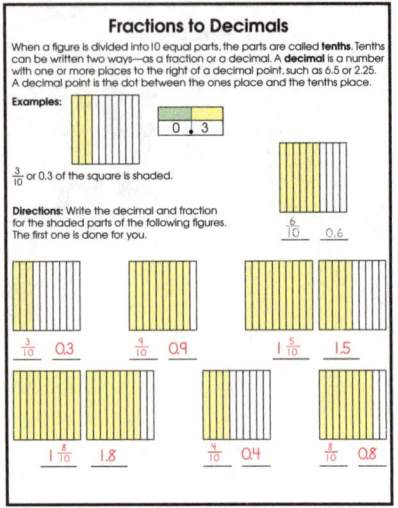

Page 57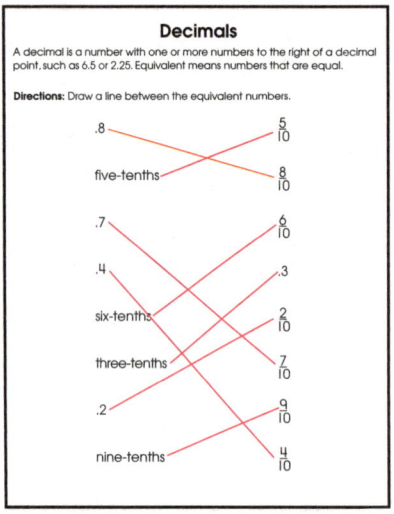

Page 58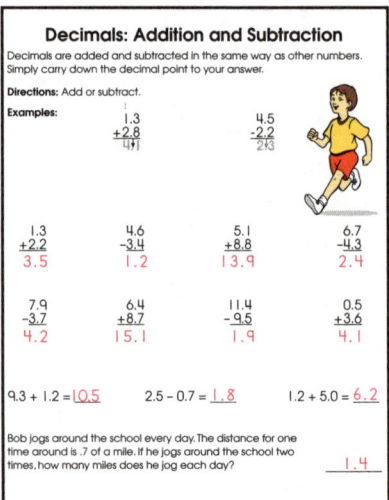

Page 59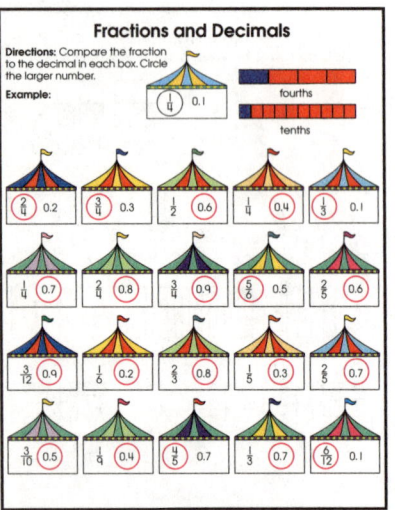

Page 60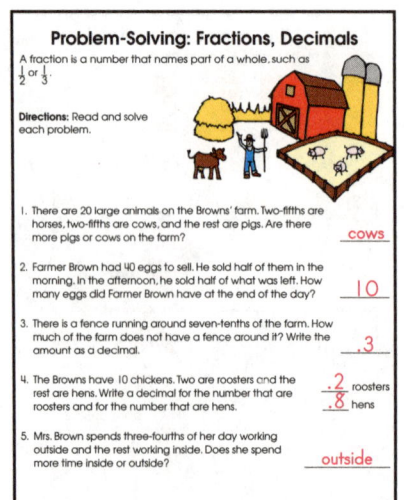

Page 61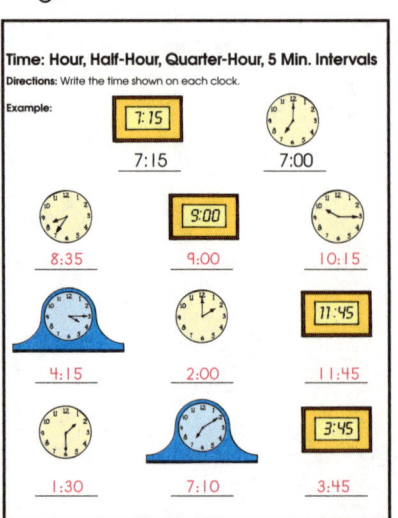

Page 62

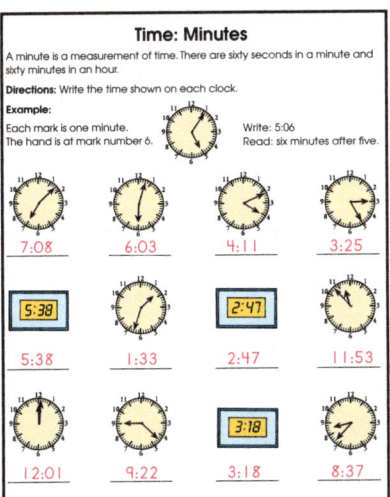

Page 63

Page 64

Page 65

Page 66

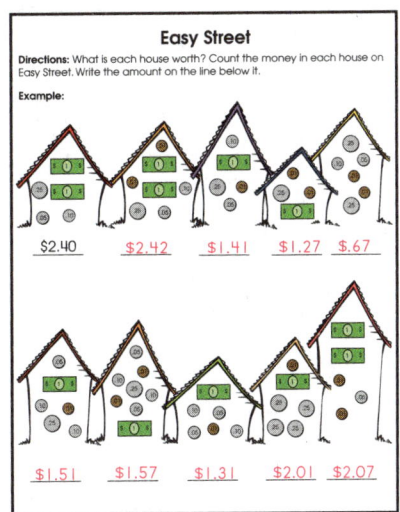

Page 67

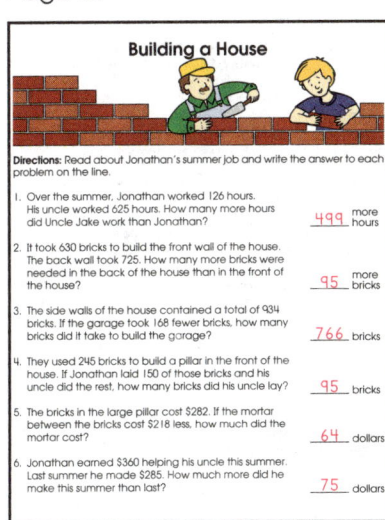

Page 68

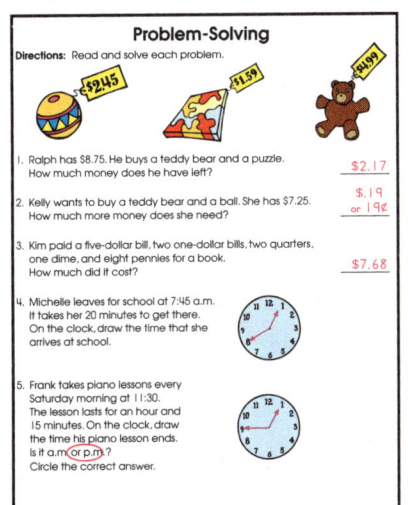

Page 69

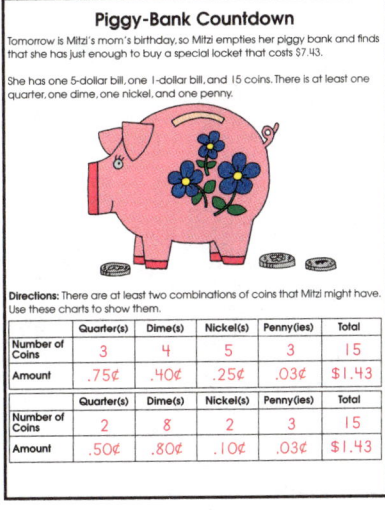

Page 70

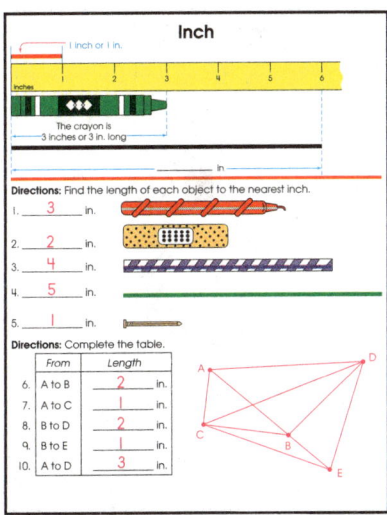

95

Summer Link Super Edition Grade 4

Page 71
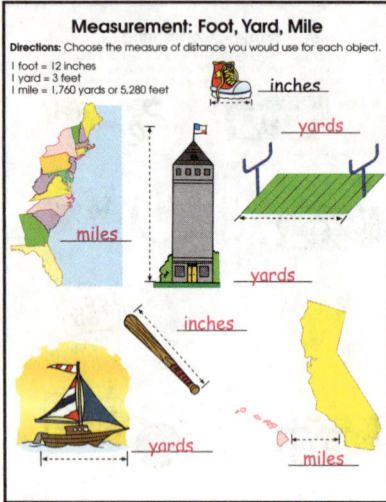

Page 72

Page 73
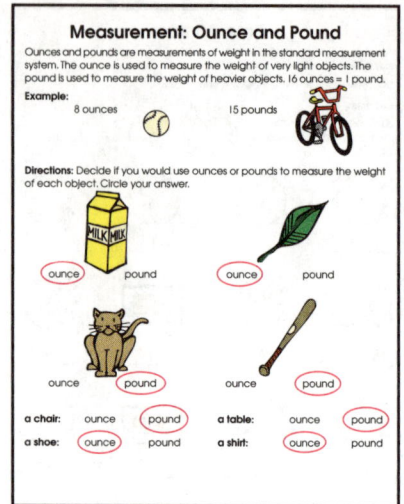

Page 74
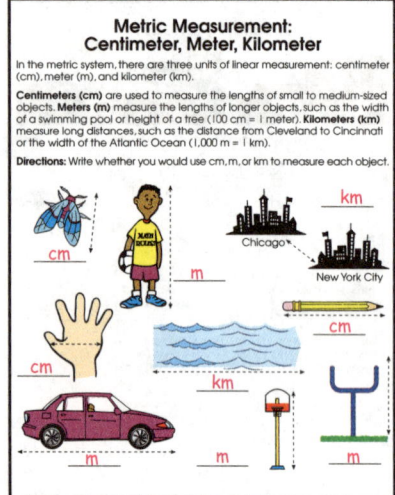

Page 75
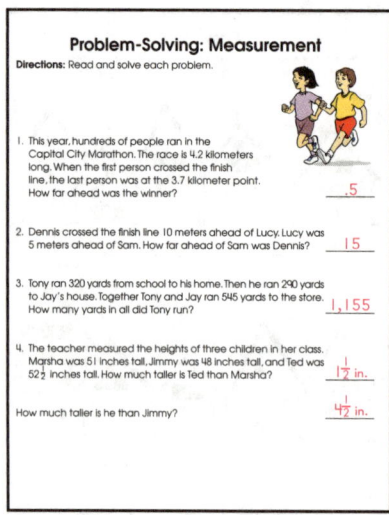

Page 76
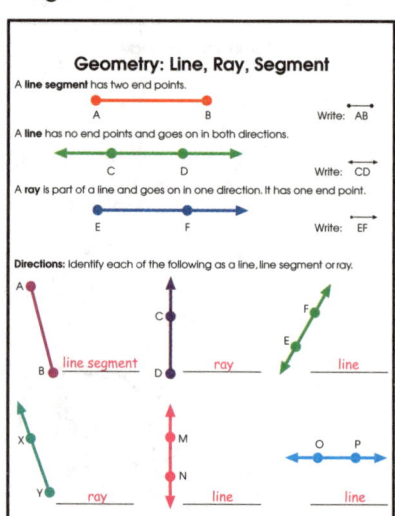

Page 77
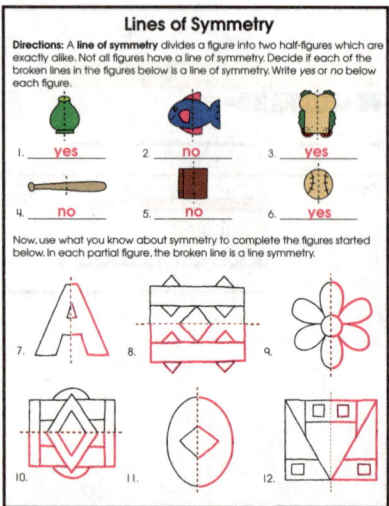

Page 78
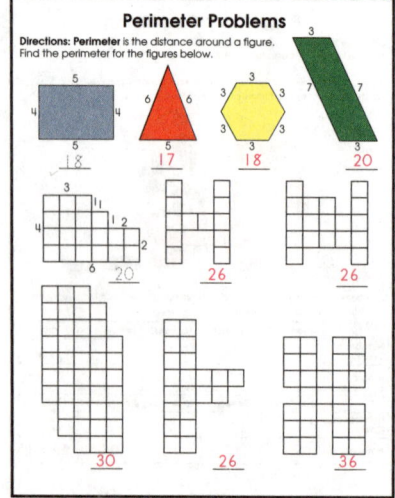

Page 79
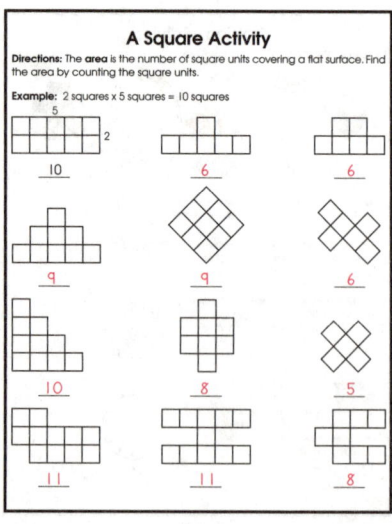

Page 80

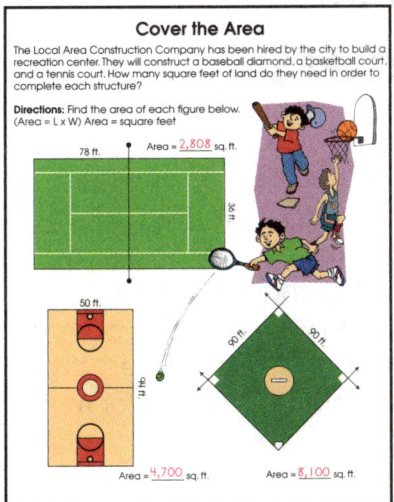

Page 81

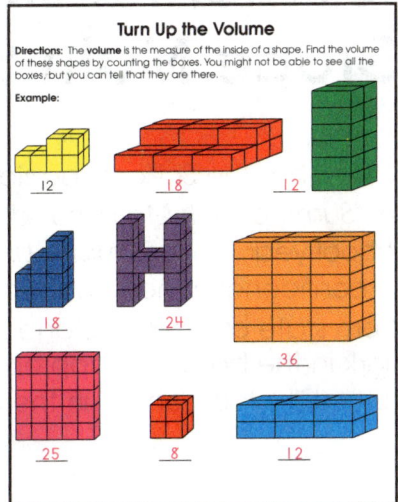

Page 82

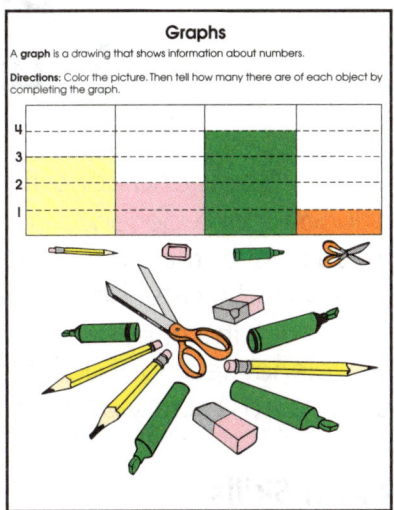

Page 83

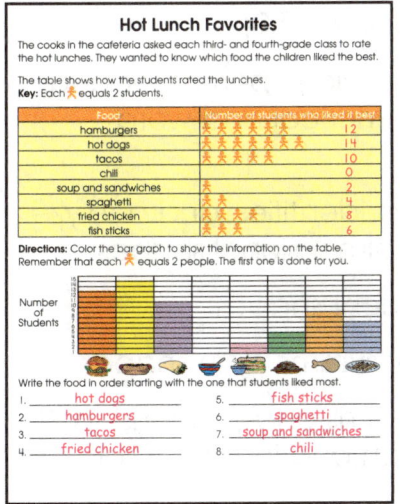

Page 84

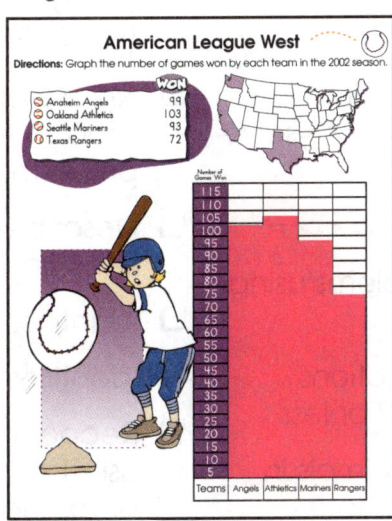

Page 85

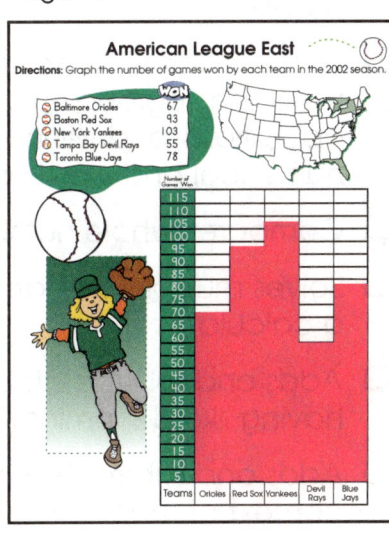

Page 86

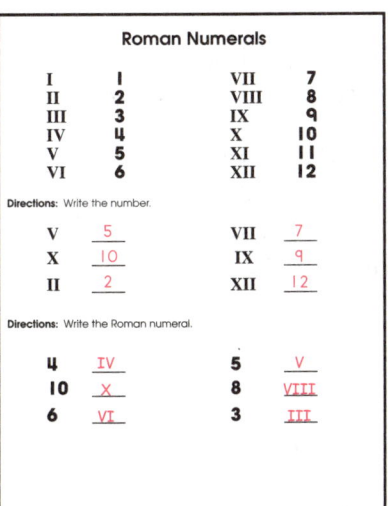

Page 87

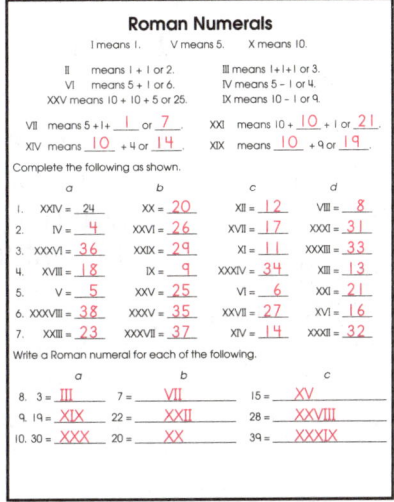

Developmental Skills for Fourth Grade Math Success

Parents and educators alike know that the School Specialty name ensures outstanding educational experience and content. *Summer Link Math* was designed to help your child retain those skills learned during the past school year. With *Summer Link Math*, your child will be ready to review and master new material with confidence when he or she returns to school in the fall.

Use this checklist—compiled from state curriculum standards—to help your child prepare for proficiency testing. Place a check mark in the box if the appropriate skill has been mastered. If your child needs more work with a particular skill, place an "R" in the box and come back to it for review.

Math Skills

- ❑ Understands place value through 999,999.
- ❑ Uses problem-solving strategies—such as rounding, regrouping, using multiple operations, and Venn diagrams—to solve numerical and word problems.
- ❑ Compares whole numbers using < > =.
- ❑ Solves multiple-operation problems using a calculator.
- ❑ Adds and subtracts proper fractions having like denominators of 12 or less.
- ❑ Adds and subtracts simple decimals in context of money with and without regrouping.
- ❑ Tells and writes time shown on traditional and digital clocks.
- ❑ Uses customary system to measure length, mass, volume, and temperature.
- ❑ Uses metric system to measure length, mass, volume, and temperature.
- ❑ Selects the appropriate operational and relational symbols to make an expression true ($4 \times 3 = 12$).
- ❑ Recognizes and uses commutative and associative properties of multiplication ($5 \times 7 = 35$...What is 7×5?).
- ❑ Measures length, width, perimeter, and area to solve numerical and word problems.
- ❑ Describes, draws, identifies, and analyzes two- and three-dimensional shapes.
- ❑ Identifies congruent shapes.
- ❑ Identifies lines of symmetry in shapes.
- ❑ Recognizes patterns and relationships using a bar graph and locating points on a grid.
- ❑ Analyzes and solves simple probability problems.
- ❑ Adds and subtracts with two and three digits, regrouping when necessary.
- ❑ Multiplies two-digit numbers with regrouping, and divides one and two-digit numbers by divisors of 6 – 10, with and without remainders.

READING

Recommended Reading
Summer Before Grade 4

- Art and Civilization Series: Ancient Rome; Medieval Times; Prehistory — McGraw-Hill Children's Publishing
- The Bad Beginning — Lemony Snicket
- Because of Winn-Dixi — Kate Dicamillo
- Cam Jansen and the Mystery of the Television Dog — David Adler
- The Castle in the Attic — Elizabeth Winthrop
- Charlie and the Chocolate Factory; Roald Dahl's Revolting Rhymes — Roald Dahl
- Charlotte's Web; Stuart Little — E.B. White
- Crispen: The Cross of Lead — Avi
- Eleanor, Ellatony, Ellencake, and Me — C.M. Rubin
- Encyclopedia Brown Takes the Cake — Donald J. Sobol
- Esperanza Rising — Pam Munoz Ryan
- Gray Feather and the Big Dog — Cesar Vidal
- How to Eat Fried Worms — Thomas Rockwell
- The Incredible Journey to the Mummy's Tomb — Nicholas Harris
- Insectlopedia: Poems and Paintings — Douglas Florian
- It's Raining Pigs and Noodles — Jack Prelutsky
- Lunch Box Mail and Other Poems — Jenny Whitehead
- Magic School Bus: Inside a Hurricane — Joanna Cole
- Meet Kaya — Janet Shaw
- The Mouse and the Motorcycle — Beverly Cleary
- Myth Series: Egyptian; Greek; Roman; Celtic — McGraw-Hill Children's Publishing
- My America: A Poetry Atlas of the U.S. — Lee Bennett Hopkins
- On the Far Side of the Mountain — Jean Craighead George
- Raiders and Traders; Emperors and Gladiators; Athletes and Actors — Anita Ganeri
- Ramona's World; Ramona and Her Father — Judy Blume
- The Rough Face Girl — Rafe Martin
- Sarah Plain and Tall — Patricia MacLachlan
- Sideways Stories from Wayside School — Louis Sachar
- So You Want to be President? — Judith St. George
- The Stinky Cheeseman and Other Fairly Stupid Tales — Jon Scieszka
- Tales of a Fourth Grade Nothing — Judy Blume
- Valdores — Patricia Peterson

Summer Link Super Edition Grade 4

Name _____

Capital Letters and Periods

The first letter of a person's first, last, and middle name is always capitalized.

Example: **E**lizabeth **J**ane **M**arks is my best friend.

The first letter of a person's title is always capitalized. If the title is abbreviated, the title is followed by a period.

Examples: Her mother is **Dr**. Susan Jones Marks.
               Ms. Jessica Joseph was a visitor.

Directions: Write **C** if the sentence is punctuated and capitalized correctly. Draw an **X** if the sentence is not punctuated and capitalized correctly. The first one has been done for you.

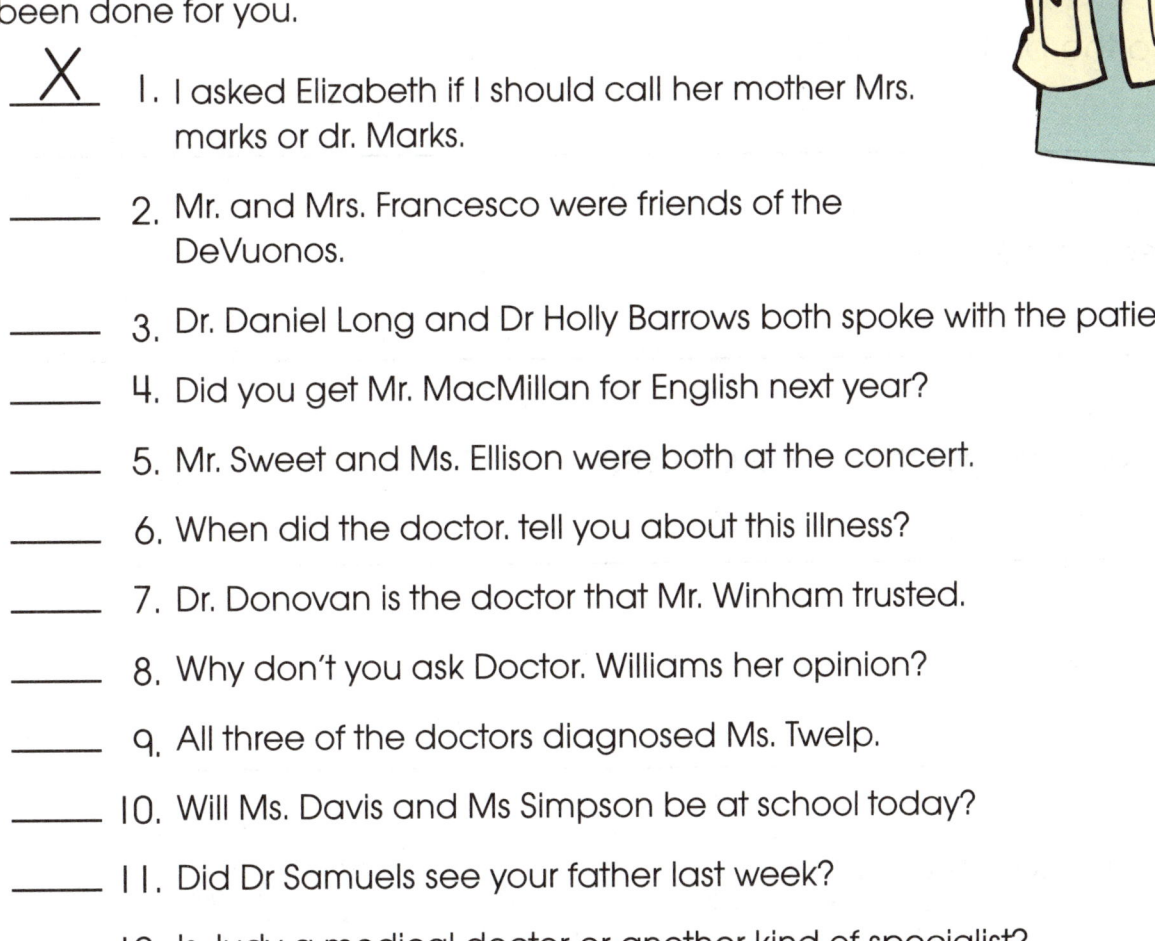

__X__ 1. I asked Elizabeth if I should call her mother Mrs. marks or dr. Marks.

_____ 2. Mr. and Mrs. Francesco were friends of the DeVuonos.

_____ 3. Dr. Daniel Long and Dr Holly Barrows both spoke with the patient.

_____ 4. Did you get Mr. MacMillan for English next year?

_____ 5. Mr. Sweet and Ms. Ellison were both at the concert.

_____ 6. When did the doctor. tell you about this illness?

_____ 7. Dr. Donovan is the doctor that Mr. Winham trusted.

_____ 8. Why don't you ask Doctor. Williams her opinion?

_____ 9. All three of the doctors diagnosed Ms. Twelp.

_____ 10. Will Ms. Davis and Ms Simpson be at school today?

_____ 11. Did Dr Samuels see your father last week?

_____ 12. Is Judy a medical doctor or another kind of specialist?

_____ 13. We are pleased to introduce Ms King and Mr. Graham.

Quotation Marks

Directions: Put quotation marks around the correct words in the sentences below.

1. Can we go for a bike ride? asked Katrina.

2. Yes, said Mom.

3. Let's go to the park, said Mike.

4. Great idea! said Mom.

5. How long until we get there? asked Katrina.

6. Soon, said Mike.

7. Here we are! exclaimed Mom.

Articles

Articles are words used before nouns. **A**, **an**, and **the** are articles. We use **a** before words that begin with a consonant. We use **an** before words that begin with a vowel.

Example: a peach  an apple

Directions: Write a or an in the sentences below.

Example: My bike had ___a___ flat tire.

1. They brought _____ goat to the farm.

2. My mom wears _____ old pair of shoes to mow the lawn.

3. We had _____ party for my grandfather.

4. Everybody had _____ ice-cream cone after the game.

5. We bought _____ picnic table for our backyard.

6. We saw _____ lion sleeping in the shade.

7. It was _____ evening to be remembered.

8. He brought _____ blanket to the game.

9. _____ exit sign was above the door.

10. They went to _____ orchard to pick apples.

11. He ate _____ orange for lunch.

Name _____

Articles and Commas

Directions: Write **a** or **an** in each blank. Put commas where they are needed in the paragraphs below.

Owls

_____ owl is _____ bird of prey. This means it hunts small animals. Owls catch insects fish and birds. Mice are _____ owl's favorite dinner. Owls like protected places, such as trees burrows or barns. Owls make noises that sound like hoots screeches or even barks. _____ owl's feathers may be black brown gray or white.

  ## A Zoo for You

_____ zoo is _____ excellent place for keeping animals. Zoos have mammals birds reptiles and amphibians. Some zoos have domestic animals, such as rabbits sheep and goats. Another name for this type of zoo is _____ petting zoo. In some zoos, elephants lions and tigers live in open country. This is because _____ enormous animal needs open space for roaming.

Name _____

Homophones

Homophones are words that sound the same but have different spellings and meanings.

Directions: Complete each sentence using a word from the box.

| blew | night | blue | knight | hour | in | ant | inn |
| our | aunt | meet | too | two | to | meat |

1. A red _____ crawled up the wall.
2. It will be one _____ before we can go back home.
3. Will you _____ us later?
4. We plan to stay at an _____ during our trip.
5. The king had a _____ who fought bravely.
6. The wind _____ so hard that I almost lost my hat.
7. His jacket was _____.
8. My _____ plans to visit us this week.
9. I will come _____ when it gets too cold outside.
10. It was late at _____ when we finally got there.
11. _____ of us will go with you.
12. I will mail a note _____ someone at the bank.
13. Do you eat red _____?
14. We would like to join you, _____.
15. Come over to see _____ new cat.

Homophones

Directions: Circle the words that are not used correctly. Write the correct word above the circled word. Use the words in the box to help you. The first one has been done for you.

| road | see | one | be | so | I | brakes | piece | there |
| wait | not | some | hour | would | no | deer | you | heard |

Jake and his family were getting close to Grandpa's. It had taken them nearly an (our) to get their, but Jake knew it was worth it. In his mind, he could already sea the pond and could almost feel the cool water. It had been sew hot this summer in the apartment.

"Wood ewe like a peace of my apple, Jake?" asked his big sister Clare. "Eye can't eat any more."

"Know, thank you," Jake replied. "I still have sum of my fruit left."

Suddenly, Dad slammed on the breaks. "Did you see that dear on the rode? I always herd that if you see won, there might bee more."

"Good thinking, Dad. I'm glad you are a safe driver. We're knot very far from Grandpa's now. I can't weight!"

Homophones

Directions: Use the homophones in the box to answer the riddles below.

| main | meat | peace | dear | to |
| mane | meet | piece | deer | too |

1. Which word has the word pie in it? _____

2. Which word rhymes with ear and is an animal? _____

3. Which word rhymes with shoe and means also? _____

4. Which word has the word eat in it and is something you might eat? _____

5. Which word has the same letters as the word read but in a different order? _____

6. Which word rhymes with train and is something on a pony? _____

7. Which word, if it began with a capital letter, might be the name of an important street? _____

8. Which word sounds like a number but has only two letters? _____

9. Which word rhymes with and is a synonym for greet? _____

10. Which word rhymes with the last syllable in police and can mean quiet? _____

Name _____

Homophones

Directions: Write a word from the box to complete each sentence.

main	meat	peace	dear	two
mane	meet	piece	deer	too

1. The horse had a long, beautiful _____ .

   The _____ idea of the paragraph was boats.

2. Let's _____ at my house to do our homework.

   The lion was fed _____ at mealtime.

3. We had _____ kittens.

   Mike has a red bike. Tom does, _____ .

4. The _____ ran in front of the car.

   I begin my letters with " _____ Mom."

Summer Link Super Edition Grade 4

Proofreading

Directions: Read more about Key West. Proofread and correct the errors. There are eight errors in capitalization, seven misspelled words, and three missing words.

More About Key West

a good way to lern more about key West is to ride the trolley. Key West has a great troley system. The trolley will take on a tour of the salt ponds. You can also three red brick forts. The troley tour goes by a 110-foot high lighthouse. It is rite in the middle of the city. Key west is the only city with a Lighthouse in the midle of it! It is also the southernmost city in the United States.

If you have time, the new Ship Wreck Museum. Key west was also the hom of former president Harry truman. During his presidency, Trueman spent many vacations on key west.

Name _____

Nouns

Nouns are words that tell the names of people, places or things.

Directions: Read the words below. Then write them in the correct column.

goat	Mrs. Jackson	girl
beach	tree	song
mouth	park	Jean Rivers
finger	flower	New York
Kevin Jones	Elm City	Frank Gates
Main Street	theater	skates
River Park	father	boy

Person   Place   Thing

_____   _____   _____
_____   _____   _____
_____   _____   _____
_____   _____   _____
_____   _____   _____
_____   _____   _____
_____   _____   _____

Common Nouns

Common nouns are nouns that name any member of a group of people, places, or things, rather than specific people, places, or things.

Directions: Read the sentences below and write the common noun found in each sentence.

Example: ___socks___ My socks do not match.

1. _____ The bird could not fly.
2. _____ Ben likes to eat jelly beans.
3. _____ I am going to meet my mother.
4. _____ We will go swimming in the lake tomorrow.
5. _____ I hope the flowers will grow quickly.
6. _____ We colored eggs together.
7. _____ It is easy to ride a bicycle.
8. _____ My cousin is very tall.
9. _____ Ted and Jane went fishing in their boat.
10. _____ They won a prize yesterday.
11. _____ She fell down and twisted her ankle.
12. _____ My brother was born today.
13. _____ She went down the slide.
14. _____ Ray went to the doctor today.

Name _____

Possessive Nouns

Possessive nouns tell who or what is the owner of something. With singular nouns, we use an apostrophe **before** the **s**. With plural nouns, we use an apostrophe **after** the **s**.

Example:
singular: one elephant
The **elephant's** dance was wonderful.

plural: more than one elephant
The **elephants'** dance was wonderful.

Directions: Put the apostrophe in the correct place in each bold word. Then write the word in the blank.

1. The **lions** cage was big. _____

2. The **bears** costumes were purple. _____

3. One **boys** laughter was very loud. _____

4. The **trainers** dogs were dancing about. _____

5. The **mans** popcorn was tasty and good. _____

6. **Marks** cotton candy was delicious. _____

7. A little **girls** balloon burst in the air. _____

8. The big **clowns** tricks were very funny. _____

9. **Lauras** sister clapped for the clowns. _____

10. The **womans** money was lost in the crowd. _____

11. **Kellys** mother picked her up early. _____

Summer Link Super Edition Grade 4

Plural Nouns

Directions: The **singular form** of a word shows one person, place, or thing. Write the singular form of each noun on the lines below.

cherries _____

lunches _____

countries _____

leaves _____

churches _____

arms _____

boxes _____

men _____

wheels _____

pictures _____

cities _____

places _____

ostriches _____

glasses _____

Name _____

Proper Nouns

Proper nouns are names of specific people, places, or things. Proper nouns begin with a capital letter.

Directions: Read the sentences below and circle the proper nouns found in each sentence.

Example: (Aunt Frances) gave me a puppy for my birthday.

1. We lived on Jackson Street before we moved to our new house.

2. Angela's birthday party is tomorrow night.

3. We drove through Cheyenne, Wyoming on our way home.

4. Dr. Charles always gives me a treat for not crying.

5. George Washington was our first president.

6. Our class took a field trip to the Johnson Flower Farm.

7. Uncle Jack lives in New York City.

8. Amy and Elizabeth are best friends.

9. We buy doughnuts at the Grayson Bakery.

10. My favorite movie is *E.T.*

11. We flew to Miami, Florida in a plane.

12. We go to Riverfront Stadium to watch the baseball games.

13. Mr. Fields is a wonderful music teacher.

14. My best friend is Tom Dunlap.

Proper Nouns

Directions: Rewrite each sentence, capitalizing the proper nouns.

1. mike's birthday is in september.

2. aunt katie lives in detroit, michigan.

3. In july, we went to canada.

4. kathy jones moved to utah in january.

5. My favorite holiday is valentine's day in february.

6. On friday, mr. polzin gave the smith family a tour.

7. saturday, uncle cliff and I will go to the mall of america in minnesota.

Name _____

Adjectives

Directions: Look at each picture. Then add adjectives to the sentences. Use colors, numbers, words from the box, and any other words you need to describe each picture.

Example:

The boy shared his pencil.

| polite neat careless |
| shy   selfish |

The polite boy shared his red pencil.

The girl dropped her _____

_____

The boy played with _____

_____

The boy put books _____

_____

Summer Link Super Edition Grade 4

Verbs

Directions: Write the verb that answers each question. Write a sentence using that verb.

| stir   clap   drag   hug   plan |

Which verb means to put your arms around someone?

_____

_____

Which verb means to mix something with a spoon?

_____

_____

Which verb means to pull something along the ground?

_____

_____

Which verb means to take something suddenly?

_____

_____

Present-Tense Verbs

When something is happening right now, it is in the **present tense**. There are two ways to write verbs in the present tense:

Examples: The dog **walks**.   The cats **play**.
The dog **is walking**.   The cats **are playing**.

Directions: Write each sentence again, writing the verb a different way.

Example:

He lists the numbers.

He is listing the numbers.

1. She is pounding the nail.

_____

2. My brother toasts the bread.

_____

3. They search for the robber.

_____

4. The teacher lists the pages.

_____

5. They are spilling the water.

_____

6. Ken and Amy load the packages.

_____

Name _____

Present-Tense Verbs

Directions: Write two sentences for each verb below. Tell about something that is happening now and write the verb as both simple present tense and present tense with a helping verb.

Example: run
Mia runs to the store.   Mia is running to the store.

1. hatch

2. check

3. spell

4. blend

5. lick

6. cry

7. write

8. dream

Name _____

Present-Tense Verbs

Present tense verbs can be written two ways: The bird sing**s**. The bird is sing**ing**.

Directions: Write each sentence again, using the verb **is** and writing the **ing** form of the verb.

Example: He cooks the cheeseburgers.

<u>　He is cooking the cheeseburgers.　</u>

1. Sharon dances to that song.

_____

2. Frank washed the car.

_____

3. Mr. Benson smiles at me.

_____

Write a verb for the sentences below that tells something that is happening now. Be sure to use the verb **is** and the **ing** form of the verb.

Example: The big, brown dog <u>　is barking　</u>.

1. The little baby _____.

2. Most nine-year-olds _____.

3. The monster on television _____.

Summer Link Super Edition Grade 4

Past-Tense Verbs

When you write about something that already happened, you add **ed** to most verbs. Here is another way to write about something in the past tense.

Examples: The dog walked.   The dog was walking.
　　　　　　　The cats played.   The cats were playing.

Directions: Write each sentence again, writing the verb a different way.

Example: The baby pounded the pans.

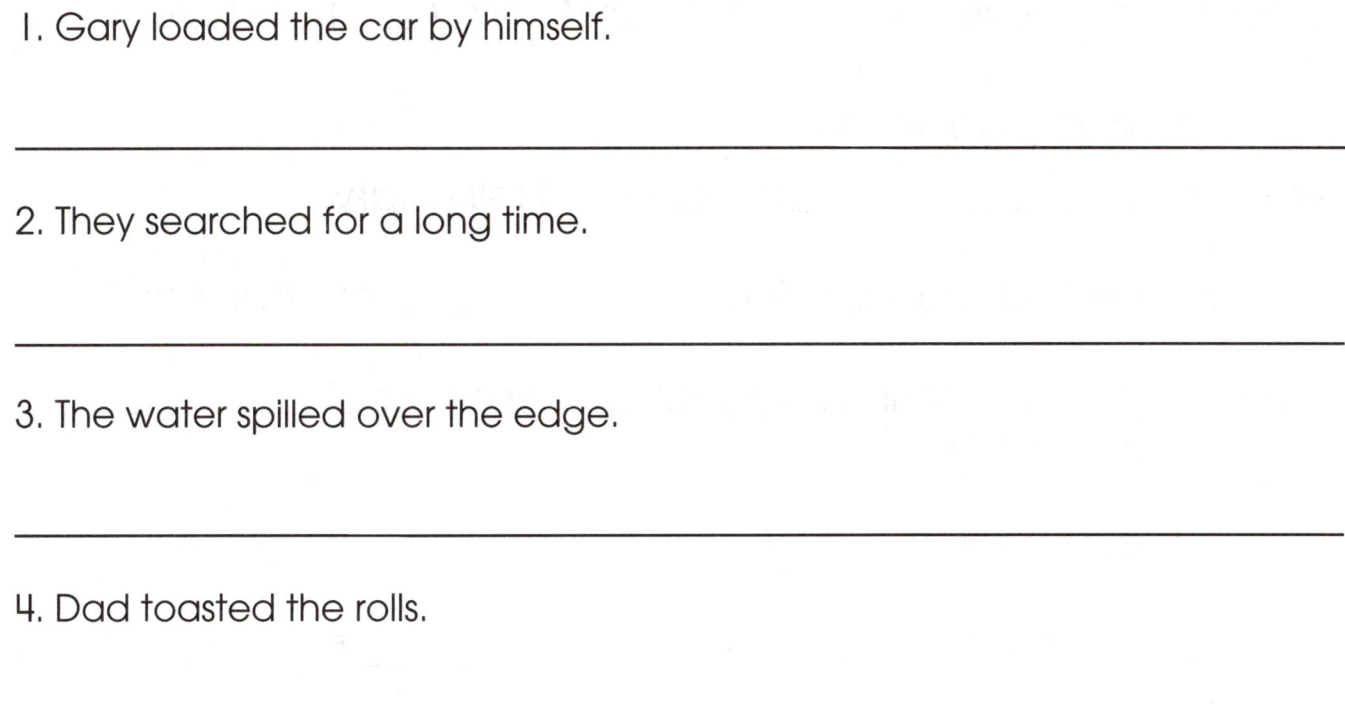

The baby was pounding the pans.

1. Gary loaded the car by himself.

_____

2. They searched for a long time.

_____

3. The water spilled over the edge.

_____

4. Dad toasted the rolls.

_____

Name _____

Past-Tense Verbs

For some verbs that have a short vowel and end in one consonant, you double the consonant before adding **ed**.

Examples:

He hug**ged** his pillow.   The dog grab**bed** the stick.
She stir**red** the carrots.   We plan**ned** to go tomorrow.
They clap**ped** for me.   They drag**ged** their bags on the ground.

Directions: Use the verb from the first sentence to complete the second sentence. Change the verb in the second part to the past tense. Double the consonant and add **ed**.

Example:

We skip to school. Yesterday, we ____**skipped**____ the whole way.

1. It's not nice to grab things.

   When you _____ my cookie, I felt angry.

2. Did anyone hug you today? Dad _____ me this morning.

3. We plan our vacations every year. Last year, we _____ to go to the beach.

4. Is it my turn to stir the pot? You _____ it last time.

5. Let's clap for Andy, just like we _____ for Amy.

6. My sister used to drag her blanket everywhere.

   Once, she _____ it to the store.

Past-Tense Verbs

To tell about something that already happened, add **ed** to most verbs. If the verb already ends in **e**, just add **d**.

Examples:

We enter**ed** the contest last week.
I fold**ed** the paper wrong.
He add**ed** two boxes to the pile.

We tast**ed** the cupcakes.
They decid**ed** quickly.
She shar**ed** her cupcake.

Directions: Use the verb from the first sentence to complete the second sentence. Add **d** or **ed** to show that something already happened.

Example:
My mom looks fine today. Yesterday, she ___looked___ tired.

1. You enter through the middle door.

   We _____ that way last week.

2. Please add this for me. I already _____ it twice.

3. Will you share your cookie with me?

   I _____ my apple with you yesterday.

4. It's your turn to fold the clothes. I _____ them yesterday.

5. May I taste another one? I already _____ one.

6. You need to decide. We _____ this morning.

Name _____

Past-Tense Verbs

Directions: Write sentences that tell about each picture using the words **is**, **are**, **was**, and **were**. Use words from the box as either nouns or verbs.

| pound | spill | toast | list | load | search |

Past-Tense Verbs

Directions: Use the verb from the first sentence to complete the second sentence.

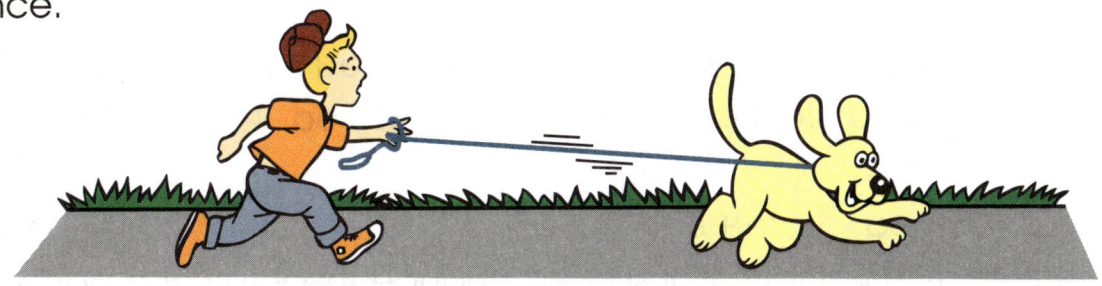

Please walk the dog.　　　　I already walked her.

1. The flowers look good.　　　They _____ better yesterday.

2. Please accept my gift.　　　I _____ it for my sister.

3. I wonder who will win.　　　I _____ about it all night.

4. He will saw the wood.　　　He _____ some last week.

5. Fold the paper neatly.　　　She _____ her paper.

6. Let's cook outside tonight.　　We _____ outside last night.

7. Do not block the way.　　　They _____ the entire street.

8. Form the clay this way.　　　He _____ it into a ball.

9. Follow my car.　　　　　　We _____ them down the street.

10. Glue the pages like this.　　She _____ the flowers on.

Adding "ed" to Make Verbs Past Tense

To make many verbs past tense, add **ed**.
Examples:
   cook + ed = cooked   wish + ed = wished   play + ed = played

When a verb ends in a **silent e**, drop the **e** and add **ed**.
Examples:
   hope + ed = hoped   hate + ed = hated

When a verb ends in **y** after a consonant, change the **y** to **i** and add **ed**.
Examples:
   hurry + ed = hurried   marry + ed = married

When a verb ends in a single consonant after a single short vowel, double the final consonant before adding **ed**.
Examples:
   stop + ed = stopped   hop + ed = hopped

Directions: Write the past tense of the verb correctly. The first one has been done for you.

1. call _____
2. copy _____
3. frown _____
4. smile _____
5. live _____
6. talk _____
7. name _____
8. list _____
9. spy _____
10. phone _____

11. reply _____
12. top _____
13. clean _____
14. scream _____
15. clap _____
16. mop _____
17. soap _____
18. choke _____
19. scurry _____
20. drop _____

Name _____

Future-Tense Verbs

The **future tense** of a verb tells about something that has not happened yet but will happen in the future. Will or shall are usually used with future tense.

Directions: Change the verb tense in each sentence to future tense.

Example:

She cooks dinner.

She will cook dinner.

1. He plays baseball.

   _____

2. She walks to school.

   _____

3. Bobby talks to the teacher.

   _____

4. I remember to vote.

   _____

5. Jack mows the lawn every week.

   _____

6. We go on vacation soon.

   _____

Helping Verbs

A **helping verb** is a word used with an action verb.

Examples: **might**, **shall**, and **are**

Directions: Write a helping verb from the box with each action verb.

can	could	must	might
may	would	should	will
shall	did	does	do
had	have	has	am
are	were	is	
be	being	been	

Example:

Tomorrow, I ___might___ play soccer.

1. Mom _____ buy my new soccer shoes tonight.

2. Yesterday, my old soccer shoes _____ ripped by the cat.

3. I _____ going to ask my brother to go to the game.

4. He usually _____ not like soccer.

5. But, he _____ go with me because I am his sister.

6. He _____ promised to watch the entire soccer game.

7. He has _____ helping me with my homework.

8. I _____ spell a lot better because of his help.

9. Maybe I _____ finish the semester at the top of my class.

Summer Link Super Edition Grade 4

Irregular Verbs

Irregular verbs are verbs that do not change from the present tense to the past tense in the regular way with **d** or **ed**.

Example: sing, **sang**

Directions: Read the sentence and underline the verbs. Choose the past-tense form from the box and write it next to the sentence.

blow — blew	fly — flew
come — came	give — gave
take — took	wear — wore
make — made	sing — sang
grow — grew	

Example:
Dad will <u>make</u> a cake tonight.   ___made___

1. I will probably <u>grow</u> another inch this year.   _____

2. I will <u>blow</u> out the candles.   _____

3. Everyone will <u>give</u> me presents.   _____

4. I will <u>wear</u> my favorite red shirt.   _____

5. My cousins will <u>come</u> from out of town.   _____

6. It will <u>take</u> them four hours.   _____

7. My Aunt Betty will <u>fly</u> in from Cleveland.   _____

8. She will <u>sing</u> me a song when she gets here.   _____

Using ing Verbs

Remember, use **is** and **are** when describing something happening right now. Use **was** and **were** when describing something that already happened.

Directions: Use the verb in bold to complete each sentence. Add **ing** to the verb and use **is**, **are**, **was**, or **were**.

Examples:

When it started to rain, we <u>were raking</u> the leaves.
rake

When the soldiers marched up that hill, Captain Stevens <u>was commanding</u> them.
command

1. Now, the police _____ them of stealing the money.
   accuse

2. Look! The eggs _____ .
   hatch

3. A minute ago, the sky _____ .
   glow

4. My dad says he _____ us to ice cream!
   treat

5. She _____ the whole time we were at the mall.
   sneeze

6. While we were playing outside at recess, he _____ our tests.
   grade

7. I hear something. Who _____ ?
   groan

8. As I watched, the workers _____ the wood into little chips.
   grind

Summer Link Super Edition Grade 4

Name _____

Verb Tense

Directions: Read the following sentences. Underline the verbs. Above each verb, write whether it is past, present, or future tense.

1. The crowd <u>was booing</u> the referee. *(past)*

2. Sally will compete on the balance beam.

3. Matt marches with the band.

4. Nick is marching, too.

5. The geese swooped down to the pond.

6. Dad will fly home tomorrow.

7. They were looking for a new book.

8. Presently, they are going to the garden.

9. The children will pick the ripe vegetables.

10. Grandmother canned the green beans.

Directions: Write six sentences of your own using the correct verb tense.

Past tense:
_____
_____

Present tense:
_____
_____

Future tense:
_____
_____

Verb Tense

Verb tenses can be in the past, present, or future.

Directions: Match each sentence with the correct verb tense. (**Think:** When did each thing happen?)

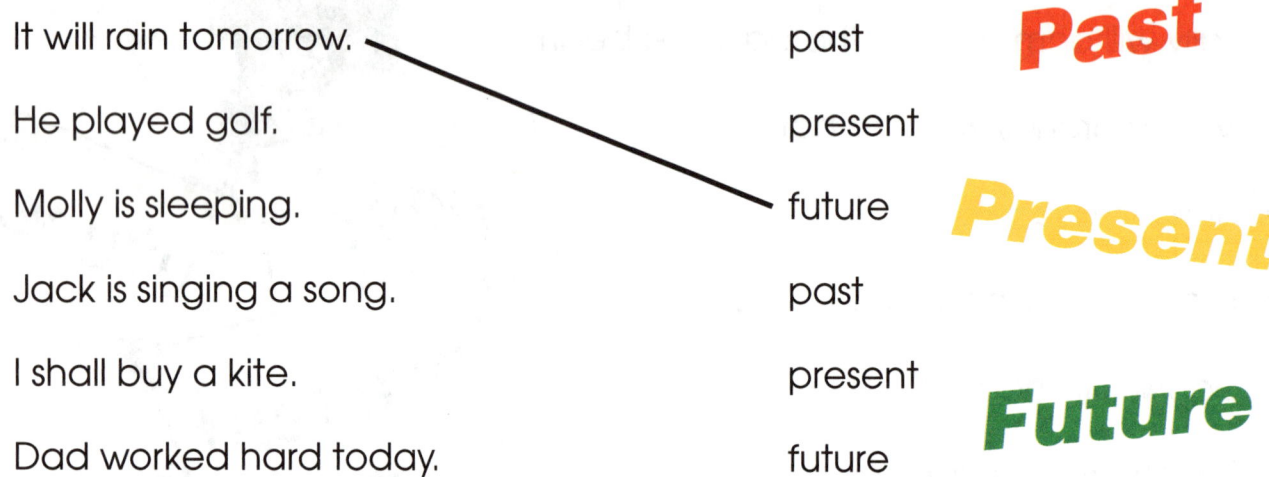

It will rain tomorrow. — past
He played golf. — present
Molly is sleeping. — future
Jack is singing a song. — past
I shall buy a kite. — present
Dad worked hard today. — future

Directions: Change the verb to the tense shown.

1. Jenny played with her new friend. (present)

_____

2. Bobby is talking to him. (future)

_____

3. Holly and Angie walk here. (past)

_____

Simple Predicates

A **simple predicate** is the main verb or verbs in the complete predicate.

Directions: Draw a line between the complete subject and the complete predicate. Circle the simple predicate.

Example: The ripe apples |(fell) to the ground.

1. The farmer scattered feed for the chickens.

2. The horses galloped wildly around the corral.

3. The baby chicks were staying warm by the light.

4. The tractor was baling hay.

5. The silo was full of grain.

6. The cows were being milked.

7. The milk truck drove up to the barn.

8. The rooster woke everyone up.

Name _____

Pronouns

We use the pronouns **I** and **we** when talking about the person or people doing the action.

Example: **I** can roller skate. **We** can roller skate.

We use **me** and **us** when talking about something that is happening to a person or people.

Example: They gave **me** the roller skates.
They gave **us** the roller skates.

Directions: Circle the correct pronoun and write it in the blank.

Example:

__We__ are going to the picnic together.   (We), Us

1. _____ am finished with my science project.   I, Me
2. Eric passed the football to _____ .   me, I
3. They ate dinner with _____ last night.   we, us
4. _____ like spinach better than ice cream.   I, Me
5. Mom came in the room to tell _____ good night.   me, I
6. _____ had a pizza party in our backyard.   Us, We
7. They told _____ the good news.   us, we
8. Tom and _____ went to the store.   me, I
9. She is taking _____ with her to the movies.   I, me
10. Katie and _____ are good friends.   I, me

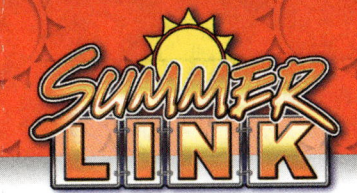

Adverbs

Adverbs are words that describe verbs. They tell where, how, or when.

Directions: Circle the adverb in each of the following sentences.

Example: The doctor worked (carefully).

1. The skater moved gracefully across the ice.

2. Their call was returned quickly.

3. We easily learned the new words.

4. He did the work perfectly.

5. She lost her purse somewhere.

Directions: Complete the sentences below by writing your own adverbs in the blanks.

Example: The bees worked _____busily_____.

1. The dog barked _____.

2. The baby smiled _____.

3. She wrote her name _____.

4. The horse ran _____.

Name _____

Prepositions

Prepositions show relationships between the noun or pronoun and another noun in the sentence. The preposition comes before that noun.

Example: The book is on the table.

Common Prepositions

above	behind	by	near	over
across	below	in	off	through
around	beside	inside	on	under

Directions: Circle the prepositions in each sentence.

1. The dog ran fast around the house.
2. The plates in the cupboard were clean.
3. Put the card inside the envelope.
4. The towel on the sink was wet.
5. I planted flowers in my garden.
6. My kite flew high above the trees.
7. The chair near the counter was sticky.
8. Under the ground, worms lived in their homes.
9. I put the bow around the box.
10. Beside the pond, there was a playground.

Summer Link Super Edition Grade 4

Subjects and Predicates

Directions: Write the words for the subject to answer the **who** or **what** questions. Write the words for the predicate to answer the **does, did, is,** or **has** questions.

Example:

My friend has two pairs of sunglasses.   **who?** My friend

has? has two pairs of sunglasses.

1. John's dog went to school with him.   **what?** _____

   did? _____

2. The Eskimo traveled by dog sled.   **who?** _____

   did? _____

3. Alex slept in his treehouse last night.   **who?** _____

   did? _____

4. Cherry pie is my favorite kind of pie.   **what?** _____

   is? _____

5. The mail carrier brings the mail to the door.   **who?** _____

   does? _____

6. We have more than enough bricks to build the wall.   **who?** _____

   has? _____

7. The bird has a worm in its beak.   **what?** _____

   has? _____

Compound Predicates

Directions: Underline the simple predicates (verbs) in each predicate.

Example: The fans <u>clapped</u> and <u>cheered</u> at the game.

1. The coach <u>talks</u> and <u>encourages</u> the team.

2. The cheerleaders <u>jump</u> and <u>yell</u>.

3. The basketball players <u>dribble</u> and <u>shoot</u> the ball.

4. The basketball <u>bounces</u> and <u>hits</u> the backboard.

5. The ball <u>rolls</u> around the rim and <u>goes</u> into the basket.

6. Everyone <u>leaps</u> up and <u>cheers</u>.

7. The team <u>scores</u> and <u>wins</u>!

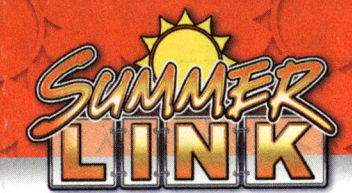

Compound Predicates

Compound predicates have two or more verbs that have the same subject.

Directions: Combine the predicates to create one sentence with a compound predicate.

Example: We went to the zoo.
We watched the monkeys.
We went to the zoo and watched the monkeys.

1. Students read their books. Students do their work.

_____

2. Dogs can bark loudly. Dogs can do tricks.

_____

3. The football player caught the ball. The football player ran.

_____

4. My dad sawed wood. My dad stacked wood.

_____

5. My teddy bear is soft. My teddy bear likes to be hugged.

_____

Name _____

Subjects and Predicates

Directions: Every sentence has two main parts—the subject and the predicate. Draw one line under the subject and two lines under the predicate in each sentence below.

Example:

<u>Porcupines</u> <u><u>are related to mice and rats.</u></u>

1. They are large rodents.

2. Porcupines have long, sharp quills.

3. The quills stand up straight when it is angry.

4. Most animals stay away from porcupines.

5. Their quills hurt other animals.

6. Porcupines sleep under rocks or bushes.

7. They sleep during the day.

8. Porcupines eat plants at night.

9. North America has some porcupines.

10. They are called New World porcupines.

11. New World porcupines can climb trees.

Predicates

A **predicate** tells what the subject is doing, has done or will do.

Directions: Underline the predicate in the following sentences.

Example: Woodpeckers <u>live in trees.</u>

1. They hunt for insects in the trees.

2. Woodpeckers have strong beaks.

3. They can peck through the bark.

4. The pecking sound can be heard from far away.

Directions: Circle the groups of words that can be predicates.

have long tongues

hole in bark

help it to climb trees

pick up insects

sticky substance

tree bark

Now, choose the correct predicates from above to finish these sentences.

1. Woodpeckers _____.

2. They use their tongues to _____.

3. Its strong feet _____.

Parts of Speech

Directions: Write the part of speech of each underlined word.

NOUN   PRONOUN   VERB   ADJECTIVE   ADVERB   PREPOSITION

There ①<u>are</u> many ②<u>different</u> kinds of animals. Some animals live in the wild. Some animals live in the ③<u>zoo</u>. And still others live in homes. The animals that ④<u>live</u> in homes are called pets.

There are many types of pets. Some pets without fur are fish, turtles, snakes and hermit crabs. Trained birds can fly ⑤<u>around</u> ⑥<u>your</u> house. Some ⑦<u>furry</u> animals are cats, dogs, rabbits, ferrets, gerbils or hamsters. Some animals can ⑧<u>successfully</u> learn tricks that ⑨<u>you</u> teach them. Whatever your favorite animal is, animals can be ⑩<u>special</u> friends!

1. _____   4. _____

2. _____   5. _____   7. _____   9. _____

3. _____   6. _____   8. _____   10. _____

Parts of Speech

Nouns, pronouns, verbs, adjectives, adverbs, and prepositions are all **parts of speech.**

Directions: Label the words in each sentence with the correct part of speech.

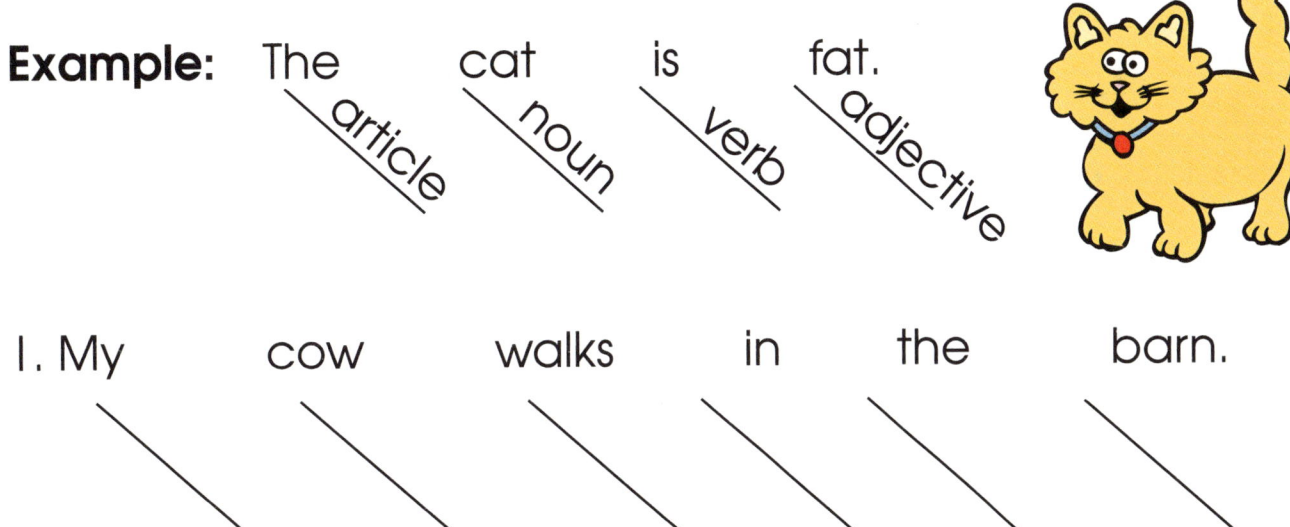

Example: The cat is fat.
article / noun / verb / adjective

1. My cow walks in the barn.

2. Red flowers grow in the garden.

3. The large dog was excited.

Parts of Speech

Directions: Ask someone to give you nouns, verbs, adjectives, and pronouns where shown. Write them in the blanks. Read the story to your friend when you finish.

The _____ Adventure
          (adjective)

I went for a _____ . I found a really big _____ .
                (noun)   (noun)

It was so _____ that I _____ all the way
            (adjective)   (verb)

home. I put it in my _____ . To my amazement, it began
                          (noun)

to _____ . I _____ . I took it to my
      (verb)   (past-tense verb)

_____ . I showed it to all my _____ .
    (place)   (plural noun)

I decided to _____ it in a box and wrap it up with
                 (verb)

_____ paper. I gave it to _____ for a
   (adjective)   (person)

present. When _____ opened it, _____
                 (pronoun)   (pronoun)

_____ . _____ shouted, "Thank you! This
 (past-tense verb)   (pronoun)

is the best _____ I've ever had!"
                (noun)

"Your" and "You're"

The word **your** shows possession.

Examples:

Is that **your** book?

I visited **your** class.

The word **you're** is a contraction for **you are**. A **contraction** is two words joined together as one. An apostrophe shows where letters have been left out.

Examples:

You're doing well on that painting.

If **you're** going to pass the test, you should study.

Directions: Write **your** or **you're** in the blanks to complete the sentences correctly. The first one has been done for you.

<u> You're </u> 1. Your/You're the best friend I have!

_____ 2. Your/You're going to drop that!

_____ 3. Your/You're brother came to see me.

_____ 4. Is that your/you're cat?

_____ 5. If your/you're going, you'd better hurry!

_____ 6. Why are your/you're fingers so red?

_____ 7. It's none of your/you're business!

_____ 8. Your/You're bike's front tire is low.

_____ 9. Your/You're kidding!

_____ 10. Have it your/you're way.

_____ 11. I thought your/you're report was great!

_____ 12. He thinks your/you're wonderful!

_____ 13. What is your/you're first choice?

_____ 14. What's your/you're opinion?

_____ 15. If your/you're going, so am I!

_____ 16. Your/You're welcome.

"Good" and "Well"

Use the word **good** to describe a noun. Good is an adjective.

Example: She is a **good** teacher.

Use the word **well** to tell or ask how something is done or to describe someone's health. Well is an adverb. It describes a verb.

Example: She is not feeling **well**.

Directions: Write **good** or **well** in the blanks to complete the sentences correctly. The first one has been done for you.

<u>good</u>   1. Our team could use a good/well captain.

_____ 2. The puny kitten doesn't look good/well.

_____ 3. He did his job so good/well that everyone praised him.

_____ 4. Whining isn't a good/well habit.

_____ 5. I might just as good/well do it myself.

_____ 6. She was one of the most well-/good- liked girls at school.

_____ 7. I did the book report as good/well as I could.

_____ 8. The television works very good/well.

_____ 9. You did a good/well job repairing the TV!

_____ 10. Thanks for a job good/well done!

_____ 11. You did a good/well job fixing the computer.

_____ 12. You had better treat your friends good/well.

_____ 13. Can your grandmother hear good/well?

_____ 14. Your brother will be well/good soon.

Summer Link Super Edition Grade 4

Name _____

Synonyms

Directions: Cut out the sails below. Glue each one to the boat whose synonym matches it.

- fast
- dirty
- happy
- mad
- noisy

cut

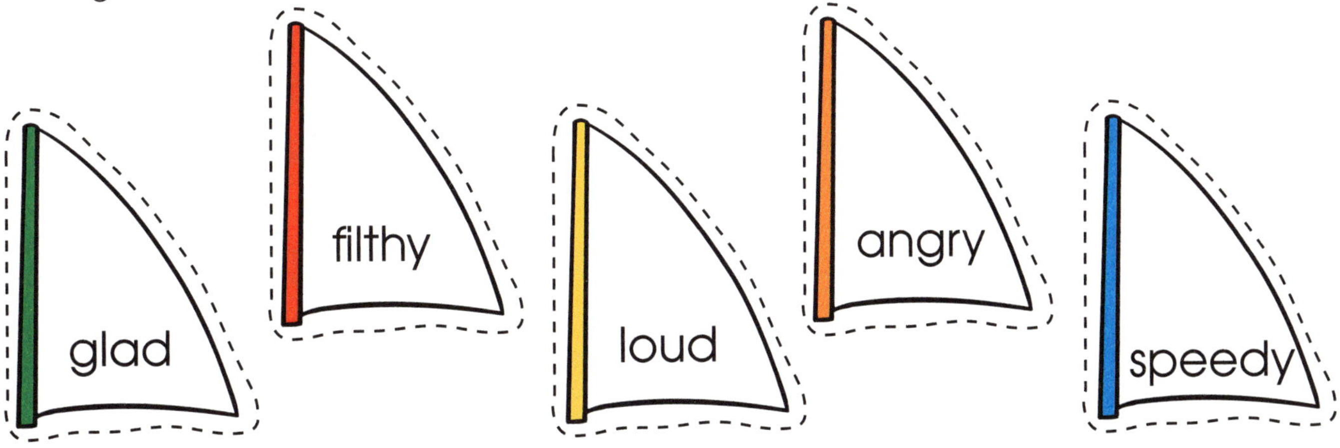

- glad
- filthy
- loud
- angry
- speedy

This page is blank for cutting exercise on previous page.

Antonyms

Antonyms are words that have opposite meanings.

Example: neat — sloppy

Directions: Cut out each frog below and glue it to the lily pad with its antonym.

cut ✂ -

This page is blank for cutting exercise on previous page.

Antonyms

Examples:

child  adult  hot  cold

Directions: Match the words that have opposite meanings. Draw a line between each pair of antonyms.

thaw	same
huge	sad
crying	friend
happy	open
enemy	freeze
asleep	thin
closed	hide
fat	tiny
seek	awake
different	laughing

Antonyms

Directions: Use antonyms from the box to complete the sentences below.

| speedy | clean | quiet | thoughtful | happy |

1. If we get too loud, the teacher will ask us to get _____ .

2. She was sad to lose her puppy, but she was _____ to find it again.

3. Mark got dirty, so he had to scrub himself _____ .

4. Janna was too _____ when she did her homework, so she tried to be slow when she did it over.

5. Dave was too selfish to share his cookies, but Deborah was _____ enough to share hers.

Think of another pair of antonyms. Write them on the lines.

_____   _____

Summer Link Super Edition Grade 4

Alliteration

Alliteration is the repeated use of beginning sounds. Alliterative sentences are sometimes referred to as tongue twisters.

Example:

She sells sea shells by the seashore.
Peter Piper picked a peck of pickled peppers.

Directions: Use alliteration to write your own tongue twisters.

1. _____

2. _____

3. _____

Word Order

Word order is the logical order of words in sentences.

Directions: Put the words in order so that each sentence tells a complete idea.

Example: outside put cat the

Put the cat outside.
_____

1. mouse the ate snake the

_____

2. dog John his walk took a for

_____

3. birthday Maria the present wrapped

_____

4. escaped parrot the cage its from

_____

5. to soup quarts water three of add the

_____

6. bird the bushes into the chased cat the

_____

Summer Link Super Edition Grade 4

Topic Sentences

A **topic sentence** is usually the first sentence in a paragraph. It tells what the story will be about.

Directions: Read the following sentences. Circle the topic sentence that should go first in the paragraph that follows.

Rainbows have seven colors.

There's a pot of gold.

I like rainbows.

The colors are red, orange, yellow, green, blue, indigo, and violet. Red forms the outer edge, with violet on the inside of the rainbow.

He cut down a cherry tree.

His wife was named Martha.

George Washington was a good president.

He helped our country get started. He chose intelligent leaders to help him run the country.

Mark Twain was a great author.

Mark Twain was unhappy sometimes.

Mark Twain was born in Missouri.

One of his most famous books is *Huckleberry Finn.* He wrote many other great books.

Middle Sentences

Middle sentences support the topic sentence. They tell more about it.

Directions: Underline the middle sentences that support each topic sentence below.

Topic Sentence:

   Penguins are birds that cannot fly.

Pelicans can spear fish with their sharp bills.

Many penguins waddle or hop about on land.

Even though they cannot fly, they are excellent swimmers.

Pelicans keep their food in a pouch.

Topic Sentence:

   Volleyball is a team sport in which the players hit the ball over the net.

There are two teams with six players on each team.

My friend John would rather play tennis with Lisa.

Players can use their heads or their hands.

I broke my hand once playing handball.

Topic Sentence:

   Pikes Peak is the most famous of all the Rocky Mountains.

Some mountains have more trees than other mountains.

Many people like to climb to the top.

Many people like to ski and camp there, too.

The weather is colder at the top of most mountains.

Summer Link Super Edition Grade 4

Ending Sentences

Ending sentences are sentences that tie the story together.

Directions: Choose the correct ending sentence for each story from the sentences below. Write it at the end of the paragraph.

A new pair of shoes!
All the corn on the cob I could eat!
A new eraser!

Corn on the Cob

    Corn on the cob used to be my favorite food. That is, until I lost my four front teeth. For one whole year, I had to sit and watch everyone else eat my favorite food without me. Mom gave me creamed corn, but it just wasn't the same. When my teeth finally came in, Dad said he had a surprise for me. I thought I was going to get a bike or a new C.D. player or something. I was just as happy to get what I did.

_____

I would like to take a train ride every year.
Trains move faster than I thought they would.
She had brought her new gerbil along for the ride.

A Train Ride

    When our family took its first train ride, my sister brought along a big box. She would not tell anyone what she had in it. In the middle of the trip, we heard a sound coming from the box. "Okay, Jan, now you have to open the box," said Mom. When she opened the box we were surprised.

_____

Parts of a Paragraph

A **paragraph** is a group of sentences that all tell about the same thing. Most paragraphs have three parts: a **beginning**, a **middle**, and an **end**.

Directions: Write **beginning**, **middle**, or **end** next to each sentence in the scrambled paragraphs below. There can be more than one middle sentence.

Example:

__middle__ We took the tire off the car.

__beginning__ On the way to Aunt Louise's, we had a flat tire.

__middle__ We patched the hole in the tire.

__end__ We put the tire on and started driving again.

_____ I took all the ingredients out of the cupboard.

_____ One morning, I decided to bake a pumpkin pie.

_____ I forgot to add the pumpkin!

_____ I mixed the ingredients together, but something was missing.

_____ The sun was very hot and our throats were dry.

_____ We finally decided to turn back.

_____ We started our hike very early in the morning.

_____ It kept getting hotter as we walked.

Statements and Questions

Statements are sentences that tell about something. Statements begin with a capital letter and end with a period. **Questions** are sentences that ask about something. Questions begin with a capital letter and end with a question mark.

Directions: Rewrite the sentences using capital letters and either a period or a question mark.

Example: walruses live in the Arctic

Walruses live in the Arctic.

1. are walruses large sea mammals or fish

_____

2. they spend most of their time in the water and on ice

_____

3. are floating sheets of ice called ice floes

_____

4. are walruses related to seals

_____

5. their skin is thick, wrinkled and almost hairless

_____

Kinds of Sentences

Remember: a **statement** tells something, a **question** asks something, and a **command** tells someone to do something.

Directions: On each line, write a statement, question, or command. Use a word from the box in each sentence.

glue	share	decide
enter	add	fold

Example:

Question:

Can he add anything else?

1. Statement:

_____

2. Question:

_____

3. Command:

_____

4. Statement:

_____

5. Question:

_____

Name _____

Kinds of Sentences

A **statement** is a sentence that tells something.
A **question** is a sentence that asks something.
A **command** is a sentence that tells someone to do something.

Commands begin with a verb or **please**. They usually end with a period. The noun is **you** but it does not need to be part of the sentence.

Example: "Come here, please." means "**You** come here, please."

Examples of commands: Stand next to me.
   Please give me some paper.

Directions: Write **S** in front of the statements, **Q** in front of the questions and **C** in front of the commands. End each sentence with a period or a question mark.

Example:

_____C_____   Stop and look before you cross the street.

_____   1. Did you do your math homework

_____   2. I think I lost my math book

_____   3. Will you help me find it

_____   4. I looked everywhere

_____   5. Please open your math books to page three

_____   6. Did you look under your desk

_____   7. I looked, but it's not there

_____   8. Who can add seven and four

_____   9. Come up and write the answer on the board

_____   10. Chris, where is your math book

_____   11. I don't know for sure

_____   12. Please share a book with a friend

Name _____

Four Kinds of Sentences

Directions: Write **S** for statement, **Q** for question, **C** for command, or **E** for exclamation. End each sentence with a period, question mark, or exclamation mark.

Example: __E__ You better watch out!

_____ 1. My little brother insists on coming with us

_____ 2. Tell him movies are bad for his health

_____ 3. He says he's fond of movies

_____ 4. Does he know there are monsters in this movie

_____ 5. He says he needs facts for his science report

_____ 6. He's writing about something that hatched from an old egg

_____ 7. Couldn't he just go to the library

_____ 8. Could we dress him like us so he'll blend in

_____ 9. Are you kidding

_____ 10. Would he sit by himself at the movie

_____ 11. That would be too dangerous

_____ 12. Mom said she'd give us money for candy if we took him with us

_____ 13. Why didn't you say that earlier

_____ 14. Get your brother and let's go

Summer Link Super Edition Grade 4

Name _____

Four Kinds of Sentences

Directions: For each pair of words, write two kinds of sentences (any combination of question, command, statement or exclamation). Use one or both words in each sentence. Name each kind of sentence you wrote.

Example: pump   crop

Question: What kind of crops did you plant?

Command: Pump the water as fast as you can.

1. pinch   health

   _____ : _____

   _____ : _____

2. fond   fact

   _____ : _____

   _____ : _____

3. insist   hatch

   _____ : _____

   _____ : _____

Complete the Sentences

Directions: Write your own endings to make the sentences tell a complete idea.

Example:

   The Wizard of Oz is a story about <u>Dorothy and her dog, Toto</u>.

1. Dorothy and Toto live on _____.

2. A big storm _____.

3. Dorothy and Toto are carried off to _____.

4. Dorothy meets _____.

5. Dorothy, Toto, and their friends follow the _____.

6. Dorothy tries to find _____.

7. The Wizard turns out to be _____.

8. A scary person in the story is _____.

9. The wicked witch is killed by _____.

10. The hot air balloon leaves without _____.

11. Dorothy uses her magic shoes to _____.

Complete the Sentences

Directions: Write your own endings to make the sentences tell a complete idea.

Example:

Cinderella is a story about   <u>Cinderella, her stepmother, stepsisters, and the prince.</u>

1. Cinderella lives with _____

2. Her stepmother and her stepsisters _____

3. Cinderella's stepsisters receive _____

4. Cinderella cannot go to the ball because _____
_____

5. The fairy godmother comes _____

6. The prince dances with _____

7. When the clock strikes midnight, _____

8. The prince's men look for _____

9. The slipper fits _____

10. Cinderella and the prince live _____

Run-On Sentences

A **run-on sentence** occurs when two or more sentences are joined together without punctuation.

Examples:

Run-on sentence: I lost my way once did you?
Two sentences with correct punctuation: I lost my way once. Did you?
Run-on sentence: I found the recipe it was not hard to follow.
Two sentences with correct punctuation: I found the recipe. It was not hard to follow.

Directions: Rewrite the run-on sentences correctly with periods, exclamation points, and question marks. The first one has been done for you.

1. Did you take my umbrella I can't find it anywhere!

   <u>Did you take my umbrella? I can't find it anywhere!</u>

2. How can you stand that noise I can't!

   _____

3. The cookies are gone I see only crumbs.

   _____

4. The dogs were barking they were hungry.

   _____

5. She is quite ill please call a doctor immediately!

   _____

6. The clouds came up we knew the storm would hit soon.

   _____

7. You weren't home he stopped by this morning.

   _____

Name _____

Sentences and Non-Sentences

A **sentence** tells a complete idea.

Directions: Circle the groups of words that tell a complete idea.

1. Sharks are fierce hunters.

2. Afraid of sharks.

3. The great white shark will attack people.

4. Other kinds will not.

5. Sharks have an outer row of teeth for grabbing food.

6. When the outer teeth fall out, another row of teeth moves up.

7. Keep the ocean clean by eating dead animals.

8. Not a single bone in its body.

9. Cartilage.

10. Made of the same material as the tip of your nose.

11. Unlike other fish, sharks cannot float.

12. In motion constantly.

13. Even while sleeping.

Using Fewer Words

Writing can be more interesting when fewer words are used. Combining sentences is easy when the subjects are the same. Notice how the comma is used.

Example: Sally woke up. Sally ate breakfast. Sally brushed her teeth.

Sally woke up, ate breakfast, and brushed her teeth.

Combining sentences with more than one subject is a little more complicated. Notice how commas are used to "set off" information.

Examples: Jane went to the store. Jane is Sally's sister.

Jane went to the store with Sally, her sister.

Eddy Eddie likes to play with cars. Eddie is my younger brother.

Eddie, my younger brother, likes to play with cars.

Directions: Write each pair of sentences as one sentence.

1. Jerry played soccer after school. He played with his best friend, Tom.

2. Spot likes to chase cats. Spot is my dog.

3. Lori and Janice both love ice cream. Janice is Lori's cousin.

4. Jayna is my cousin. Jayna helped me move into my new apartment.

5. Romeo is a big tomcat. Romeo loves to hunt mice.

Name _____

Contractions

A **contraction** is a short way to write two words together. Some letters are left out, but an apostrophe takes their place.

Directions: Write the words from the box that answer the questions.

| hasn't | you've | aren't | we've | weren't |

1. Write the correct contractions below.

    Example:
    I have ____I've____   was not ____wasn't____

    we have _____   you have _____

    are not _____   were not _____

    has not _____

2. Write two words from the box that are contractions using **have**.

    _____   _____

3. Write three words from the box that are contractions using **not**.

    _____   _____   _____

Name _____

And

Directions: Write each pair of sentences as one sentence.

Example: Jim will deal the cards one at a time. Jim will give four cards to everyone.

Jim will deal the cards one at a time <u>and</u> give four cards to everyone.

1. Amy won the contest.　　　　　Amy claimed the prize.
   _____

2. We need to find the scissors.　　We need to buy some tape.
   _____

3. The stream runs through the woods.　The stream empties into the East River.
   _____
   _____

4. Katie tripped on the steps.　　Katie has a pain in her left foot.
   _____
   _____

5. Grandpa took me to the store.　Grandpa bought me a treat.
   _____

6. Charity ran 2 miles.　　　　　She walked 1 mile to cool down afterwards.
   _____
   _____

And and But

We can use **and** or **but** to make one longer sentence from two short ones.

Directions: Use **and** or **but** to make two short sentences into a longer, more interesting one. Write the new sentence on the line below the two short sentences.

Example:

The skunk has black fur. The skunk has a white stripe.

The skunk has black fur and a white stripe.

1. The skunk has a small head. The skunk has small ears.

_____

2. The skunk has short legs. Skunks can move quickly.

_____

3. Skunks sleep in hollow trees. Skunks sleep underground.

_____

4. Skunks are chased by animals. Skunks do not run away.

_____

5. Skunks sleep during the day. Skunks hunt at night.

_____

Cause and Effect

A **cause** is the reason for an event. An **effect** is what happens as a result of a cause.

Directions: Circle the cause and underline the effect in each sentence. They may be in any order. The first one has been done for you.

1. (The truck hit an icy patch) and <u>skidded off the road</u>.

2. When the door slammed shut, the baby woke up crying.

3. Our soccer game was cancelled when it began to storm.

4. Dad and Mom are adding a room onto the house since our family is growing.

5. Our car ran out of gas on the way to town, so we had to walk.

6. The home run in the ninth inning helped our team win the game.

7. We had to climb the stairs because the elevator was broken.

8. We were late to school because the bus had a flat tire.

Comprehension: The Moon

Our moon is not the only moon in the solar system. Some other planets have moons also. Saturn has 10 moons! Our moon is Earth's closest neighbor in the solar system. Sometimes our moon is 225,727 miles away. Other times, it is 252,002 miles away. Why? Because the Moon revolves around Earth. It does not go around Earth in a perfect circle. So, sometimes its path takes it further away from our planet.

When our astronauts visited the Moon, they found dusty plains, high mountains and huge craters. There is no air or water on the Moon. That is why life cannot exist there. The astronauts had to wear space suits to protect their skin from the bright Sun. They had to take their own air to breathe. They had to take their own food and water. The Moon was an interesting place to visit. Would you want to live there?

Directions: Answer these questions about the Moon.

1. Circle the main idea:

    The Moon travels around Earth, and the astronauts visited the Moon.

    Astronauts found that the Moon—Earth's closest neighbor— has no air or water and cannot support life.

2. Write three things our astronauts found on the Moon.

    1) _____ 2) _____ 3) _____

3. Make a list of what to take on a trip to the Moon.

    _____

    _____

Comprehension: Troy Aikman

Troy Aikman, Dallas Cowboy, was born on November 21, 1966. As a young boy, he enjoyed doing the usual things, like fishing or hunting with his dad. He also loved playing sports with his friends.

Troy Aikman knows a lot about change. When he was a young boy of 12 living in a city, he knew he wanted to be a baseball player. But when his family moved to a 172-acre ranch near Henryetta, Oklahoma, he felt like he would have to give up that dream. He soon learned that the people of Oklahoma loved football more than any other sport. Troy soon learned to love football, too. And he learned he was very good at it.

You can be a champion, too, in spite of changes in your life. You just have to be willing to make those changes work for you!

Directions: Answer these questions about Troy Aikman.

1. Why did Troy Aikman change from playing baseball to playing football?
   _____

2. How old was he when his family moved?
   _____

3. For what NFL team does he play?
   _____

4. How can changes in your life be a good thing?
   _____
   _____

Poetry

Shape poems are words that form the shape of the thing being written about.

Example:

Directions: Create your own shape poem below.

Poetry: Cinquains

A cinquain is a type of poetry. The form is:

Noun
Adjective, adjective
Verb + ing, verb + ing, verb + ing
Four-word phrase
Synonym for noun in line 1.

Example:

Books
Creative, fun
Reading, choosing, looking
I love to read!
Novels

Directions: Write your own cinquain!

_____
noun

_____, _____
adjective   adjective

_____, _____, _____
verb + ing   verb + ing   verb + ing

_____
four-word phrase

_____
synonym for noun in first line

Reading a Schedule

There are many different kinds of reading. When reading a magazine, you probably skim over pictures, captions, and headlines. You stop to read carefully when you see something of interest. If your teacher assigns a chapter in a science textbook, you read it carefully so you don't miss important details. A **schedule** is a chart with lists of times. Would you read slowly or quickly to get information from a schedule? If you did not read carefully, you might get on the wrong bus or miss the bus altogether!

Directions: Look carefully at the bus schedule, then answer the questions.

City Transit System

Bus	Leaves		Arrives	
#10	Pine Street	7:35 A.M.	Oak Street	7:58 A.M.
#17	James Road	7:46 A.M.	Main Street	8:10 A.M.
#10	Oak Street	8:05 A.M.	Charles Road	8:25 A.M.
#29	Pine Street	9:12 A.M.	Oak Street	9:35 A.M.

1. Which bus goes to Main Street in the morning? _____

2. If you miss the #10 bus to Oak Street, could you still get there by noon? _____ How? _____

3. What time does bus #29 arrive at Oak Street? _____

4. Can you travel from Pine Street to Charles Road? _____ On which bus? _____

5. Bus #17 leaves _____ at 7:46 A.M. and arrives at Main Street at _____ A.M.

Reading a Schedule

Here is a schedule for the day's activities at Camp Do-A-Lot. Lisa and Jessie need help to decide what they will do on their last day.

Directions: Use this schedule to answer the questions on page 179.

CAMP DO-A-LOT
Saturday, July 8, 2000

Activity	Time	Location
Breakfast	6:30 A.M.	Dining Hall
Archery	7:30 A.M.	Field behind the Hall
Canoeing	7:30 A.M.	Blue Bottom Lake
Landscape Painting	7:30 A.M.	Rainbow Craft Shed
Horseback Riding	8:45 A.M.	Red Barn
Landscape Painting	8:45 A.M.	Rainbow Craft Shed
Scavenger Hunt	8:45 A.M.	Dining Hall
Cabin Clean-up	10:45 A.M.	Assigned Cabins
Lunch	11:45 A.M.	Dining Hall
Canoeing	1:00 P.M.	Blue Bottom Lake
Archery	1:00 P.M.	Field behind the Hall
Scavenger Hunt	1:00 P.M.	Dining Hall
Awards Ceremony	2:45 P.M.	Outdoor Theater
Dismissal	3:30 P.M.	

Name _____

Reading a Schedule

Directions: Use the schedule of activities on page 178 to answer the questions

1. Where do Lisa and Jessie need to go to take part in archery?
   _____

2. Both girls want to go canoeing. What are the two times that canoeing is offered? _____ and _____

3. Lisa and Jessie love to go on scavenger hunts. They agree to go on the hunt at 1:00 P.M. When will they have to go canoeing? _____

4. Only one activity on the last day of camp takes place at the Outdoor Theater. What is it? _____

5. What happens at 10:45 A.M.? _____

6. If you went to the Rainbow Craft Shed at 7:30 A.M., what activity would you find there? _____

Pretend you are at Camp Do-A-Lot with Lisa and Jessie. On the line next to each time, write which activity you would choose to do.

7:30 A.M. _____
_____

8:45 A.M. _____
_____

1:00 P.M. _____
_____

Glossary of Reading and Language Arts Terms

adjective: a describing word that tells more about a noun

adverb: tells when, where, or how about the verb of a sentence

antonym: words with opposite, or nearly opposite, meanings

articles: any one of the words *a*, *an*, or *the* used to modify a noun

autobiography: a written account of your life

base word (also called root word): the word left after you take off a prefix or a suffix

character: a person, animal, or object that a story is about

climax: the most thrilling part of the story where the problem will or will not be solved

conclusion: a final decision about something, or the part of a story that tells what happens to the characters

contraction: shortened forms of two words often using an apostrophe to show where letters are missing

diphthongs: two vowels together that make a new sound

fact: something known to be true

fiction: stories that are made up

homophone: a word with the same pronunciation as another, but with a different meaning, and often a different spelling, such as *son-sun*

idiom: a figure of speech or phrase that means something different than what the words actually say, such as "He changed his bad habits and *turned over a new leaf*"

nonfiction: stories that are true

noun: a word that names a person, place, or thing

opinion: a belief based on what a person thinks instead of what is known to be true

plot: explains the events in a story that create a problem

plural: a form of a word that names or refers to more than one person or thing

prefix: a part that is added to the beginning of a word that changes the word's meaning.

pronoun: a word that is used in place of a noun

punctuation: the marks that qualify sentences, such as a period, comma, question mark, exclamation point, and apostrophe

reading strategies: main idea, supporting details, context clues, fact/opinion

resolution: tells how the characters solve the story problem

setting: the place and time that a story happens

suffix: a part added to the end of a word to change the word's meaning

synonym: words that mean the same, or almost the same, thing

theme: a message or central idea of the story

verb: a word that can show action

verb tense: tells whether the action is happening in the past, present, or future

Page 101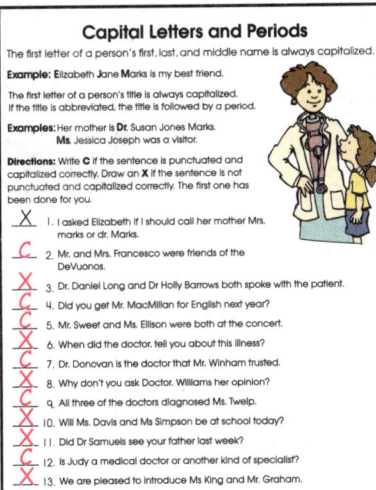
Page 102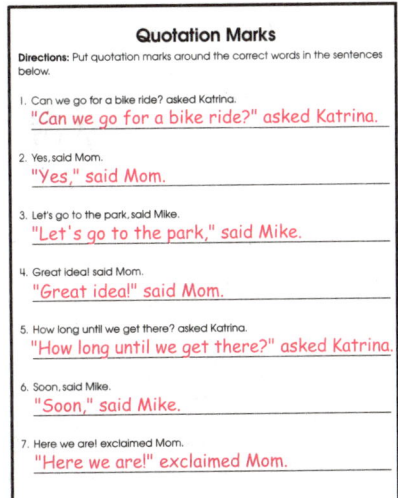
Page 103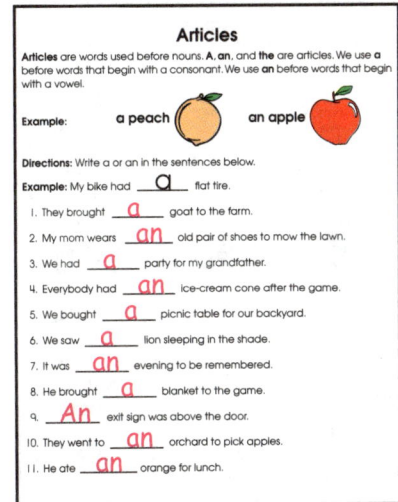
Page 104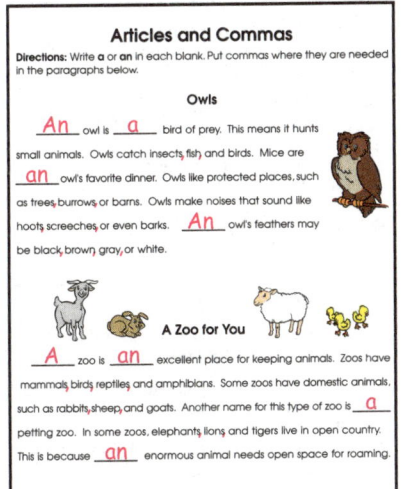
Page 105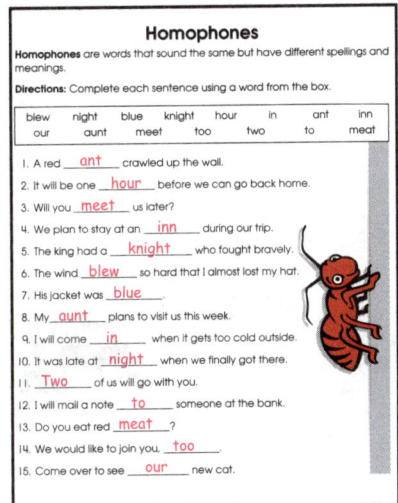
Page 106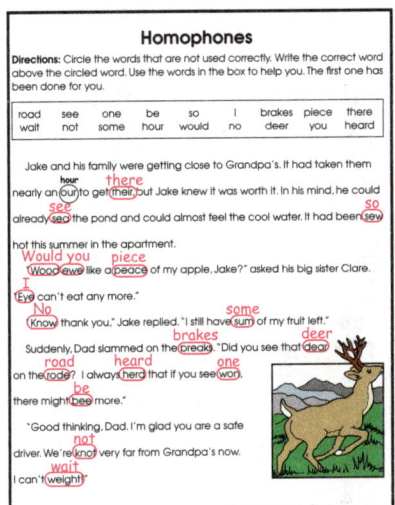
Page 107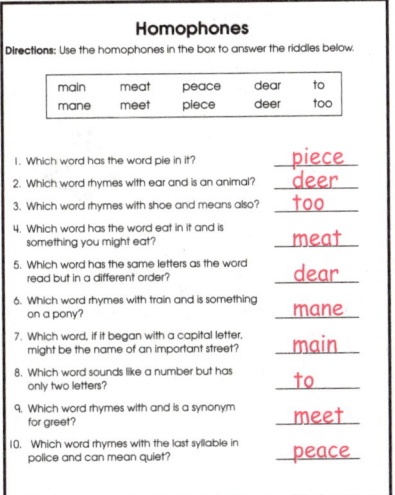
Page 108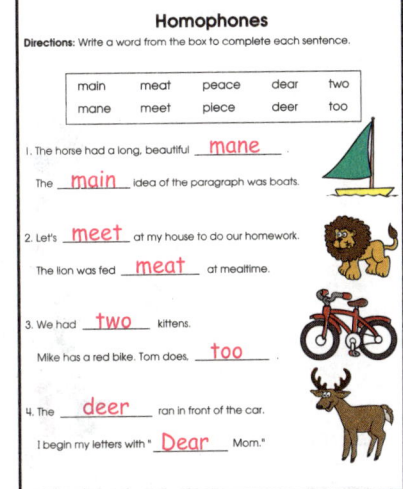
Page 109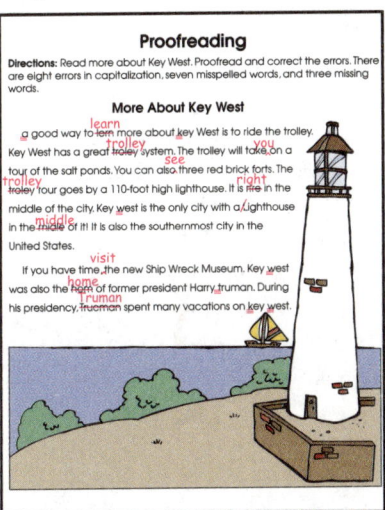

Summer Link Super Edition Grade 4

Page 110

Nouns

Nouns are words that tell the names of people, places or things.
Directions: Read the words below. Then write them in the correct column.

goat	Mrs. Jackson	girl
beach	tree	song
mouth	park	Jean Rivers
finger	flower	New York
Kevin Jones	Elm City	Frank Gates
Main Street	theater	skates
River Park	father	boy

Person
Kevin Jones
Mrs. Jackson
father
girl
Jean Rivers
Frank Gates
boy

Place
beach
Main Street
River Park
park
Elm City
theater
New York

Thing
goat
mouth
finger
tree
flower
song
skates

Page 111

Common Nouns

Common nouns are nouns that name any member of a group of people, places, or things, rather than specific people, places, or things.

Directions: Read the sentences below and write the common noun found in each sentence.

Example: _socks_ My socks do not match.

1. _bird_ The bird could not fly.
2. _jelly beans_ Ben likes to eat jelly beans.
3. _mother_ I am going to meet my mother.
4. _lake_ We will go swimming in the lake tomorrow.
5. _flowers_ I hope the flowers will grow quickly.
6. _eggs_ We colored eggs together.
7. _bicycle_ It is easy to ride a bicycle.
8. _cousin_ My cousin is very tall.
9. _boat_ Ted and Jane went fishing in their boat.
10. _prize_ They won a prize yesterday.
11. _ankle_ She fell down and twisted her ankle.
12. _brother_ My brother was born today.
13. _slide_ She went down the slide.
14. _doctor_ Ray went to the doctor today.

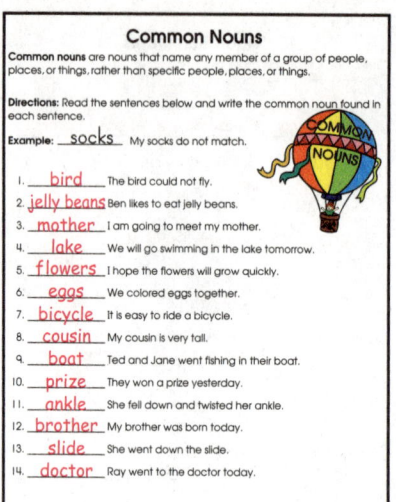

Page 112

Possessive Nouns

Possessive nouns tell who or what is the owner of something. With singular nouns, we use an apostrophe **before** the s. With plural nouns, we use an apostrophe **after** the s.

Example:
singular: one elephant
The **elephant's** dance was wonderful.
plural: more than one elephant
The **elephants'** dance was wonderful.

Directions: Put the apostrophe in the correct place in each bold word. Then write the word in the blank.

1. The **lions** cage was big. _lion's or lions'_
2. The **bears** costumes were purple. _bears'_
3. One **boys** laughter was very loud. _boy's_
4. The **trainers** dogs were dancing about. _trainer's or trainers'_
5. The **mans** popcorn was tasty and good. _man's_
6. **Marks** cotton candy was delicious. _Mark's_
7. A little **girls** balloon burst in the air. _girl's_
8. The big **clowns** tricks were very funny. _clown's or clowns'_
9. **Lauras** sister clapped for the clowns. _Laura's_
10. The **womans** money was lost in the crowd. _woman's_
11. **Kellys** mother picked her up early. _Kelly's_

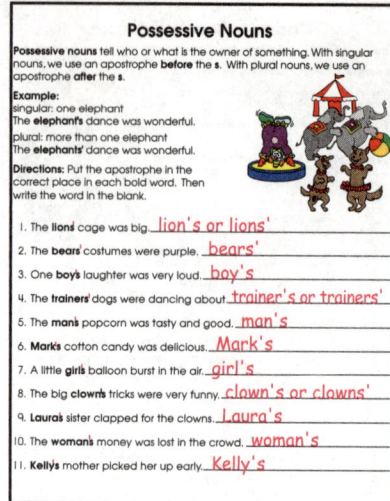

Page 113

Plural Nouns

Directions: The **singular** form of a word shows one person, place, or thing. Write the singular form of each noun on the lines below.

cherries	cherry
lunches	lunch
countries	country
leaves	leaf
churches	church
arms	arm
boxes	box
men	man
wheels	wheel
pictures	picture
cities	city
places	place
ostriches	ostrich
glasses	glass

Page 114

Proper Nouns

Proper nouns are names of specific people, places, or things. Proper nouns begin with a capital letter.

Directions: Read the sentences below and circle the proper nouns found in each sentence.

Example: (Aunt Frances) gave me a puppy for my birthday.

1. We lived on (Jackson Street) before we moved to our new house.
2. (Angela's) birthday party is tomorrow night.
3. We drove through (Cheyenne, Wyoming) on our way home.
4. (Dr. Charles) always gives me a treat for not crying.
5. (George Washington) was our first president.
6. Our class took a field trip to the (Johnson Flower Farm).
7. (Uncle Jack) lives in (New York City).
8. (Amy) and (Elizabeth) are best friends.
9. We buy doughnuts at the (Grayson Bakery).
10. My favorite movie is (E.T.).
11. We flew to (Miami, Florida) in a plane.
12. We go to (Riverfront Stadium) to watch the baseball games.
13. (Mr. Fields) is a wonderful music teacher.
14. My best friend is (Tom Dunlap).

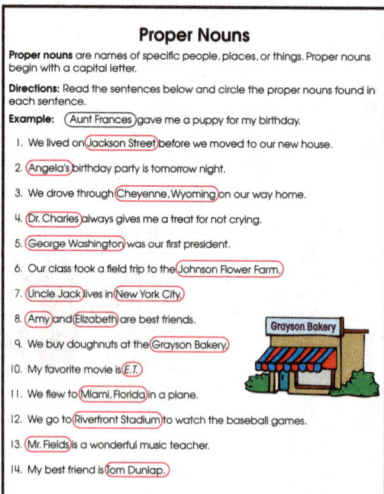

Page 115

Proper Nouns

Directions: Rewrite each sentence, capitalizing the proper nouns.

1. mike's birthday is in september.
Mike's birthday is in September.

2. aunt katie lives in detroit, michigan.
Aunt Katie lives in Detroit, Michigan.

3. In july, we went to canada.
In July, we went to Canada.

4. kathy jones moved to utah in january.
Kathy Jones moved to Utah in January.

5. My favorite holiday is valentine's day in february.
My favorite holiday is Valentine's Day in February.

6. On friday, mr. polzin gave the smith family a tour.
On Friday, Mr. Polzin gave the Smith family a tour.

7. saturday, uncle cliff and I will go to the mall of america in minnesota.
Saturday, Uncle Cliff and I will go to the Mall of America in Minnesota.

Page 116

Adjectives

Directions: Look at each picture. Then add adjectives to the sentences. Use colors, numbers, words from the box, and any other words you need to describe each picture.

polite   neat   careless
shy   selfish

Example:
The boy shared his pencil.
The polite boy shared his red pencil.

The girl dropped her
Answers will vary.

The boy played with
Answers will vary.

The boy put books
Answers will vary.

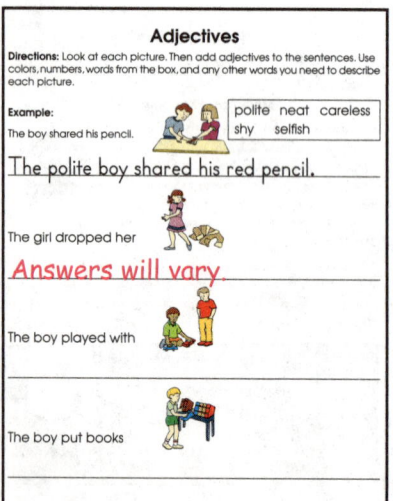

Page 117

Verbs

Directions: Write the verb that answers each question. Write a sentence using that verb.

| stir | clap | drag | hug | plan |

Which verb means to put your arms around someone?
hug
Answers will vary.

Which verb means to mix something with a spoon?
stir
Answers will vary.

Which verb means to pull something along the ground?
drag
Answers will vary.

Which verb means to take something suddenly?
grab
Answers will vary.

Page 118

Present-Tense Verbs

When something is happening right now, it is in the **present tense**. There are two ways to write verbs in the present tense:

Examples: The dog **walks**.   The cats **play**.
The dog **is walking**.   The cats **are playing**.

Directions: Write each sentence again, writing the verb a different way.

Example:
He lists the numbers.
He is listing the numbers.

1. She is pounding the nail.
She pounds the nail.

2. My brother toasts the bread.
He is toasting the bread.

3. They search for the robber.
They are searching for the robber.

4. The teacher lists the pages.
The teacher is listing the pages.

5. They are spilling the water.
They spill the water.

6. Ken and Amy load the packages.
They are loading the packages.

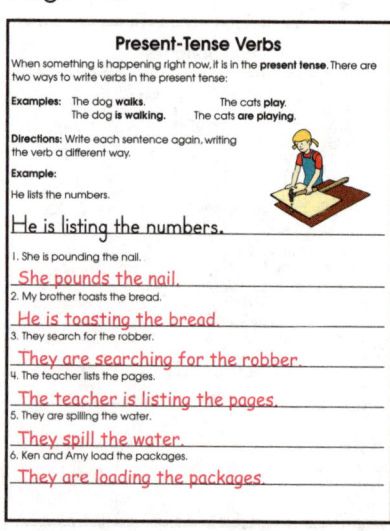

Page 119

Present-Tense Verbs

Directions: Write two sentences for each verb below. Tell about something that is happening now and write the verb as both simple present tense and present tense with a helping verb.

Example: run
Mia runs to the store.   Mia is running to the store.

1. hatch
2. check
3. spell
4. blend
5. lick
6. cry
7. write
8. dream

Sentences will vary.

Page 120

Present-Tense Verbs

Present tense verbs can be written two ways: The bird sings. The bird is singing.
Directions: Write each sentence again, using the verb **is** and writing the **ing** form of the verb.
Example: He cooks the cheeseburgers.
He is cooking the cheeseburgers.

1. Sharon dances to that song.
   Sharon is dancing to that song.
2. Frank washed the car.
   Frank is washing the car.
3. Mr. Benson smiles at me.
   Mr. Benson is smiling at me.

Write a verb for the sentences below that tells something that is happening now. Be sure to use the verb **is** and the **ing** form of the verb.

Example: The big, brown dog is barking .

1. The little baby _____
2. Most nine-year-olds _____
3. The monster on television _____

Answers will vary.

Page 121

Past-Tense Verbs

When you write about something that already happened, you add **ed** to most verbs. Here is another way to write about something in the past tense.

Examples: The dog walked.   The dog was walking.
The cats played.   The cats were playing.

Directions: Write each sentence again, writing the verb a different way.

Example: The baby pounded the pans.
The baby was pounding the pans.

1. Gary loaded the car by himself.
   Gary was loading the car by himself.
2. They searched for a long time.
   They were searching for a long time.
3. The water spilled over the edge.
   The water was spilling over the edge.
4. Dad toasted the rolls.
   Dad was toasting the rolls.

Page 122

Past-Tense Verbs

For some verbs that have a short vowel and end in one consonant, you double the consonant before adding **ed**.

Examples:
He hugged his pillow.   The dog grabbed the stick.
She stirred the carrots.   We planned to go tomorrow.
They clapped for me.   They dragged their bags on the ground.

Directions: Use the verb from the first sentence to complete the second sentence. Change the verb in the second part to the past tense. Double the consonant and add **ed**.

Example:
We skip to school. Yesterday, we skipped the whole way.

1. It's not nice to grab things. When you grabbed my cookie, I felt angry.
2. Did anyone hug you today? Dad hugged me this morning.
3. We plan our vacations every year. Last year, we planned to go to the beach.
4. Is it my turn to stir the pot? You stirred it last time.
5. Let's clap for Andy, just like we clapped for Amy.
6. My sister used to drag her blanket everywhere. Once, she dragged it to the store.

Page 123

Past-Tense Verbs

To tell about something that already happened, add **ed** to most verbs. If the verb already ends in **e**, just add **d**.

Examples:
We entered the contest last week.   We tasted the cupcakes.
I folded the paper wrong.   They decided quickly.
He added two boxes to the pile.   She shared her cupcake.

Directions: Use the verb from the first sentence to complete the second sentence. Add **d** or **ed** to show that something already happened.

Example:
My mom looks fine today. Yesterday, she looked tired.

1. You enter through the middle door. We entered that way last week.
2. Please add this for me. I already added it twice.
3. Will you share your cookie with me? I shared my apple with you yesterday.
4. It's your turn to fold the clothes. I folded them yesterday.
5. May I taste another one? I already tasted one.
6. You need to decide. We decided this morning.

Page 124

Past-Tense Verbs

Directions: Write sentences that tell about each picture using the words **is**, **are**, **was**, and **were**. Use words from the box as either nouns or verbs.

| pound | spill | toast | list | load | search |

Answers will vary.

Page 125

Past-Tense Verbs

Directions: Use the verb from the first sentence to complete the second sentence.

Example:
Please walk the dog.   I already walked her.

1. The flowers look good.   They looked better yesterday.
2. Please accept my gift.   I accepted it for my sister.
3. I wonder who will win.   I wondered about it all night.
4. He will saw the wood.   He sawed some last week.
5. Fold the paper neatly.   She folded her paper.
6. Let's cook outside tonight.   We cooked outside last night.
7. Do not block the way.   They blocked the entire street.
8. Form the clay this way.   He formed it into a ball.
9. Follow my car.   We followed them down the street.
10. Glue the pages like this.   She glued the flowers on.

Page 126

Adding "ed" to Make Verbs Past Tense

To make many verbs past tense, add **ed**.
Examples:
cook + ed = cooked   wish + ed = wished   play + ed = played
When a verb ends in a **silent e**, drop the **e** and add **ed**.
Examples:
hope + ed = hoped   hate + ed = hated
When a verb ends in **y** after a consonant, change the **y** to **i** and add **ed**.
Examples:
hurry + ed = hurried   marry + ed = married
When a verb ends in a single consonant after a single short vowel, double the final consonant before adding **ed**.
Examples:
stop + ed = stopped   hop + ed = hopped

Directions: Write the past tense of the verb correctly. The first one has been done for you.

1. call — called
2. copy — copied
3. frown — frowned
4. smile — smiled
5. live — lived
6. talk — talked
7. name — named
8. list — listed
9. spy — spied
10. phone — phoned
11. reply — replied
12. top — topped
13. clean — cleaned
14. scream — screamed
15. clap — clapped
16. mop — mopped
17. soap — soaped
18. choke — choked
19. scurry — scurried
20. drop — dropped

Page 127

Future-Tense Verbs

The **future tense** of a verb tells about something that has not happened yet but will happen in the future. **Will** or **shall** are usually used with future tense.
Directions: Change the verb tense in each sentence to future tense.
Example:
She cooks dinner.
She will cook dinner.

1. He plays baseball.
   He will play baseball.
2. She walks to school.
   She will walk to school.
3. Bobby talks to the teacher.
   Bobby will talk to the teacher.
4. I remember to vote.
   I will remember to vote.
5. Jack mows the lawn every week.
   Jack will mow the lawn every week.
6. We go on vacation soon.
   We will go on vacation soon.

Page 128

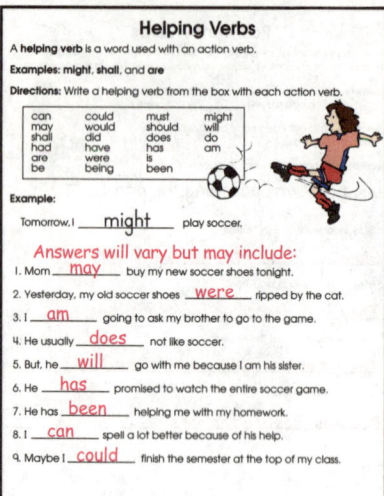

Page 129

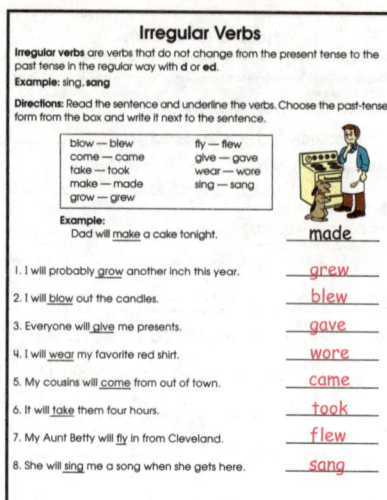

Page 130

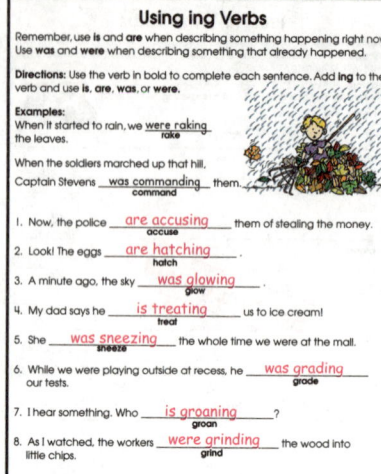

Page 131

Page 132

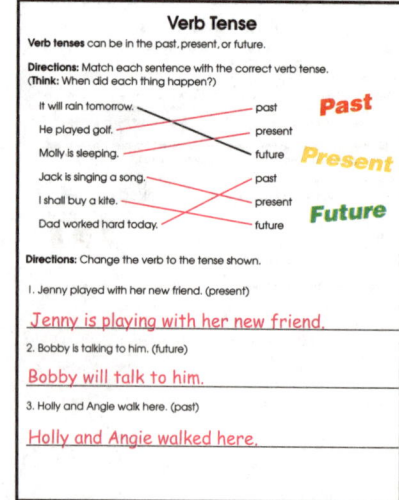

Page 133

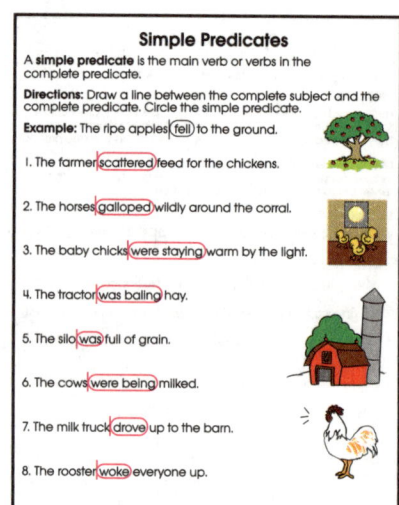

Page 134

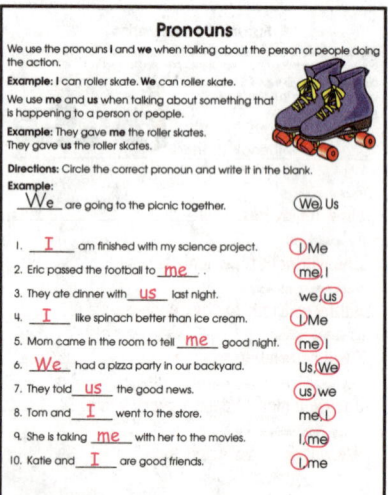

Page 135

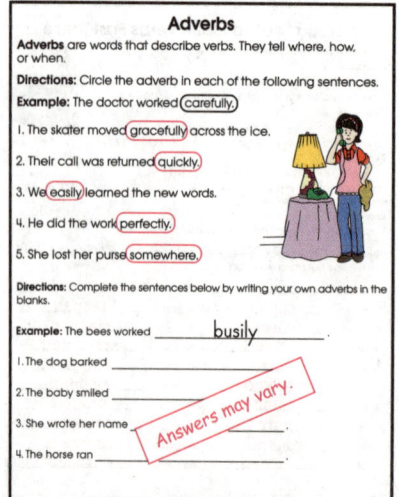

Page 136

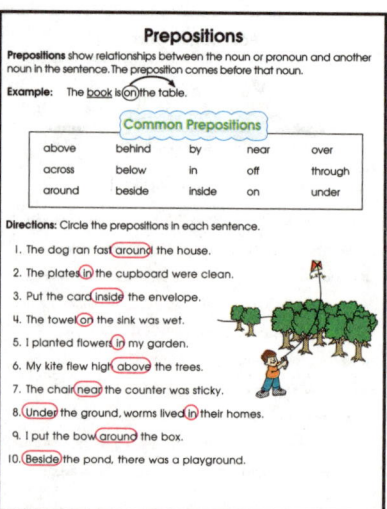

Page 137
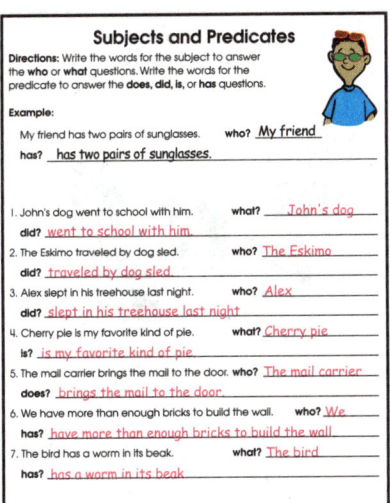

Page 138
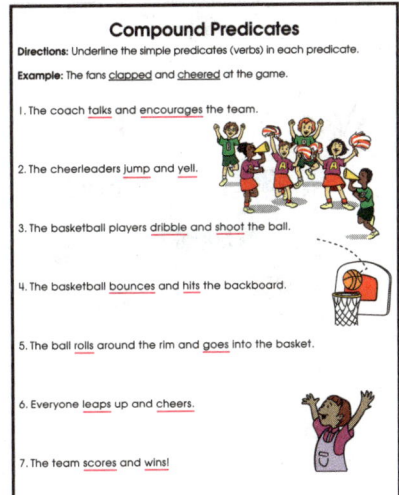

Page 139
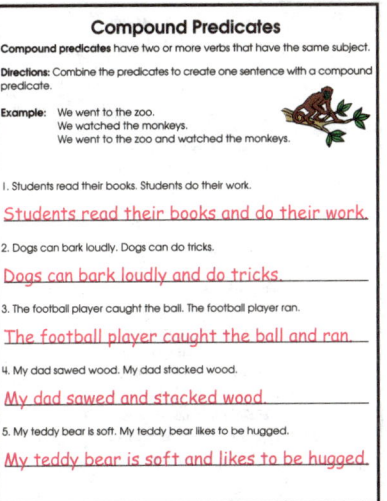

Page 140
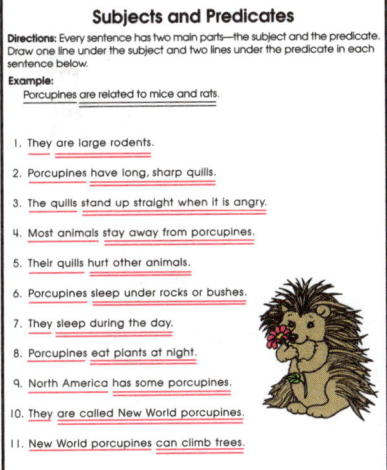

Page 141
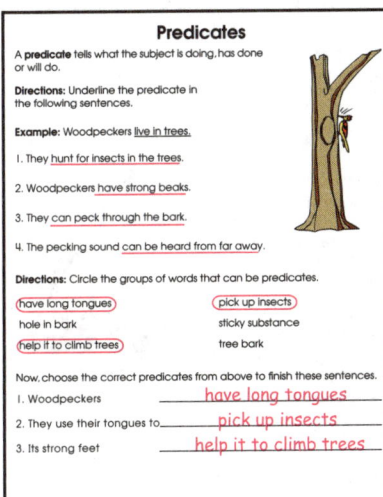

Page 142
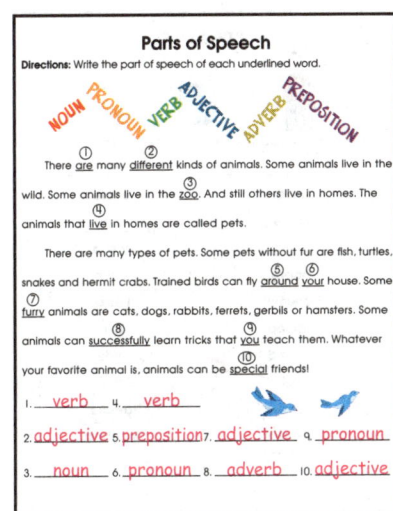

Page 143
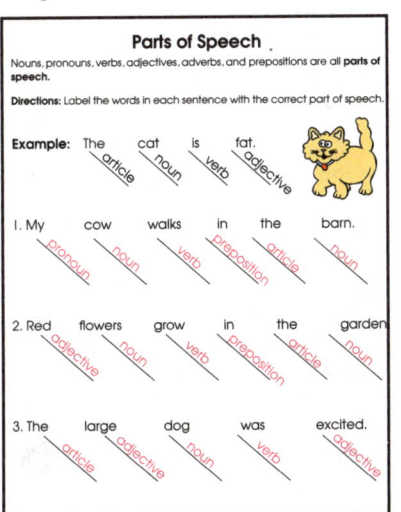

Page 144
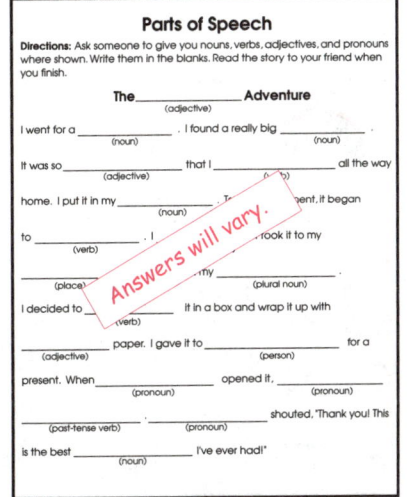

Page 145
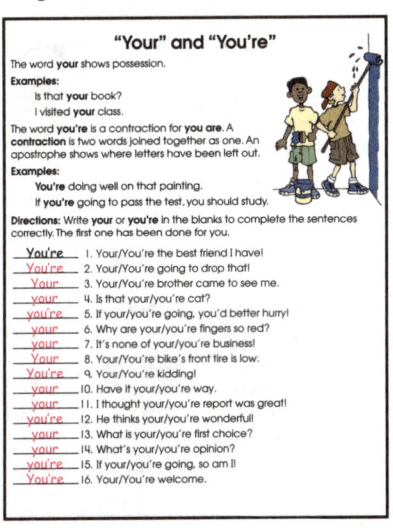

185

Summer Link Super Edition Grade 4

Page 146

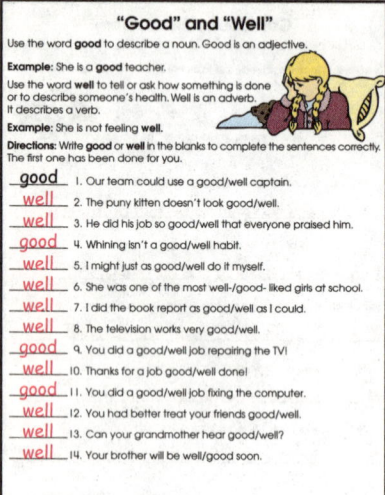

Page 147

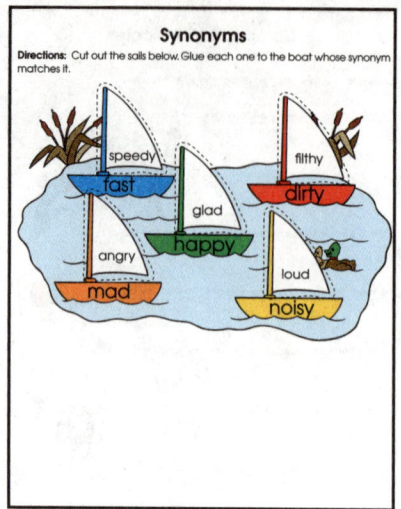

Page 149

Page 151

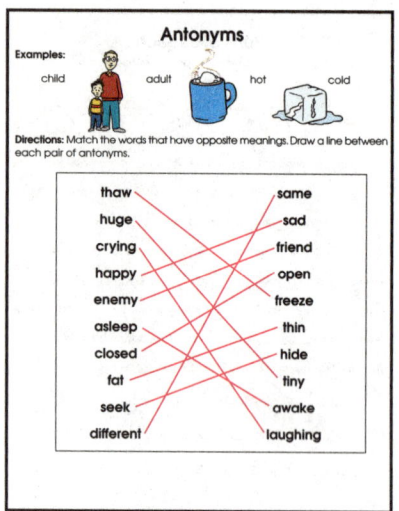

Page 152

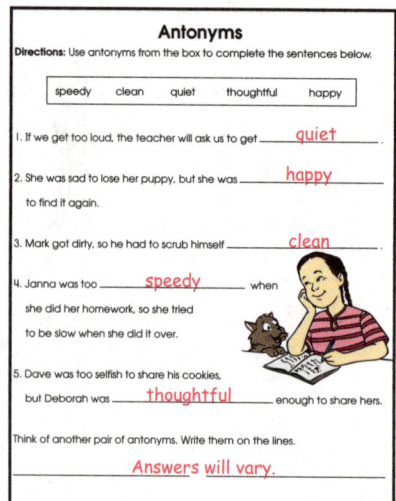

Page 153

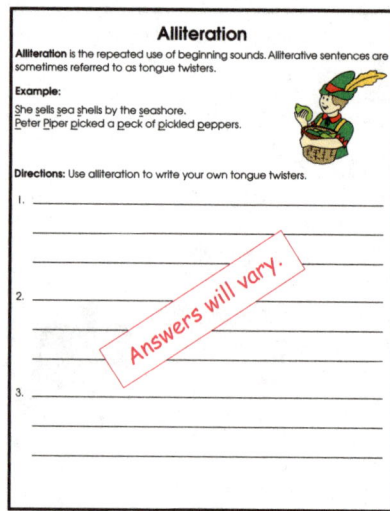

Page 154

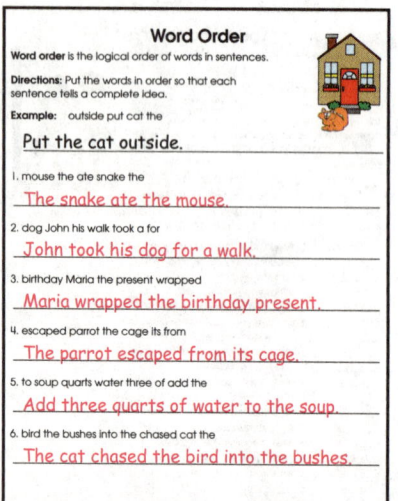

Page 155

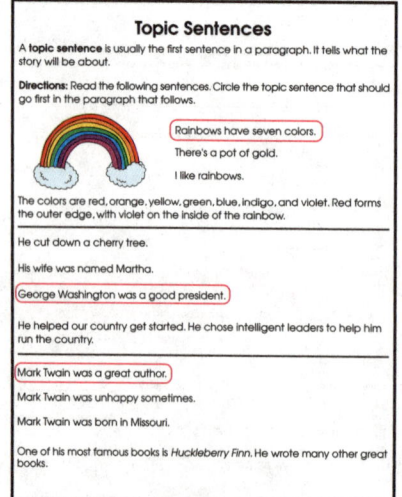

Page 156

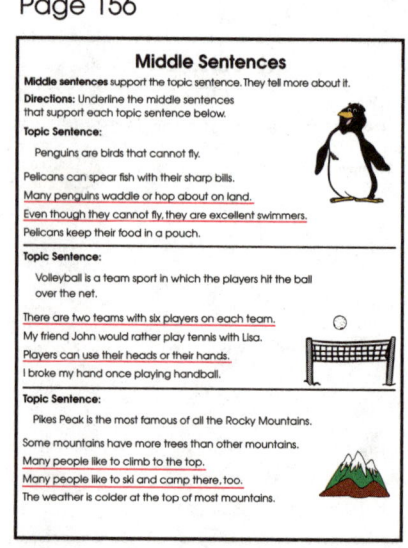

Summer Link Super Edition Grade 4

Page 166

Run-On Sentences

A **run-on sentence** occurs when two or more sentences are joined together without punctuation.

Examples:
Run-on sentence: I lost my way once did you?
Two sentences with correct punctuation: I lost my way once. Did you?
Run-on sentence: I found the recipe it was not hard to follow.
Two sentences with correct punctuation: I found the recipe. It was not hard to follow.

Directions: Rewrite the run-on sentences correctly with periods, exclamation points, and question marks. The first one has been done for you.

1. Did you take my umbrella I can't find it anywhere!
   Did you take my umbrella? I can't find it anywhere!
2. How can you stand that noise I can't!
   How can you stand that noise? I can't!
3. The cookies are gone I see only crumbs.
   The cookies are gone. I see only crumbs.
4. The dogs were barking they were hungry.
   The dogs were barking. They were hungry.
5. She is quite ill please call a doctor immediately!
   She is quite ill. Please call a doctor immediately!
6. The clouds came up we knew the storm would hit soon.
   The clouds came up. We knew the storm would hit soon.
7. You weren't home he stopped by this morning.
   You weren't home. He stopped by this morning.

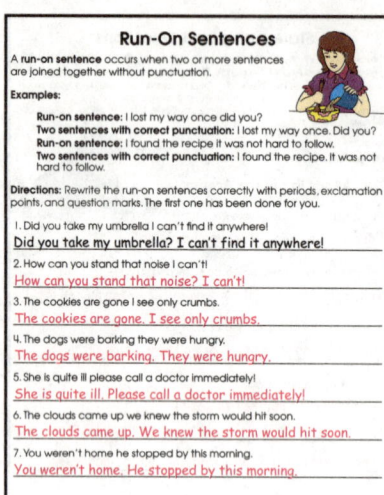

Page 167

Sentences and Non-Sentences

A **sentence** tells a complete idea.

Directions: Circle the groups of words that tell a complete idea.

1. (Sharks are fierce hunters.)
2. Afraid of sharks.
3. (The great white shark will attack people.)
4. (Other kinds will not.)
5. (Sharks have an outer row of teeth for grabbing food.)
6. (When the outer teeth fall out, another row of teeth moves up.)
7. Keep the ocean clean by eating dead animals.
8. Not a single bone in its body.
9. Cartilage.
10. Made of the same material as the tip of your nose.
11. (Unlike other fish, sharks cannot float.)
12. In motion constantly.
13. Even while sleeping.

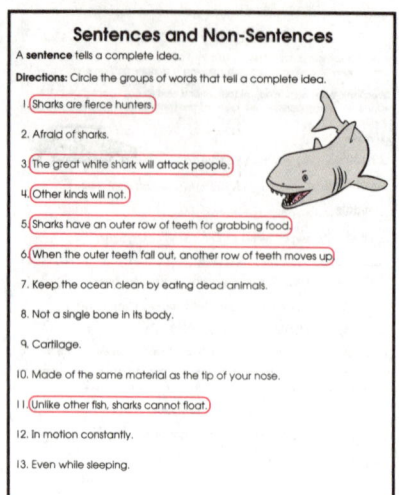

Page 168

Using Fewer Words

Writing can be more interesting when fewer words are used. Combining sentences is easy when the subjects are the same. Notice how the comma is used.

Example: Sally woke up. Sally ate breakfast. Sally brushed her teeth.
Sally woke up, ate breakfast, and brushed her teeth.

Combining sentences with more than one subject is a little more complicated. Notice how commas are used to "set off" information.

Examples: Jane went to the store. Jane is Sally's sister.
Jane went to the store with Sally, her sister.
Eddy Eddie likes to play with cars. Eddie is my younger brother.
Eddie, my younger brother, likes to play with cars.

Directions: Write each pair of sentences as one sentence.

1. Jerry played soccer after school. He played with his best friend, Tom.
   Jerry played soccer after school with his best friend, Tom.
2. Spot likes to chase cats. Spot is my dog.
   Spot, my dog, likes to chase cats.
3. Lori and Janice both love ice cream. Janice is Lori's cousin.
   Lori and Janice, Lori's cousin, both like ice cream.
4. Jayna is my cousin. Jayna helped me move into my new apartment.
   Jayna, my cousin, helped me move into my new apartment.
5. Romeo is a big tomcat. Romeo loves to hunt mice.
   Romeo, a big tomcat, loves to hunt mice.

Page 169

Contractions

A **contraction** is a short way to write two words together. Some letters are left out, but an apostrophe takes their place.

Directions: Write the words from the box that answer the questions.

| hasn't | you've | aren't | we've | weren't |

1. Write the correct contractions below.

Example:
I have — I've   was not — wasn't
we have — we've   you have — you've
are not — aren't   were not — weren't
has not — hasn't

2. Write two words from the box that are contractions using **have**.
   you've   we've

3. Write three words from the box that are contractions using **not**.
   hasn't   aren't   weren't

Page 170

And

Directions: Write each pair of sentences as one sentence.
Example: Jim will deal the cards one at a time. Jim will give four cards to everyone.
Jim will deal the cards one at a time <u>and</u> give four cards to everyone.

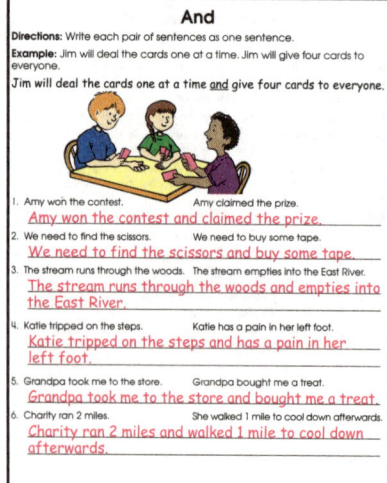

1. Amy won the contest. Amy claimed the prize.
   Amy won the contest and claimed the prize.
2. We need to find the scissors. We need to buy some tape.
   We need to find the scissors and buy some tape.
3. The stream runs through the woods. The stream empties into the East River.
   The stream runs through the woods and empties into the East River.
4. Katie tripped on the steps. Katie has a pain in her left foot.
   Katie tripped on the steps and has a pain in her left foot.
5. Grandpa took me to the store. Grandpa bought me a treat.
   Grandpa took me to the store and bought me a treat.
6. Charity ran 2 miles. She walked 1 mile to cool down afterwards.
   Charity ran 2 miles and walked 1 mile to cool down afterwards.

Page 171

And and But

We can use **and** or **but** to make one longer sentence from two short ones.
Directions: Use **and** or **but** to make two short sentences into a longer, more interesting one. Write the new sentence on the line below the two short sentences.
Example:
The skunk has black fur. The skunk has a white stripe.
The skunk has black fur and a white stripe.

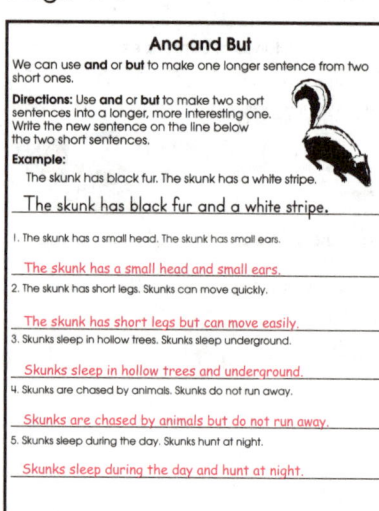

1. The skunk has a small head. The skunk has small ears.
   The skunk has a small head and small ears.
2. The skunk has short legs. Skunks can move quickly.
   The skunk has short legs but can move easily.
3. Skunks sleep in hollow trees. Skunks sleep underground.
   Skunks sleep in hollow trees and underground.
4. Skunks are chased by animals. Skunks do not run away.
   Skunks are chased by animals but do not run away.
5. Skunks sleep during the day. Skunks hunt at night.
   Skunks sleep during the day and hunt at night.

Page 172

Cause and Effect

A **cause** is the reason for an event. An **effect** is what happens as a result of a cause.

Directions: Circle the cause and underline the effect in each sentence. They may be in any order. The first one has been done for you.

1. (The truck hit an icy patch) and skidded off the road.
2. (When the door slammed shut) the baby woke up crying.
3. Our soccer game was cancelled (when it began to storm).
4. (Dad and Mom are adding a room onto the house) since our family is growing.
5. (Our car ran out of gas on the way to town) so we had to walk.
6. (The home run in the ninth inning) helped our team win the game.
7. We had to climb the stairs (because the elevator was broken).
8. We were late to school (because the bus had a flat tire).

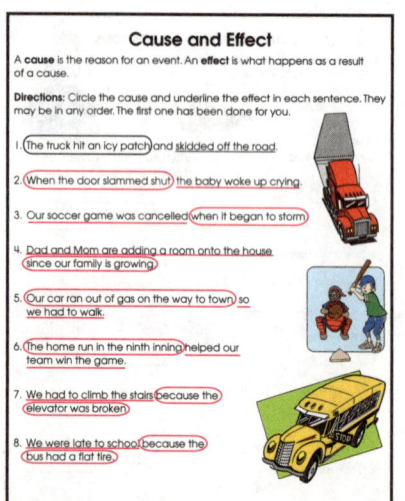

Page 173

Comprehension: The Moon

Our moon is not the only moon in the solar system. Some other planets have moons also. Saturn has 10 moons! Our moon is 225,727 miles away. Other times, it is 252,002 miles away. Why? Because the Moon revolves around Earth. It does not go around Earth in a perfect circle. So, sometimes its path takes it further away from our planet.

When our astronauts visited the Moon, they found dusty plains, high mountains and huge craters. There is no air or water on the Moon. That is why life cannot exist there. The astronauts had to wear space suits to protect their skin from the bright Sun. They had to take their own air to breathe. They had to take their own food and water. The Moon was an interesting place to visit. Would you want to live there?

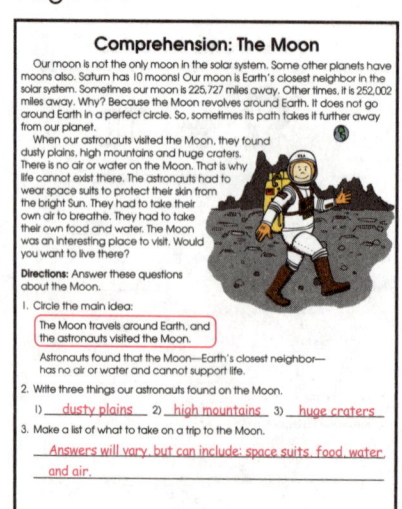

Directions: Answer these questions about the Moon.

1. Circle the main idea:
   (The Moon travels around Earth, and the astronauts visited the Moon.)
   Astronauts found that the Moon—Earth's closest neighbor—has no air or water and cannot support life.
2. Write three things our astronauts found on the Moon.
   1) dusty plains   2) high mountains   3) huge craters
3. Make a list of what to take on a trip to the Moon.
   Answers will vary, but can include: space suits, food, water, and air.

Page 174

Comprehension: Troy Aikman

Troy Aikman, Dallas Cowboy, was born on November 21, 1966. As a young boy, he enjoyed doing the usual things, like fishing or hunting with his dad. He also loved playing sports with his friends.

Troy Aikman knows a lot about change. When he was a young boy of 12 living in a city, he knew he wanted to be a baseball player. But when his family moved to a 172-acre ranch near Henryetta, Oklahoma, he felt like he would have to give up that dream. He soon learned that the people of Oklahoma loved football more than any other sport. Troy soon learned to love football, too. And he learned he was very good at it.

You can be a champion, too, in spite of changes in your life. You just have to be willing to make those changes work for you!

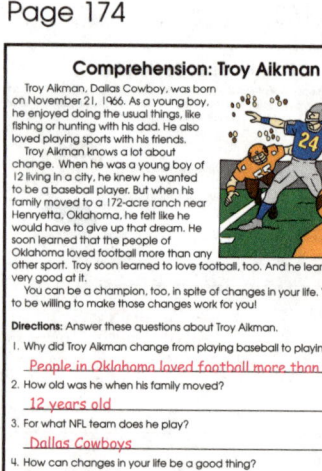

Directions: Answer these questions about Troy Aikman.

1. Why did Troy Aikman change from playing baseball to playing football?
   People in Oklahoma loved football more than baseball.
2. How old was he when his family moved?
   12 years old
3. For what NFL team does he play?
   Dallas Cowboys
4. How can changes in your life be a good thing?
   You can make them work for you.

Summer Link Super Edition Grade 4

Page 175

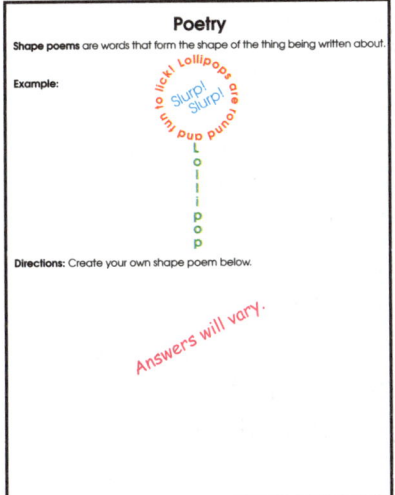

Page 176

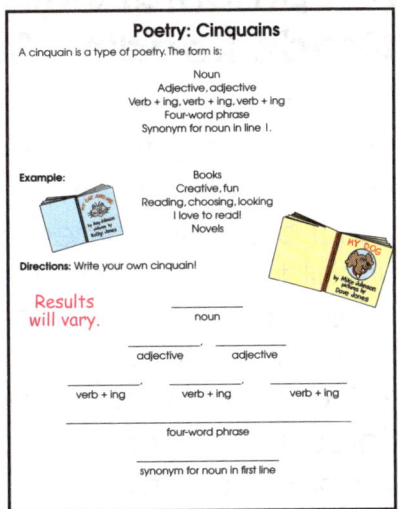

Page 177

Page 179

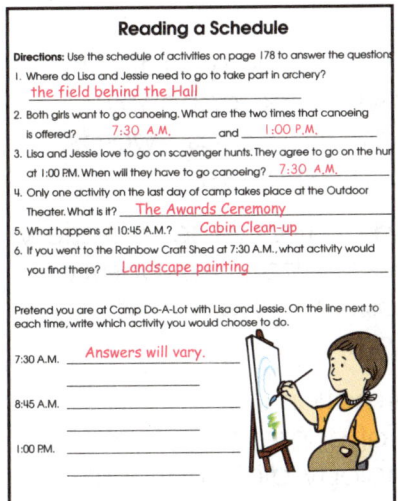

Developmental Skills for Fourth Grade Reading Success

Parents and educators alike know that the School Specialty name ensures outstanding educational experience and content. *Summer Link Reading* was designed to help your child retain those skills learned during the past school year. With *Summer Link Reading,* your child will be ready to review and master new material with confidence when he or she returns to school in the fall.

Use this checklist—compiled from state curriculum standards—to help your child prepare for proficiency testing. Place a check mark in the box if the appropriate skill has been mastered. If your child needs more work with a particular skill, place an "R" in the box and come back to it for review.

Language Arts Skills

❑ Recognizes and correctly uses parts of speech: nouns, pronouns, verbs, adjectives, adverbs, articles.

❑ Understands and correctly uses language conventions: spelling, noun plurals, verb tenses, complete sentences using subject and predicate, contractions, syllables, prefixes, suffixes, base words, idioms.

❑ Understands and correctly uses mechanics conventions: capitalization, period, comma, question mark, exclamation point, apostrophe.

❑ Uses a variety of vocabulary strategies: synonyms, antonyms, homophones, compound words, affixes, base words, phonics clues, context clues.

❑ Understands and correctly uses a variety of writing purposes: letters, lists, poetry, narrative composition, note taking, outlining, webbing.

❑ Can locate information in reference materials: table of contents, indexes, glossaries, technology, dictionaries, etc.

Reading Skills

❑ Uses reading strategies to understand meaning: sequence, context clues, cause and effect, compare/contrast, classification.

❑ Reads for different purposes: main idea, supporting details, following directions, predicting outcomes, making inferences, distinguishing fact/opinion, drawing conclusions.

❑ Recognizes story elements: character, setting, plot, conflict, resolution.

❑ Distinguishes between fiction and nonfiction.

❑ Recognizes a variety of literature forms: biography, poetry, fable, fairytales, historical/science fiction, etc.

Summer Link Test Practice
Table of Contents

Just for Parents

About the Tests 193
How to Help Your Child Prepare for Standardized Testing 197

For All Students

Taking Standardized Tests 199
Terms to Know 203
Practice Test and Final Test Information 206

Kinds of Questions

Multiple Choice Questions 207
Fill-in-the-Blank Questions 208
True/False Questions 209
Matching Questions 210
Analogy Questions 211
Short Answer Questions 212

Subject Help

Reading 213
Writing 214
Language Arts 215
Mathematics 217
Social Studies 219
Science 221

Practice Test and Final Test

Practice Test 223
Final Test 267
Answer Key 301
Record Your Scores 311
Test Practice Worksheet 313

About the Tests

What Are Standardized Achievement Tests?

Achievement tests measure what children know in particular subject areas such as reading, language arts, and mathematics. They do not measure your child's intelligence or ability to learn.

When tests are standardized, or *normed,* children's test results are compared with those of a specific group who have taken the test, usually at the same age or grade.

Standardized achievement tests measure what children around the country are learning. The test makers survey popular textbook series, as well as state curriculum frameworks and other professional sources, to determine what content is covered widely.

Because of variations in state frameworks and textbook series, as well as grade ranges on some test levels, the tests may cover some material that children have not yet learned. This is especially true if the test is offered early in the school year. However, test scores are compared to those of other children who take the test at the same time of year, so your child will not be at a disadvantage if his or her class has not covered specific material yet.

Different School Districts, Different Tests

There are many flexible options for districts when offering standardized tests. Many school districts choose not to give the full test battery, but select certain content and scoring options. For example, many schools may test only in the areas of reading and mathematics. Similarly, a state or district may use one test for certain grades and another test for other grades. These decisions are often based on the amount of time and money a district wishes to spend on test administration. Some states choose to develop their own statewide assessment tests.

On pages 194 and 195 you will find information about these five widely used standardized achievement tests:

- California Achievement Tests (CAT)
- Terra Nova/CTBS
- Iowa Test of Basic Skills (ITBS)
- Stanford Achievement Test (SAT9)
- Metropolitan Achievement Test (MAT).

However, this book contains strategies and practice questions for use with a variety of tests. Even if your state does not give one of the five tests listed above, your child will benefit from doing the practice questions in this book. If you're unsure about which test your child takes, contact your local school district to find out which tests are given.

Types of Test Questions

Traditionally, standardized achievements tests have used only multiple choice questions. Today, many tests may include constructed response (short answer) and extended response (essay) questions as well.

In addition, many tests include questions that tap students' higher-order thinking skills. Instead of simple recall questions, such as identifying a date in history, questions may require students to make comparisons and contrasts or analyze results among other skills.

What the Tests Measure

These tests do not measure your child's level of intelligence, but they do show how well your child knows material that he or she has learned and that

is also covered on the tests. It's important to remember that some tests cover content that is not taught in your child's school or grade. In other instances, depending on when in the year the test is given, your child may not yet have covered the material.

If the test reports you receive show that your child needs improvement in one or more skill areas, you may want to seek help from your child's teacher and find out how you can work with your child to improve his or her skills.

California Achievement Tests (CAT/5)

What Is the *California Achievement Test?*

The *California Achievement Test* is a standardized achievement test battery that is widely used with elementary through high school students.

Parts of the Test

The CAT includes tests in the following content areas:

Reading
- Word Analysis
- Vocabulary
- Comprehension

Spelling

Language Arts
- Language Mechanics
- Language Usage

Mathematics

Science

Social Studies

Your child may take some or all of these subtests if your district uses the *California Achievement Test.*

Terra Nova/CTBS (Comprehensive Tests of Basic Skills)

What Is the *Terra Nova/CTBS?*

The *Terra Nova/Comprehensive Tests of Basic Skills* is a standardized achievement test battery used in elementary through high school grades.

While many of the test questions on the *Terra Nova* are in the traditional multiple choice form, your child may take parts of the *Terra Nova* that include some open-ended questions (constructed-response items).

Parts of the Test

Your child may take some or all of the following subtests if your district uses the *Terra Nova/CTBS:*

Reading/Language Arts
Mathematics
Science
Social Studies

Supplementary tests include:
- Word Analysis
- Vocabulary
- Language Mechanics
- Spelling
- Mathematics Computation

Critical thinking skills may also be tested.

Iowa Tests of Basic Skills (ITBS)

What Is the ITBS?

The *Iowa Test of Basic Skills* is a standardized achievement test battery used in elementary through high school grades.

Parts of the Test

Your child may take some or all of these subtests if your district uses the *ITBS*, also known as the *Iowa:*

Reading
- Vocabulary
- Reading Comprehension

Language Arts
- Spelling
- Capitalization
- Punctuation
- Usage and Expression

Math
- Concepts/Estimate
- Problems/Data Interpretation

Social Studies

Science

Sources of Information

Stanford Achievement Test (SAT9)

What Is the Stanford Achievement Test?

The *Stanford Achievement Test, Ninth Edition (SAT9)* is a standardized achievement test battery used in elementary through high school grades.

Note that the *Stanford Achievement Test (SAT9)* is a different test from the *SAT* used by high school students for college admissions.

While many of the test questions on the *SAT9* are in traditional multiple choice form, your child may take parts of the *SAT9* that include some open-ended questions (constructed-response items).

Parts of the Test

Your child may take some or all of these subtests if your district uses the *Stanford Achievement Test.*

Reading
- Vocabulary
- Reading Comprehension

Mathematics
- Problem Solving
- Procedures

Language Arts

Spelling

Study Skills

Listening

Critical thinking skills may also be tested.

Metropolitan Achievement Test (MAT7 and MAT8)

What Is the Metropolitan Achievement Test?

The *Metropolitan Achievement Test* is a standardized achievement test battery used in elementary through high school grades.

Parts of the Test

Your child may take some or all of these subtests if your district uses the *Metropolitan Achievement Test*.

Reading
- Vocabulary
- Reading Comprehension

Math
- Concepts and Problem Solving
- Computation

Language Arts
- Pre-writing
- Composing
- Editing

Science
Social Studies
Research Skills
Thinking Skills
Spelling

Statewide Assessments

Today the majority of states give statewide assessments. In some cases these tests are known as *high-stakes assessments*. This means that students must score at a certain level in order to be promoted. Some states use minimum competency or proficiency tests. Often these tests measure more basic skills than other types of statewide assessments.

Statewide assessments are generally linked to state curriculum frameworks. Frameworks provide a blueprint, or outline, to ensure that teachers are covering the same curriculum topics as other teachers in the same grade level in the state. In some states, standardized achievement tests (such as the five described in this book) are used in connection with statewide assessments.

When Statewide Assessments Are Given

Statewide assessments may not be given at every grade level. Generally, they are offered at one or more grades in elementary school, middle school, and high school. Many states test at grades 4, 8, and 10.

State-by-State Information

You can find information about statewide assessments and curriculum frameworks at your state Department of Education Web site. To find the address for your individual state go to www.ed.gov, click on Topics A–Z, and then click on State Departments of Education. You will find a list of all the state departments of education, mailing addresses, and Web sites.

How to Help Your Child Prepare for Standardized Testing

Preparing All Year Round

Perhaps the most valuable way you can help your child prepare for standardized achievement tests is by providing enriching experiences. Keep in mind also, that test results for younger children are not as reliable as for older students. If a child is hungry, tired, or upset, this may result in a poor test score. Here are some tips on how you can help your child do his or her best on standardized tests.

Read aloud with your child. Reading aloud helps develop vocabulary and fosters a positive attitude toward reading. Reading together is one of the most effective ways you can help your child succeed in school.

Share experiences. Baking cookies together, planting a garden, or making a map of your neighborhood are examples of activities that help build skills that are measured on the tests such as sequencing and following directions.

Become informed about your state's testing procedures. Ask about or watch for announcements of meetings that explain about standardized tests and statewide assessments in your school district.

Talk to your child's teacher about your child's individual performance on these state tests during a parent-teacher conference.

Help your child know what to expect. Read and discuss with your child the test-taking tips in this book. Your child can prepare by working through a couple of strategies a day so that no practice session takes too long.

Help your child with his or her regular school assignments. Set up a quiet study area for homework. Supply this area with pencils, paper, markers, a calculator, a ruler, a dictionary, scissors, glue, and so on. Check your child's homework and offer to help if he or she gets stuck. But remember, it's your child's homework, not yours. If you help too much, your child will not benefit from the activity.

Keep in regular contact with your child's teacher. Attend parent-teacher conferences, school functions, PTA or PTO meetings, and school board meetings. This will help you get to know the educators in your district and the families of your child's classmates.

Learn to use computers as an educational resource. If you do not have a computer and Internet access at home, try your local library.

Remember—simply getting your child comfortable with testing procedures and helping him or her know what to expect can improve test scores!

Getting Ready for the Big Day

There are lots of things you can do on or immediately before test day to improve your child's chances of testing success. What's more, these strategies will help your child prepare him or herself for school tests, too, and promote general study skills that can last a lifetime.

Provide a good breakfast on test day. Instead of sugar cereal, which provides immediate but not long-term energy, have your child eat a breakfast with protein or complex carbohydrates such as an egg, whole grain cereal or toast, or a banana-yogurt shake.

Assure your child that he or she is not expected to know all of the answers on the test. Explain that other children in higher grades may take the same test, and that the test may measure things your child has not yet learned in school. Help your child understand that you expect him or her to put forth a good effort—and that this is enough. Your child should not try to cram for these tests. Also avoid threats or bribes; these put undue pressure on children and may interfere with their best performance.

Promote a good night's sleep. A good night's sleep before the test is essential. Try not to overstress the importance of the test. This may cause your child to lose sleep because of anxiety. Doing some exercise after school and having a quiet evening routine will help your child sleep well the night before the test.

Keep the mood light and offer encouragement. To provide a break on test days, do something fun and special after school—take a walk around the neighborhood, play a game, read a favorite book, or prepare a special snack together. These activities keep your child's mood light—even if the testing sessions have been difficult—and show how much you appreciate your child's effort.

Taking Standardized Tests

No matter what grade you're in, this is information you can use to prepare for standardized tests. Here is what you'll find:

- Test-taking tips and strategies to use on test day and year-round.
- Important terms to know for Language Arts, Reading, Math, Science, and Social Studies.
- A checklist of skills to complete to help you understand what you need to know in Language Arts, Reading Comprehension, Writing, and Math.
- General study/homework tips.

By opening this book, you've already taken your first step towards test success. The rest is easy—all you have to do is get started!

What You Need to Know

There are many things you can do to increase your test success. Here's a list of tips to keep in mind when you take standardized tests—and when you study for them, too.

Keep up with your school work. One way you can succeed in school and on tests is by studying and doing your homework regularly. Studies show that you remember only about one-fifth of what you memorize the night before a test. That's one good reason not to try to learn it all at once! Keeping up with your work throughout the year will help you remember the material better. You also won't be as tired or nervous as if you try to learn everything at once.

Feel your best. One of the ways you can do your best on tests and in school is to make sure your body is ready. To do this, get a good night's sleep each night and eat a healthy breakfast (not sugary cereal that will leave you tired by the middle of the morning). An egg or a milkshake with yogurt and fresh fruit will give you lasting energy. Also, wear comfortable clothes, maybe your lucky shirt or your favorite color on test day. It can't hurt, and it may even keep you relax.

Be prepared. Do practice questions and learn about how standardized tests are organized. Books like this one will help you know what to expect when you take a standardized test.

When you are taking the test, follow the directions. It is important to listen carefully to the directions your teacher gives and to read the written instructions carefully. Words like *not, none, rarely, never,* and *always* are very important in test directions and questions. You may want to circle words like these.

Look at each page carefully before you start answering. In school you usually read a passage and then answer questions about it. But when you take a test, it's helpful to follow a different order.

If you are taking a Reading test, first read the directions. Then read the *questions* before you read the passage. This way you will know exactly what kind of information to look for as you read. Next, read the passage carefully. Finally, answer the questions.

On math and science tests, look at the labels on graphs and charts. Think about what each graph or chart shows. Questions often will ask you to draw conclusions about the information.

Manage your time. *Time management* means using your time wisely on a test so that you can finish as much of it as possible and do your best. Look over the test or the parts that you are allowed to do at one time. Sometimes you may want to do the easier parts first. This way, if you run out of time before you finish, you will have completed a good chunk of the work.

For tests that have a time limit, notice what time it is when the test begins and figure out when you need to stop. Check a few times as you work through the test to be sure you are making good progress and not spending too much time on any particular section.

You don't have to keep up with everyone else. You may notice other students in the class finishing before you do. Don't worry about this. Everyone works at a different pace. Just keep going, trying not to spend too long on any one question.

Fill in answer circles properly. Even if you know every answer on a test, you won't do well unless you fill in the circle next to the correct answer.

Fill in the entire circle, but don't spend too much time making it perfect. Make your mark dark, but not so dark that it goes through the paper! And be sure you only choose one answer for each question, even if you are not sure. If you choose two answers, both will be marked as wrong.

It's usually not a good idea to change your answers. Usually your first choice is the right one. Unless you realize that you misread the question, the directions, or some facts in a passage, it's usually safer to stay with your first answer. If you are pretty sure it's wrong, of course, go ahead and change it. Make sure you completely erase the first choice and neatly fill in your new choice.

Use context clues to figure out tough questions. If you come across a word or idea you don't understand, use context clues—the words in the sentences nearby—to help you figure out its meaning.

Sometimes it's good to guess. Should you guess when you don't know an answer on a test? That depends. If your teacher has made the test, usually you will score better if you answer as many questions as possible, even if you don't really know the answers.

On standardized tests, here's what to do to score your best. For each question, most of these tests let you choose from four or five answer choices. If you decide that a couple of answers are clearly wrong but you're still not sure about the answer, go ahead and make your best guess. If you can't narrow down the choices at all, then you may be better off skipping the question. Tests like these take away extra points for wrong answers, so it's better to leave them blank. Be sure you skip over the answer space for these questions on the answer sheet, though, so you don't fill in the wrong spaces.

Sometimes you should skip a question and come back to it. On many tests, you will score better if you answer more questions. This means that you should not spend too much time on any single question. Sometimes it gets tricky, though, keeping track of questions you skipped on your answer sheet.

If you want to skip a question because you don't know the answer, put a very light pencil mark next to the question in the test booklet. Try to choose an answer, even if you're not sure of it. Fill in the answer lightly on the answer sheet.

Check your work. On a standardized test, you can't go ahead or skip back to another section of the test. But you may go back and review your answers on the section you just worked on if you have extra time.

First, scan your answer sheet. Make sure that you answered every question you could. Also, if you are using a bubble-type answer sheet, make sure that you filled in only one bubble for each question. Erase any extra marks on the page.

Finally—avoid test anxiety! If you get nervous about tests, don't worry. *Test anxiety* happens to lots of good students. Being a little nervous actually sharpens your mind. But if you get very nervous about tests, take a few minutes to relax the night before or the day of the test. One good way to relax is to get some exercise, even if you just have time to stretch, shake out your fingers, and wiggle your toes. If you can't move around, it helps just to take a few slow, deep breaths and picture yourself doing a great job!

Terms to Know

Here's a list of terms that are good to know when taking standardized tests. Don't be worried if you see something new. You may not have learned it in school yet.

acute angle: an angle of less than 90°

adjective: a word that describes a noun (*yellow duckling, new bicycle*)

adverb: a word that describes a verb (*ran fast, laughing heartily*)

analogy: a comparison of the relationship between two or more otherwise unrelated things (*Carrot is to vegetable as banana is to fruit.*)

angle: the figure formed by two lines that start at the same point, usually shown in degrees

antonyms: words with opposite meanings (*big and small, young and old*)

area: the amount of space inside a flat shape, expressed in square units

article: a word such as *a*, *an*, or *the* that goes in front of a noun (*the chicken, an apple*)

cause/effect: the reason that something happens

character: a person in a story, book, movie, play, or TV show

compare/contrast: to tell what is alike and different about two or more things

compass rose: the symbol on a map that shows where North, South, East, and West are

conclusion: a logical decision you can make based on information from a reading selection or science experiment

congruent: equal in size or shape

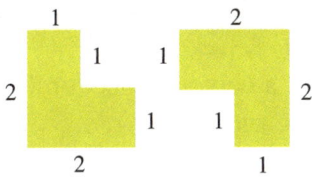

context clues: language and details in a piece of writing that can help you figure out difficult words and ideas

denominator: in a fraction, the number under the line, shows how many equal parts a whole has been divided into ($\frac{1}{2}, \frac{6}{7}$)

direct object: in a sentence, the person or thing that receives the action of a verb (*John hit the ball hard.*)

equation: in math, a statement where one set of numbers or values is equal to another set ($6 + 6 = 12, 4 \times 5 = 20$)

factor: a whole number that can be divided exactly into another whole number (*1, 2, 3, 4, and 6 are all factors of 12.*)

genre: a category of literature that contains writing with common features (*drama, fiction, nonfiction, poetry*)

hypothesis: in science, the possible answer to a question; most science experiments begin with a hypothesis

indirect object: in a sentence, the noun or pronoun that tells to or for whom the action of the verb is done (*Louise gave a flower to her sister.*)

infer: to make an educated guess about a piece of writing, based on information contained in the selection and what you already know

main idea: the most important idea or message in a writing selection

203 Summer Link Super Edition Grade 4

map legend: the part of a map showing symbols that represent natural or human-made objects

noun: a person, place, or thing (*president, underground, train*)

numerator: in a fraction, the number above the line, shows how many equal parts are to be taken from the denominator ($\frac{3}{4}, \frac{1}{5}$)

operation: in math, tells what must be done to numbers in an equation (such as add, subtract, multiply, or divide)

parallel: lines or rays that, if extended, could never intersect

percent: fraction of a whole that has been divided into 100 parts, usually expressed with % sign ($\frac{5}{100} = 5\%$)

perimeter: distance around an object or shape

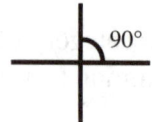

perpendicular: lines or rays that intersect to form a 90° (right) angle

predicate: in a sentence, the word or words that tell what the subject does, did, or has (*The fuzzy kitten had black spots on its belly.*)

predict: in science or reading, to use given information to decide what will happen

prefixes/suffixes: letters added to the beginning or end of a word to change its meaning (*reorganize, hopeless*)

preposition: a word that shows the relationship between a noun or pronoun and other words in a phrase or sentence (*We sat by the fire. She walked through the door.*)

probability: the likelihood that something will happen, often shown with numbers

pronoun: a word that is used in place of a noun (*She gave the present to them.*)

ratio: a comparison of two quantities, often shown as a fraction (*The ratio of boys to girls in the class is 2 to 1, or 2/1.*)

sequence: the order in which events happen or in which items can be placed in a pattern

subject: in a sentence, the word or words that tells who or what the sentence is about (*Uncle Robert baked the cake. Everyone at the party ate it.*)

summary: a restatement of important ideas from a selection in the writer's own words

synonyms: words with the same, or almost the same, meaning (*delicious and tasty, funny and comical*)

symmetry: in math and science, two or more sides or faces of an object that are mirror images of one another

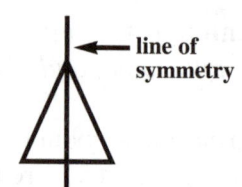

Venn diagram: two or more overlapping circles used to compare and contrast two or more things

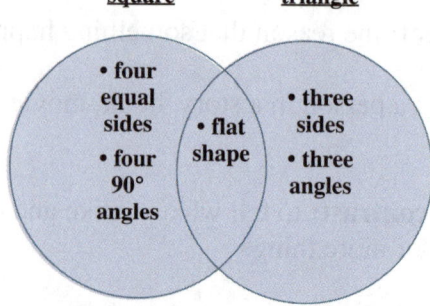

verb: a word that describes an action or state of being (*He watched the fireworks.*)

writing prompt: on a test, a question or statement that you must respond to in writing

Practice Test and Final Test Information

The remainder of this book is made up of two tests. On page 223, you will find a Practice Test. On page 267, you will find a Final Test. These tests will give you a chance to put the tips you have learned to work.

Here are some things to remember as you take these tests:

- Be sure you understand all the directions before you begin each test.
- Ask an adult questions about the directions if you do not understand them.
- Work as quickly as you can during each test. There are no time limits on the Practice Test, but you should try to make good use of your time. There are suggested time limits on the Final Test to give you practice managing your time.
- You will notice little GO and STOP signs at the bottom of the test pages. When you see a GO sign, continue on to the next page if you feel ready. The STOP sign means you are at the end of a section. When you see a STOP sign, take a break.
- When you change an answer, be sure to erase your first mark completely.
- You can guess at an answer or skip difficult items and go back to them later.
- Use the tips you have learned whenever you can.
- After you have completed your tests, check your answers with the answer key. You can record the number of questions you got correct for each unit on the recording sheet on page 311.
- It is OK to be a little nervous. You may even do better.
- When you complete all the lessons in this book, you will be on your way to test success!

This page intentionally left blank.

Multiple Choice Questions

You have probably seen multiple choice questions before. They are the most common type of question used on standardized tests. To answer a multiple choice question, you must choose one answer from a number of choices.

EXAMPLE **Another word for <u>unsafe</u> is _____.**

    A safe

    B dangerous

    C unkind

    D careful

Sometimes you will know the answer right away. Other times you won't. To answer multiple choice questions on a test, do the following:

- Read the directions carefully. If you're not sure what you're supposed to do, you might make a lot of mistakes.
- First answer any easy questions whose answers you are sure you know.
- When you come to a harder question, circle the question number. You can come back to this question after you have finished all the easier ones.
- When you're ready to answer a hard question, throw out answers that you know are wrong. You can do this by making an X after each choice you know is not correct. The last choice left is probably the correct one.

Testing It Out
Now look at the sample question more closely.

Think: I know that *safe* is the opposite of *unsafe*, so **A** cannot be the correct answer. I think that *cautious* is like being *careful*, so **D** is probably not the right answer.

Now I have to choose between **C** and **B**. Let's see: *unkind* has the word *kind* in it, and **un** usually means *not*, so I think that *unkind* means *not kind*. However, something that is *dangerous* is definitely not safe. So **B** must be the correct choice.

207   Summer Link Super Edition Grade 4

Fill-in-the-Blank Questions

On some tests, you will be given multiple choice questions where you must fill in something that's missing from a phrase, sentence, equation, or passage. These are called "fill-in-the-blank" questions.

> **EXAMPLE**   Tricia felt _____ that Robyn could not come to her party.
>
> A   disturbed
>
> B   distorted
>
> C   dissolved
>
> D   disappointed

To answer fill-in-the-blank questions:

- First read the item with a blank that needs to be filled.
- See if you can think of the answer even before you look at your choices.
- Even if the answer you first thought of is one of the choices, be sure to check the other choices. There may be an even better answer.
- For harder questions, try to fit every answer choice into the blank. Underline clue words that may help you find the correct answer. Write an **X** after answers that do not fit. Choose the answer that does fit.

Testing It Out

Now look at the sample question above more closely.

Think: Choice **A** says, "Tricia felt *disturbed* that Robyn could not come to her party." I guess someone *might* feel disturbed if a friend could not come to her party.

Choice **B** says, "Tricia felt *dissolved* that Robyn could not come to her party." That sounds silly—people don't feel dissolved. That choice is wrong.

Choice **C** says, "Tricia felt *distorted* that Robyn could not come to her party." I have never heard of anyone feeling distorted. That choice must be wrong, too.

Choice **D** says, "Tricia felt *disappointed* that Robyn could not come to her party." This is how I would feel if a friend could not come to my party. I'll choose **D**.

True/False Questions

A true/false question asks you to read a statement and decide if it is right (true) or wrong (false). Sometimes you will be asked to write **T** for true or **F** for false. Most of the time you must fill in a bubble next to the correct answer.

EXAMPLE	**Milk is the only ingredient in yogurt.**
	A true
	B false

To answer true/false questions on a test, think about the following:

- True/false sections contain more questions than other sections of a test. If there is a time limit on the test, you may need to go a little more quickly than usual. Do not spend too much time on any one question.
- First answer all of the easy questions. Circle the numbers next to harder ones and come back to them later.
- If you have time left after completing all the questions, quickly double-check your answers.
- True/false questions with words like *always, never, none, only,* and *every* are usually false. This is because they limit a statement so much.

Remember

True/false questions with words like *always, never, none, only* and *every* are usually false.

Testing It Out
Now look at the sample question more closely.

Think: I see the word *only* in this statement. I know that milk is the main ingredient in yogurt—it tastes a lot like milk. But some kinds of yogurt have fruit in them, and I think they must have sugar, too. I will mark this answer **B** for false.

Matching Questions

Matching questions ask you to find pairs of words or phrases that go together. The choices are often shown in columns.

EXAMPLE **Match items that mean the same, or almost the same, thing.**

1	happy	A	mournful	1	A B C D
2	angry	B	flabbergasted	2	A B C D
3	surprised	C	joyful	3	A B C D
4	sad	D	furious	4	A B C D

When answering matching questions on tests, there are some simple guidelines you can use:

- When you first look at a matching question, you will probably be able to spot some of the matches right away. So match the easiest choices first.
- If you come to a word you don't know, look for prefixes, suffixes, or root words to help figure out its meaning.
- Work down one column at a time. It is confusing to switch back and forth.

Testing It Out

Now look at the sample question more closely.

Think: What's a word from the second column that goes with *happy*? *Joyful* has the word *joy* in it, which is like happiness, so the answer to **1** must be **C**.

I know that *furious* is another word for *angry*, so the answer to 2 is **D**.

I'm not sure which of the remaining choices means the same as *surprised*, so I'll come back to that one.

For *sad*, I'm not sure what the best match is; however, I see that *mournful* has the word *mourn* in it, and people mourn when someone dies. Since people mourn when someone dies and they are also sad, then I'll choose **A** as the match for *sad*.

Going back to *surprised*, the only remaining choice is **B**, *flabbergasted*. That must be the correct choice, since I am fairly certain of my other answers.

Analogy Questions

Analogies are a special kind of question. In an analogy question, you are asked to figure out the relationship between two things. Then you must complete another pair with the same relationship.

EXAMPLE Carrot is to vegetable as orange is to _____.

  A celery   C apple
  B sweet   D fruit

Analogies usually have two pairs of items. In the question above the two pairs are carrot/vegetable and orange/_____. To answer analogy questions on standardized tests, do the following:

- Find the missing item that completes the second pair. To do this, you must figure out how the first pair of items relate to each other. Try to form a sentence that explains how they are related.
- Next, use your sentence to figure out the missing word in the second pair of items.
- For more difficult analogies, try each answer choice in the sentence you formed. Choose the answer that fits best.

Testing It Out

Now look at the sample question more closely.

Think: How are carrots and vegetables related? A carrot is a kind of vegetable. So if I use the word *orange* in this sentence, I'd say, an *orange* is a kind of _____.

Choice **A** is *celery*. If I use *celery* to complete the sentence, I end up with *An orange is a kind of celery*. I think that celery is a vegetable. That choice must be wrong.

Choice **B** is *sweet*. *An orange is a kind of sweet*. No, that's not right, either. Oranges are sweet, but they're not a kind of sweet.

Choice **C** is *apple*. *An orange is a kind of apple*. I know that that answer is wrong because that sentence makes no sense.

Choice **D** would be *An orange is a kind of fruit*. Yes, I think that's true. So the answer must be **D**.

211 Summer Link Super Edition Grade 4

Short Answer Questions

Some test questions don't give you answers to choose from; instead, you must write short answers in your own words. These are called "short answer" or "open response" questions. For example:

Which animal does not fit into the group?
_____

Why?
_____

When you must write short answers to questions on a standardized test:

- Make sure to respond directly to the question that is being asked.
- Your response should be short but complete. Don't waste time including unnecessary information. On the other hand, make sure to answer the entire question, not just a part of it.
- Write in complete sentences unless the directions say you don't have to.
- Double-check your answers for spelling, punctuation, and grammar mistakes.

Testing It Out

Now look at the sample question more closely.

Think: Squirrels, rabbits, and skunks are all mammals. They have fur and four legs. But butterflies are insects. So *butterfly* must be the animal that does not fit.

Since there are no instructions about what to write for each answer, I should use complete sentences. So I'll write:

Which animal does not fit into the group?

The butterfly does not fit into the group.

Why?

A butterfly is an insect. All the other animals shown are mammals.

Reading

Many standardized tests have sections called "Reading" or "Reading Comprehension." Reading Comprehension questions test your ability to read for detail, find meaning in a sentence or passage, and use context clues to figure out words or ideas you don't understand.

The following is a list of topics covered on Reading Comprehension tests. Look at the tips and examples that go with each topic.

Word Meaning
Word meaning questions test your vocabulary and your ability to figure out unfamiliar words. When answering questions about word meaning:

- Look at words carefully and see if you can find prefixes, suffixes, or root words that give clues to their meaning. If you look at the underlined word below, *unusual*, you can see it contains the prefix **un** (which means not) and a root word, *usual* (common or ordinary). So you can guess that the word means something like "not common" or "not ordinary."

> We saw some unusual animals at the zoo.

- For clues to a more difficult word's meaning, look at the other words in the sentence or passage. If you look at the example below, for instance, you can tell by the use of words like *detective* and *mystery* that solved means "found the answer to" or "explained."

> The detective solved the mystery of the missing jewels.

Characterization
What characters say, do, and feel is an important part of many reading passages. Often you can tell what a character is feeling by what he or she says or does.

> When Joey heard the winning score, he jumped up and cheered.

Cause and Effect
Look for **cause and effect** when you read. A **cause** is an event that makes another event happen. The **effect** is the event that is caused.

- Words like *before, after*, and *because* can provide clues to cause and effect.

> Sheila was mad at her sister because she had borrowed her shirt without asking.

In this sentence, Sheila's sister borrowing a shirt is the cause and Sheila being mad is the effect.

Sequence
The **sequence of events** is the order in which events take place in a story or article. Sometimes events are listed in sequence. Other times, they aren't.

213

Summer Link Super Edition Grade 4

Writing

Many tests will ask you to respond to a writing prompt. When responding to a writing prompt, follow these guidelines:

> **EXAMPLE**
>
> **Do you think Little Red Riding Hood was a smart girl? Write a paragraph explaining your answer.**

The following is a list of guidelines to use when responding to a writing prompt.

Reading the Prompt
- Read the instructions carefully. Sometimes you will be given a choice of questions or topics to write about. You don't want to end up responding to more questions than you need to.
- Read the prompt twice to be sure you understand it. Remember, there is no one right response to a writing prompt.

Prewriting
- Before you write your answer, jot down some details to include.
- You may find it helpful to use a chart, web, illustration, or outline to help you organize the information you want to include in your response.

A web is a way of organizing your thoughts. If you were writing about Little Red Riding Hood, your web might look like this:

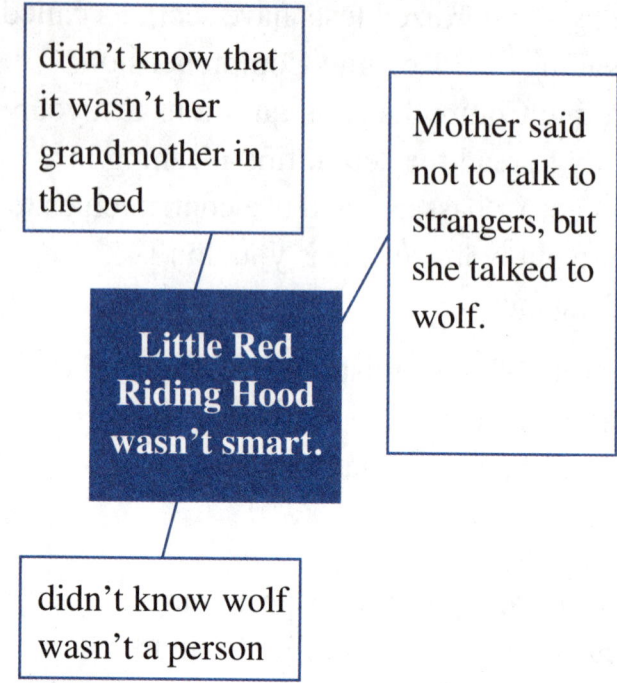

Drafting
- Begin your answer with a **topic sentence** that answers the question and gives the main idea.
- Write **supporting sentences** that give details and tell more about the main idea.
- If you are allowed, skip lines as you write. That way you'll have space to correct your mistakes once you're done writing.

Proofreading
- Make sure to proofread your draft for missing words, grammar, punctuation, capitalization, indentation, and spelling. Correct your mistakes.

Language Arts

Mechanics and Expression

Standardized tests usually include questions about spelling, grammar, punctuation, and capitalization. These questions are often grouped together in sections called "Language Mechanics and Expression" or "Language Arts."

The following is a list of the different topics included under Language Mechanics and Expression. Look at the tips and examples that go with each topic.

Grammar

Grammar is the set of rules that helps you write good, clear sentences. Whether you are answering a multiple choice question, writing a short answer, or responding to a writing prompt, you should:

- Be sure the subject and verb of each sentence agree with each other.

> Sam **brushes** his dog.
> [singular subject and verb]
>
> Sam and Gina **brush** their dog.
> [plural subject and verb]

- Remember how to use different parts of speech such as nouns, verbs, adjectives, adverbs, and pronouns.

> Lila ate quickly. She was hungry.
> [noun-verb-adverb-pronoun-verb-adjective]

Capitalization

You may be asked to identify words that should be capitalized and words that shouldn't. Remember:

- always capitalize the first word in a sentence.
- always capitalize the names of people, places, and other proper nouns.

> **T**he **R**amirez family visited the **G**rand **C**anyon in **J**uly.
>
> **T**hey sent postcards to the **S**osas and the **M**orleys.

Punctuation

You will probably be given multiple choice questions about punctuation, but you will also be required to use punctuation marks when you write answers in your own words.

- Make sure to check punctuation at the end of sentences *and* within them.

> Did you pack the food**?**
> [question mark]
>
> I think I put it in the car**.**
> [period]
>
> Wait**,** I left the food in the garage**!**
> [comma, exclamation point]
>
> We can buy fruit**,** sandwiches**,** and pop at the market. *[commas]*

Language Arts

Spelling

You may be asked to pick out misspelled words or choose the correct spelling of a word that is already misspelled. You should also check your own spelling when you write.

> The Grand Canyon is 500 **mils** from our **hom**.
> [incorrect]
>
> The Grand Canyon is 500 **miles** from our **home**.
> [correct]

Sentence Structure

Remember to use complete sentences whenever you write a short answer or paragraph. To tell if a sentence is complete:

- make sure the sentence has a subject and a verb.
- make sure the sentence starts with a capital letter and ends with the correct punctuation mark.

> barked at us as we drove by
> [fragment]
>
> The dog barked at us as we drove by.
> [complete sentence]

Also keep in mind:

- avoid beginning sentences with *And*.
- you can often make two sentences more interesting by combining them into one. However, you should be careful not to change the sentences' meaning.

> Jed went to the movie. Alice went to the movie. Sandy stayed home.
>
> Jed and Alice went to the movie, but Sandy stayed home.
> [combined]

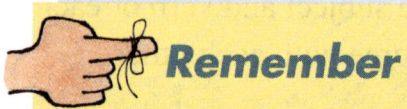

- Make sure each sentence has a subject and predicate.
- Start each sentence with a capital letter.
- End each sentence with the correct punctuation mark.

Summer Link Super Edition Grade 4

Math: Concepts

Standardized tests also test your understanding of important math concepts you will have learned about in school. The following is a list of concepts that you may be tested on:

Number Concepts
- recognizing the standard and metric units of measure used for weighing and finding length and distance.
- recognizing place value (the ones, tens, hundreds, and thousands places; the tenths and hundredths places).
- telling time to the nearest quarter-hour.
- using a calendar.
- reading a thermometer.
- rounding up and down to the nearest ten or hundred.
- recognizing the bills and coins we use for money.

Geometry
- identify flat shapes such as triangles, circles, squares, rectangles, and more.
- identify solid shapes such as prisms, spheres, cubes, cylinders, and cones.
- find the perimeter of flat shapes.
- find the line of symmetry in a flat shape.
- tell about the number of angles and sides of flat shapes.

Other Things to Keep in Mind
- If you come to a difficult problem, think of what you do know about the topic and eliminate answer choices that don't make sense.
- Also keep in mind that you may be given a problem that can't be solved because not enough information is provided. In that case, "not enough information" or "none of the above" will be an answer choice. Carefully consider each of the other answer choices before you decide that a problem is not solvable.

Math: Applications

You will often be asked to apply what you know about math to a new type of problem or set of information. Even if you aren't exactly sure how to solve a problem of this type, you can usually draw on what you already know to make the most logical choice.

When preparing for standardized tests, you may want to practice some of the following:

- how to use a number line.
- putting numbers in order from least to greatest and using greater than/less than symbols.
- recognizing basic number patterns and object patterns and extending them.
- choosing the best operation to solve a problem and writing an equation to solve the problem.
- reading bar graphs, tally charts, or pictographs.
- reading pie charts.
- reading simple line graphs.
- reading and making Venn diagrams.

Other Things to Keep in Mind
- When answering application questions, be sure to read each problem carefully. You may want to use scrap paper to work out some problems.
- Again, if you come to a problem you aren't sure how to solve or a word/idea you don't recognize, try to eliminate answer choices by using what you do know. Then go back and check your answer choice in the context of the problem.

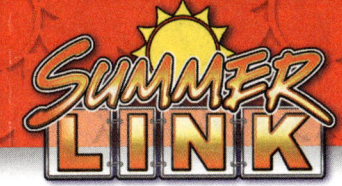

Social Studies

Standardized tests often include questions about social studies topics. You may see questions about maps, geography, history, and government.

The following is a list of topics that may be covered on the test and tips to use when answering the questions. Sample questions are also included.

Map Skills

You will probably be asked to read a map and to identify some of its parts:

- **compass rose:** shows where north, south, east, and west are
- **legend**, or **map key:** shows **symbols** (drawings) that represent natural or human-made objects
- **scale:** compares distance on the map to actual distance

You may also be asked to think about other mapping tools, such as charts, atlases, and globes, as well as map vocabulary, such as **pole**, **equator**, **hemisphere**, and **continent**.

Geography

Geography is the study of the land and its features. Keep in mind some of the basic geography words:

- **natural features:** plateau, mountain, ocean, bay, peninsula, island
- **man-made features**: bridges, roads, buildings, aqueducts

Social Studies Practice

Directions: For numbers 7 and 8, read the passage and answer the questions that follow.

August 19, 1874

Dear Will,

By the time this letter reaches you, I will have reached California. It has taken us so many weeks, and I am eager for our journey to be over.

We are passing through Blackfoot territory these days. Last week, we saw one of their villages, with their cone-shaped homes made from buffalo skin in a circle around a central fire. At night, the firelight glows through the hides, and it is quite beautiful. Though their homes are so different from ours, it made me wish for a home of our own. I cannot wait to reach the West!

Your friend,
Silas

7 Silas is probably

   A   a Blackfoot Indian.

   B   a settler moving to the East Coast.

   C   a settler moving to the West Coast.

   D   living in the Midwest

8 A Blackfoot home is called a

   F   tipi.

   G   wigwam.

   H   wetu.

   J   pueblo.

Summer Link Super Edition Grade 4

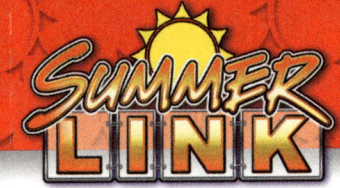

Science

Reading Graphs

Standardized tests may include graphs showing the results of an experiment. You may be asked to read the data on the graph or to use the data to make a prediction or draw a conclusion.

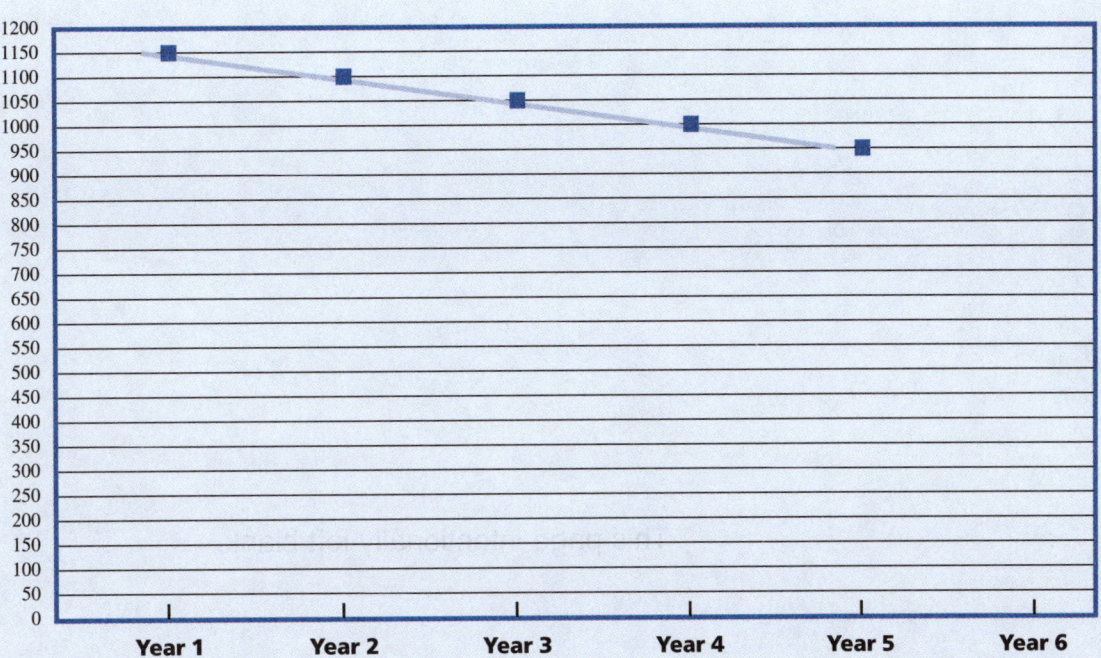

Based on the data in the graph above, what would be an accurate prediction for the panda population in year 6?

A 1,000

B 950

C 1050

D 900

Pandas decrease by 50 each year. The prediction for Year 6 would be 900, 50 less than 950 in Year 5. So the answer is **D**.

What is the difference in panda populations between year 1 and year 6?

F 150

G 250

H 1050

J 300

You know that the panda population for Year 6 is 900. In Year 1 it was 1150. 1150 – 900 is 250. So the answer is **G**.

This page intentionally left blank.

Reading

| Lesson 1 | **Story Reading** |

Suzie and Luis were up before their parents. They went outside the tent and looked at the sun coming up over the mountains.

Find the picture that shows where Suzie and Luis were.

at the beach
A

in the mountains
B

in the desert
C

Find the words that best complete the sentence.

Orange juice _____ .

tastes good
F

from trees
G

for breakfast
H

Look at each answer choice before marking the one you think is right.

Skip difficult items and come back to them later. Take your best guess when you don't know which answer is right.

For many people, morning is the best time of the day. The stories and poem you will read next will talk about some of the things that make mornings special.

GO

Directions: This is a story about a family vacation. Read the story and then do numbers 1–7.

We're Not in Kansas Anymore

"I guess we're not in Kansas any more." Suzie smiled at her younger brother and walked toward the creek. Luis ran to catch up with her and took her hand. Both were wearing heavy sweaters to keep warm in the chilly morning air.

They sat down on a boulder beside the mountain stream. Across the stream was a meadow, and beyond that was a rocky base of a huge mountain. In fact, they were surrounded by mountains, many of which still had snow on them.

"Look, Suzie, cows." Luis pointed at several animals that had wandered into the meadow.

"I don't think they are cows, Buddy. They look like elk. I think they are almost like deer, but bigger."

Luis snuggled closer to his sister. He loved it when she called him "Buddy," and he was convinced she was the smartest person in the world, or at least the smartest kid.

The family had arrived the night before at the campground. Mr. and Mrs. Montoya had set the tent up while the kids were sleeping in the back of the car. They woke the children up and helped them into their sleeping bags, but neither Suzie nor Luis had taken a look around. This morning was their first chance to see where they had camped.

As the sun rose higher over the top of the mountain, fish started dimpling the surface of the pool below the boulder on which the children sat. Each time the fish rose to the surface, they left a small ring of water that spread across the pond. As the rings bumped into one another, they made glittering patterns in the sunlight.

"I wonder what the fish are doing?" wondered Suzie out loud.

"Probably eating breakfast," answered a voice. They turned to see their mother standing behind them.

Mrs. Montoya hugged the children, and the three of them watched the fish quietly for a few minutes.

"Let's head back to the tent." suggested Mrs. Montoya. "Maybe we can convince Dad to cook us some breakfast. We have a busy day ahead of us."

1 **The children in this story seem to**

Ⓐ spend very little time together.

Ⓑ enjoy visiting their relatives.

Ⓒ love each other very much.

2 **Luis calls the elk cows because**

Ⓕ he doesn't know what elk are.

Ⓖ he is making a joke.

Ⓗ they look like deer.

3 Which of these will the children probably do next?

　Ⓐ walk over to the elk

　Ⓑ eat breakfast

　Ⓒ set up the tents

4 Find the sentence that best completes the story.

Mr. Montoya is fixing breakfast. _____ . *Then he will cook pancakes.*

　Ⓕ He is getting his fishing rod ready.

　Ⓖ The tent is large enough for the family.

　Ⓗ First he will make a fire.

5 Find the word that best completes the sentence.

Mount Wheeler is the _____ peak in New Mexico.

　Ⓐ high　　　　　　　　Ⓑ higher　　　　　　　　Ⓒ highest

6 The children wore sweaters in the chilly morning air. A word that means the *opposite* of chilly is

　Ⓕ warm　　　　　　　　Ⓖ cool　　　　　　　　Ⓗ damp

7 The meadow was at the base of a rocky cliff. Find another word that means rocky.

　Ⓐ dirty　　　　　　　　Ⓑ stony　　　　　　　　Ⓒ swampy

Summer Link Super Edition Grade 4

Name _____

Directions: This story is about a girl who spends each Saturday morning with her uncle. Read the story and then do numbers 8–12.

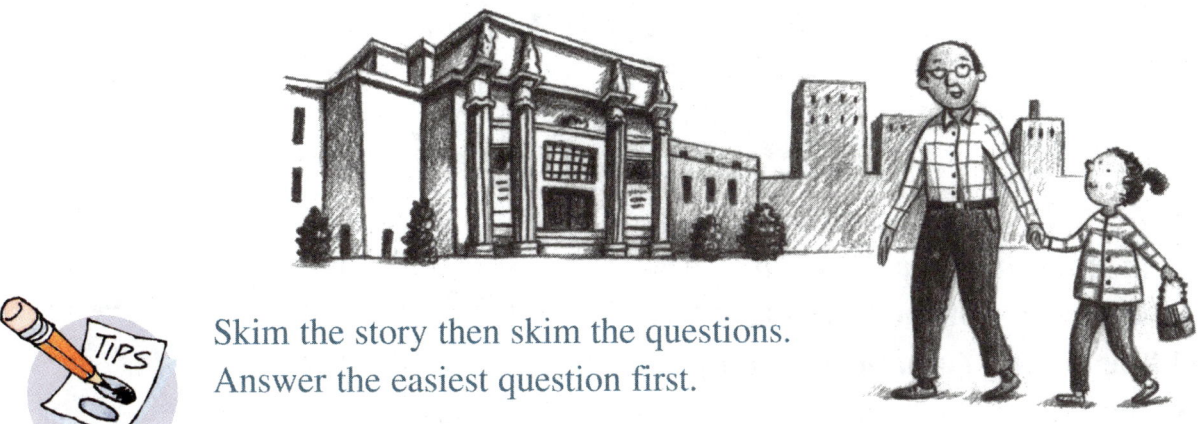

Skim the story then skim the questions. Answer the easiest question first.

A Saturday Morning Surprise

Almost every Saturday morning, Uncle Bob stopped by Vanna's apartment to pick her up. Uncle Bob was her mother's older brother and had been her father's best friend. Vanna missed her father since he died a few years ago, but she was glad she had Uncle Bob.

On this Saturday morning, Uncle Bob said he had a surprise for Vanna. After saying good-bye to her mother, they took the elevator down to the street. Instead of getting in the car, she and Uncle Bob walked down the entrance to the subway and got on the next car that came by. They rode for about 15 minutes, then got off at a stop Vanna had never visited before. They walked up the stairs to the exit, and Vanna found herself in front of a building with huge columns holding up the roof.

"This is the Museum of Natural History, Vanna. It has some of the neatest things you could imagine. I thought you might enjoy spending the day here."

Vanna was speechless as they walked up the steps and through the doors. There, in the middle of a huge hallway, was a dinosaur skeleton! She and Uncle Bob walked over to a museum guide who was telling the story of the dinosaur. Vanna hung on every word she said, and when the guide had finished, Vanna was able to ask some questions.

Uncle Bob then led her over to another room. It was warm and dark, but at the far end there was a glow of light. As they got closer, a recording said, "Welcome to the Living Volcano." This room was just like being inside a real volcano. Vanna loved science, and she was sure this was going to be one of the best mornings ever with Uncle Bob.

GO

227

Name _____

8 Look at the squares to the right. They show some of the things that might be found in a natural history museum. One of the squares is empty. Find the sentence that tells something else that might be found in a natural history museum.

- Ⓕ lightning display
- Ⓖ famous paintings
- Ⓗ old cars
- Ⓙ live animals

---

9 The story says that "Vanna was speechless." What does that probably mean?

- Ⓐ She was disappointed at the surprise.
- Ⓑ Uncle Bob didn't give her a chance to talk.
- Ⓒ She was so excited she didn't know what to say.
- Ⓓ The museum guide did all the talking.

Name _____

10 Vanna did some research about museums. Find the best topic sentence for her paragraph.

_____. Art museums and science museums are the most well-known. Museums have also been built for trains, cars, and even toys.

- Ⓕ Some museums are free.
- Ⓖ Students often take trips to museums.
- Ⓗ Art museums have many paintings.
- Ⓙ There are several kinds of museums.

11 In the story, the roof of the museum is held up by <u>columns</u>. The <u>columns</u> probably look like

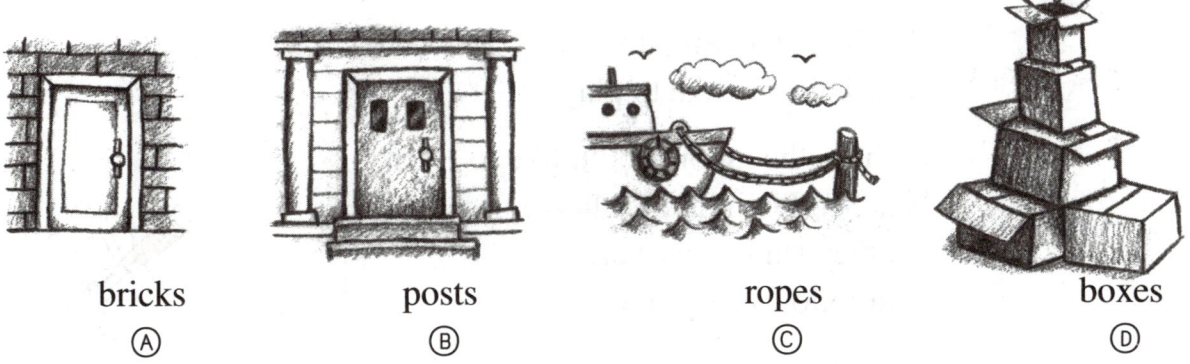

bricds Ⓐ   posts Ⓑ   ropes Ⓒ   boxes Ⓓ

12 Find the sentence that is complete and correctly written.

- Ⓕ Crowded subway in the morning.
- Ⓖ Museum opening at nine o'clock
- Ⓗ They had breakfast before leaving.
- Ⓙ Vanna getting ready early.

STOP

Name _____

Lesson 2 Poem Reading

Every Monday, as we know,
Up we get, and off we go.

The writer is probably talking about going off to

- Ⓐ school
- Ⓑ dinner
- Ⓒ shopping

Directions: Ben wrote this poem about something that couldn't happen. Read the poem and then do numbers 1–7.

What Do You Think?

I wonder if the sun gets tired
Of rising every day?
Or if the stars might want to see
How children like to play?

Perhaps the moon would like to learn
What children do in school?
Do they study very hard
And follow every rule?

Of course, these things can never be
Because it's nature's way,
For moon and stars to toil at night,
And sun to work all day.

The right answer is not always stated exactly in the poem.

1 This poem is mostly about

- Ⓐ the moon and stars changing places with the sun.
- Ⓑ children studying in school.
- Ⓒ children pretending they are the sun, moon, or stars.

2 This poem wonders if

- Ⓕ the moon is bored.
- Ⓖ the stars are funny.
- Ⓗ the sun is tired.

Summer Link Super Edition Grade 4

3 In this poem, "nature's way" means

Ⓐ the way things are now.

Ⓑ the way things should be.

Ⓒ the way things were before.

4 Choose the words that best complete this sentence.

The moon _____.

Ⓕ shining at night

Ⓖ is bright tonight

Ⓗ in the dark sky

5 The moon and stars toil in the poem. Another word for toil is

Ⓐ play.

Ⓑ travel.

Ⓒ work.

6 Find the word that can take the place of Millie and Larry in the sentence below.

Millie and Larry went for a run this morning.

Ⓕ They

Ⓖ Them

Ⓗ It

7 Find the picture that shows what the moon is doing in the poem.

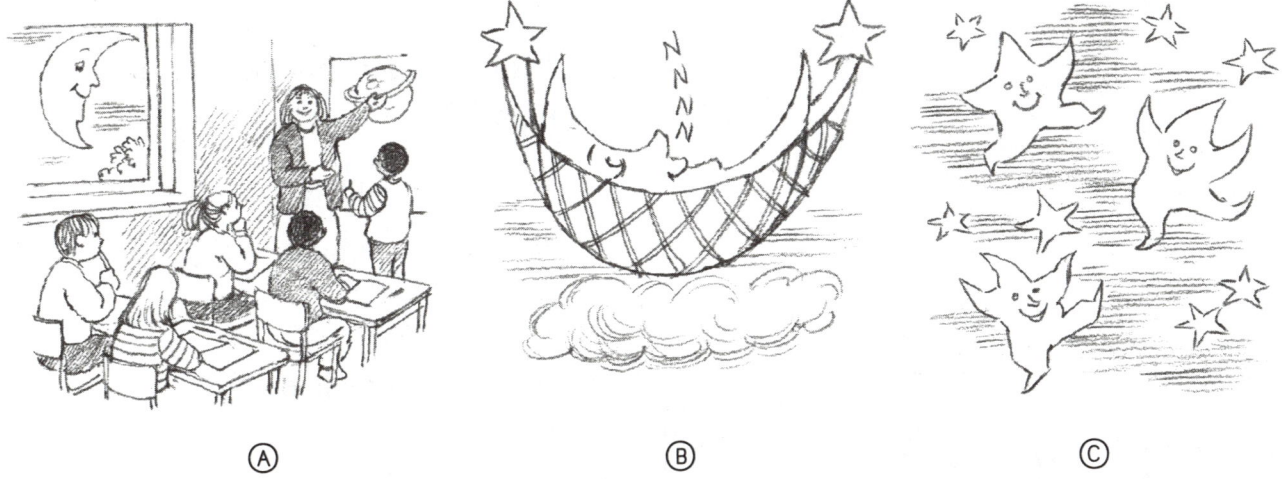

Directions: Ben started this poem. Help him finish it by choosing the right words to fill the blanks.

*A cow is such a silly thing,
It makes a silly sound, _____(8)_____
It lives on a _____(9)_____
Inside a barn
And gives us milk, _____(10)_____ .*

8   Ⓕ bark
    Ⓖ meow
    Ⓗ oink
    Ⓙ moo

9   Ⓐ beach
    Ⓑ farm
    Ⓒ street
    Ⓓ porch

10 Ⓕ too
    Ⓖ also
    Ⓗ yum
    Ⓙ wow

Directions: For numbers 11 and 12, find the answer that best fills each blank.

*A _____(11)_____ is such a pretty thing,
with eyes and coat of brown.
It lives in the _____(12)_____
And hides among trees
But rarely makes a sound.*

11 Ⓐ (food name)
    Ⓑ (person name)
    Ⓒ (animal name)
    Ⓓ (time name)

12 Ⓕ (place name)
    Ⓖ (animal name)
    Ⓗ (food name)
    Ⓙ (time name)

13 Which idea is <u>not</u> part of these poems?

    Ⓐ animal names
    Ⓑ where animals live
    Ⓒ animal sounds
    Ⓓ what animals eat

STOP

Summer Link Super Edition Grade 4

Name _____

Lesson 3 Writing

Directions: Read the paragraph about one student's favorite class. Then write one or two sentences to answer each question below.

My favorite class is art. I like to draw, and I like to paint. The teacher is very nice. He shows us how to do new things. I always look forward to this class. It would be even better if it were longer.

What is your favorite class?

_____
_____
_____

Why is it your favorite?

_____
_____

What might make this class even better?

_____
_____
_____
_____

Name _____

Directions: Read the short story about a friend's visit. Then think about a fiction story that you would like to write. Write one or two sentences to answer each question below.

Juan looked at the clock. He paced across the floor. His best friend, Bill, was coming to visit for the first time in six months. Bill had moved very far away. Juan wondered if they would still feel like good friends.

The doorbell rang, and Juan raced to answer it. Bill looked a bit unsure. Juan smiled and started talking just as he always had when they had lived near one another. He made Bill feel comfortable. As the day went on, it felt like old times.

Think about the main character. Who is it? What is he or she like?

_____
_____

Where does the story take place? When does the story take place? Now? In the past? In the future?

_____
_____

What problem will the main character have? How will he or she try to solve the problem?

_____
_____

STOP

Name _____

Lesson 4 Review

The alarm clock at seven o'clock rang.

Which of these shows the best way to write this sentence?

Ⓐ At seven o'clock rang the alarm clock.

Ⓑ Rang at seven o'clock the alarm clock.

Ⓒ The alarm clock rang at seven o'clock.

Ⓓ Best as it is.

Directions: Nick wrote this story about birds coming to the feeder in his back yard in the morning. The story has a few errors that should be corrected. Read the story and then do numbers 1–4.

A Busy Morning

[1]The finches come to the feeder early. [2]They chirp and take turns eating. [3]Later, the doves them join. [4]The doves almost never eat at the feeder. [5]Instead, they pecking at seeds on the ground. [6]Another bird that eats on the ground is the junco. [7]Juncoes, they usually arrive in flocks of about ten. [8]They are shy birds and fly away if they see me.

GO

235

Summer Link Super Edition Grade 4

Name _____

1 **Choose the best way to write Sentence 1.**

Ⓐ The finches comes to the feeder early.

Ⓑ Coming early to the feeder are the finches.

Ⓒ The finches had come to the feeder early.

Ⓓ Best as it is

2 **Which of these shows the best way to write Sentence 3?**

Ⓕ Later, the doves join they.

Ⓖ The doves join them later.

Ⓗ The doves join they later.

Ⓙ Best as it is

3 **Select the best way to write Sentence 5.**

Ⓐ Instead, they peck at seeds on the ground.

Ⓑ Them are pecking at seeds on the ground instead.

Ⓒ It pecks at seeds on the ground instead.

Ⓓ Best as it is

4 **Which of these shows the best way to write Sentence 7?**

Ⓕ Them juncoes usually arrive in flocks of about ten.

Ⓖ Juncoes are arriving usually in flocks of about ten.

Ⓗ Juncoes usually arrive in flocks of about ten.

Ⓙ Best as it is

GO

Summer Link Super Edition Grade 4

Name _____

Directions: For numbers 5 and 6, find the sentence in each of these stories that has the correct capitalization and punctuation.

5 Ⓐ The bus comes for us at 7:30

   Ⓑ terri likes to ride up front.

   Ⓒ My friends and I sit in the back.

   Ⓓ We talk about sports and television?

6 Ⓕ On saturday morning we sleep late.

   Ⓖ Mom and Dad have to wake us.

   Ⓗ the four of us have a big breakfast

   Ⓙ Last week we went to denver.

7 **One of Nick's friends wrote this story about the morning at his house. Find the best topic sentence for the story.**

_____. Both my mom and dad work, so they get in the bathroom first. My sister and I get up next. While we get ready, Dad fixes us breakfast.

   Ⓐ Morning in our house is very busy.

   Ⓑ Breakfast is my favorite meal.

   Ⓒ My sister and I like to sleep in.

   Ⓓ We take a bus to school in the morning.

237 Summer Link Super Edition Grade 4

8 Nick's sister, Alex, wrote this story. Find the sentences that best complete it.

Sometimes we go out for breakfast. Mom and Dad take us to different restaurants. _____.

- Ⓕ They work downtown. Mom drives, but Dad takes the subway.
- Ⓖ Breakfast is an important meal. You shouldn't eat too much.
- Ⓗ I always order pancakes. Nick gets waffles.
- Ⓙ Fruit is good to eat. I like bananas best.

Directions: For numbers 9 and 10, find the sentence that is complete and that is written correctly.

9
- Ⓐ Mr. Woo his store early.
- Ⓑ Always nice to us.
- Ⓒ Food and other things.
- Ⓓ We like to shop there.

10
- Ⓕ Many people in the park.
- Ⓖ Cool and smells good.
- Ⓗ They run in the morning.
- Ⓙ Later to get crowded.

11 Find the words that best complete the sentence.

_____ *all night long.*

- Ⓐ It rained
- Ⓑ Too hot to sleep
- Ⓒ Cloudy and windy
- Ⓓ A few times

STOP

Summer Link Super Edition Grade 4   238

Directions: Read the paragraph that describes a trip to the beach. Then think about a place you have visited. Write one or two sentences to answer each question below.

I'll never forget my trip to the beach last summer. We drove a long time to get there. The sun blazed overhead. The sand felt hot against my feet. I splashed in the crashing waves and ate sweet, cool ice cream. I can't wait to go back to the beach!

What is the name of the place you visited?

_____

_____

_____

Did you like this place? Why or why not?

_____

_____

_____

_____

What do you remember about its sights, sounds, tastes, and smells?

_____

_____

_____

_____

_____

Name _____

Basic Skills

Lesson 1 Word Analysis

SAMPLE A Find the word in which the underlined letters have the same sound as the picture name.

bread   black   bowl
 Ⓐ   Ⓑ   Ⓒ

 Repeat the directions to yourself as you look at the answer choices. Think carefully about what you should do.

Directions: For numbers 1–4, choose the best answer.

1 Find the word that has the same beginning sound as

- Ⓐ frame.
- Ⓑ flame.
- Ⓒ fork.

2 Find the word that has the same ending sound as

- Ⓕ meant.
- Ⓖ stand.
- Ⓗ earn.

3 Look at the first word. Find the other word that has the same vowel sound as the underlined part.

float

- Ⓐ block
- Ⓑ board
- Ⓒ chose
- Ⓓ pool

4 Look at the underlined word. Find a word that can be added to the underlined word to make a compound word.

door

- Ⓕ knock
- Ⓖ open
- Ⓗ window
- Ⓙ step

STOP

Name _____

Lesson 2 Vocabulary

Directions: For Samples A and B and numbers 1 and 2, find the answer that means the same or about the same as the underlined word.

SAMPLE A consider this idea
- Ⓐ ignore
- Ⓒ agree with
- Ⓑ think about
- Ⓓ like

SAMPLE B raise a flag
- Ⓕ lift
- Ⓖ lower
- Ⓗ fly
- Ⓙ hold

1 liberty for everyone
- Ⓐ freedom
- Ⓒ work
- Ⓑ vacation
- Ⓓ food

2 long journey
- Ⓕ story
- Ⓗ road
- Ⓖ movie
- Ⓙ trip

Think about where you heard or read the underlined word before. Try each answer in the blank.

Directions: For numbers 4 and 5, read the sentence with the missing word and then read the question. Find the best answer to the question.

4 The weather will _____ tomorrow.

Which word means the weather will get better?
- Ⓕ improve
- Ⓗ worsen
- Ⓖ change
- Ⓙ vary

Directions: For number 3, find the word that means the opposite of the underlined word.

3 thrilling ride
- Ⓐ long
- Ⓑ exciting
- Ⓒ boring
- Ⓓ interesting

5 The _____ followed the rabbit into the forest.

Which word means a dog followed the rabbit into the forest?
- Ⓐ traveler
- Ⓒ hound
- Ⓑ hunter
- Ⓓ hawk

GO

241   Summer Link Super Edition Grade 4

Name _____

Directions: For Sample C and numbers 6 and 7, read the sentences. Then choose the word that correctly completes both sentences.

SAMPLE C

The _____ swam in the pond.

You have to _____ your head here.

Ⓐ fish   Ⓑ duck   Ⓒ children   Ⓓ lower

6 Who will _____ this problem?

The _____ on the shovel is broken.

Ⓐ solve   Ⓑ blade   Ⓒ cause   Ⓓ handle

7 Can I take your _____?

She will _____ him to do it.

Ⓕ order   Ⓖ tell   Ⓗ coat   Ⓙ hat

Use the meaning of the sentence to find the answer.

Directions: For numbers 8 and 9, read the story. For each blank, look at the words with the same number. Find the word from each list that fits best in the blank.

Dogs need __(8)__ to stay healthy. They should be given an __(9)__ to play for at least 15 minutes each day.

8 Ⓐ exercise   Ⓑ leashes   Ⓒ treats   Ⓓ dishes

9 Ⓕ examination   Ⓖ assistance   Ⓗ individual   Ⓙ opportunity

STOP

Summer Link Super Edition Grade 4

Lesson 3   Language Mechanics

Directions: For Sample A and numbers 1 and 2, find the punctuation mark that is needed in the sentence.

SAMPLE A   The television is too loud

- Ⓐ ?
- Ⓑ .
- Ⓒ ,
- Ⓓ None

1 How many fish did you catch

- Ⓐ ?
- Ⓑ .
- Ⓒ ,
- Ⓓ None

2 Quick, let's get out of the rain

- Ⓕ ?
- Ⓖ .
- Ⓗ !
- Ⓙ None

Look for a mistake in capitalization or a missing punctuation mark in this part of the lesson.

Directions: For Sample B and numbers 3 and 4, which part needs a capital letter? If no capital letter is needed, mark "None."

SAMPLE B   My cousin | has a bird | named fluffy. | None
                      Ⓐ   Ⓑ   Ⓒ   Ⓓ

3 Give this | piece of pie | to connie. | None
    Ⓐ   Ⓑ   Ⓒ   Ⓓ

4 Imo's class | will go to | Orlando, Florida. | None
    Ⓕ   Ⓖ   Ⓗ   Ⓙ

GO

Name _____

Directions: Find the sentence that has the correct capitalization and punctuation.

5
Ⓐ Our picnic is tomorrow!
Ⓑ Mr. ames will cook.
Ⓒ we'll meet Jenny there.
Ⓓ Sam and I will be there.

6
Ⓕ Who is playing.
Ⓖ The park is this way!
Ⓗ Call Jeff. He wants to come with us.
Ⓙ The game starts soon. let's hurry

Remember, in this part of the lesson you should find the answer with correct capitalization and punctuation.

SAMPLE C

Find the answer choice that shows the correct capitalization and punctuation for the underlined part.

Did you finish your <u>project. Mine</u> is almost done.

Ⓐ Project mine.
Ⓑ project? Mine
Ⓒ Project. Mine
Ⓓ Correct as it is

Directions: For numbers 7 and 8, look at the underlined part of the sentence. Choose the answer that shows the best capitalization and punctuation for that part.

(7) None of <u>Winnies friends</u> told her about the surprise
(8) birthday party. She was the captain of the softball <u>team. The</u> other players wanted to do something special for her.

7
Ⓐ Winnies friend's
Ⓑ Winnies' friends
Ⓒ Winnie's friends
Ⓓ Correct as it is

8
Ⓕ team! The
Ⓖ team the
Ⓗ team, the
Ⓙ Correct as it is

STOP

Summer Link Super Edition Grade 4

244

Lesson 4 Spelling

Directions: Find the word that is spelled correctly and best fits in the blank.

1. We picked _____ in our garden.
   - Ⓐ berries
   - Ⓒ berrys
   - Ⓑ berrese
   - Ⓓ berreis

2. The _____ helped me.
   - Ⓕ nourse
   - Ⓗ nurce
   - Ⓖ nirse
   - Ⓙ nurse

3. The answer to this problem is a _____ .
   - Ⓐ frackshun
   - Ⓒ fracteon
   - Ⓑ fraction
   - Ⓓ fracton

4. Did you _____ the page?
   - Ⓕ tare
   - Ⓗ tair
   - Ⓖ tear
   - Ⓙ taer

5. This _____ was in the school paper.
   - Ⓐ artical
   - Ⓒ article
   - Ⓑ articel
   - Ⓓ articol

Directions: For Sample A and numbers 6–8, find the underlined word that is <u>not</u> spelled correctly.

SAMPLE A
- Ⓐ <u>identify</u> a bird
- Ⓑ <u>bottle</u> of juice
- Ⓒ <u>quiet</u> room
- Ⓓ All correct

6.
   - Ⓐ easy <u>lesson</u>
   - Ⓑ last <u>forevr</u>
   - Ⓒ <u>paddle</u> a canoe
   - Ⓓ All correct

7.
   - Ⓕ good <u>balance</u>
   - Ⓖ delicious <u>stew</u>
   - Ⓗ <u>private</u> property
   - Ⓙ All correct

8.
   - Ⓐ great <u>relief</u>
   - Ⓑ our <u>mayor</u>
   - Ⓒ <u>sunnie</u> day
   - Ⓓ All correct

If an item is too difficult, skip it and come back to it later.

STOP

Name _____

Lesson 5 Computation

Directions: For Samples A and B and numbers 1–4, find the answer that is the solution to the problem. If the answer is not given, choose "None of these."

 **SAMPLE A**

23
+ 16

Ⓐ 17
Ⓑ 29
Ⓒ 39
Ⓓ 84
Ⓔ None of these

 **SAMPLE B**

48
− 43

Ⓕ 10
Ⓖ 25
Ⓗ 41
Ⓙ 91
Ⓚ None of these

Pay attention to the operation sign so you know what to do.
Be sure to transfer numbers correctly to scratch paper.

1

115 + 71 =

Ⓐ 44
Ⓑ 76
Ⓒ 176
Ⓓ 186
Ⓔ None of these

3

$9.38
− 4.51

Ⓐ $4.87
Ⓑ $5.87
Ⓒ $5.32
Ⓓ $13.89
Ⓔ None of these

2

52
16
+ 5

Ⓕ 21
Ⓖ 57
Ⓗ 63
Ⓙ 83
Ⓚ None of these

4

5 × 5 =

Ⓕ 10
Ⓖ 25
Ⓗ 35
Ⓙ 55
Ⓚ None of these

STOP

Name _____

Lesson 6 Review

SAMPLE A Find the word in which the underlined letters have the same sound as the picture name.

Ⓐ s<u>k</u>ate Ⓑ <u>s</u>mile Ⓒ <u>s</u>low

1 Find the word in which the underlined letters have the same sound as the picture name.

Ⓐ <u>st</u>amp
Ⓑ <u>sk</u>irt
Ⓒ <u>sw</u>an

2 Find the word that has the same ending sound as

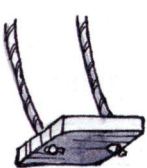

Ⓕ ei<u>ght</u>.
Ⓖ len<u>gth</u>.
Ⓗ ra<u>nge</u>.

3 Look at the word. Find the other word that has the same vowel sound as the underlined part.

cr<u>i</u>sp

Ⓐ cr<u>i</u>ed
Ⓑ st<u>ai</u>r
Ⓒ l<u>i</u>on
Ⓓ p<u>i</u>nch

4 Look at the underlined word. Find a word that can be added to the underlined word to make a compound word. <u>hair</u>

Ⓕ dark
Ⓖ cut
Ⓗ comb
Ⓙ hat

5 Find the word in which just the prefix is underlined.

Ⓐ <u>pre</u>tend
Ⓑ <u>al</u>low
Ⓒ <u>be</u>tween
Ⓓ <u>un</u>known

6 Find the word in which only the root word is underlined.

Ⓕ <u>car</u>pet
Ⓖ <u>play</u>ful
Ⓗ <u>bar</u>rel
Ⓙ <u>re</u>lease

7 Find the word in which only the suffix is underlined.

Ⓐ land<u>ed</u>
Ⓑ clos<u>et</u>
Ⓒ storm<u>s</u>
Ⓓ televi<u>sion</u>

GO

Name _____

Directions: For Sample B and numbers 8 and 9, find the answer that means the same or about the same as the underlined word.

SAMPLE B firm <u>grip</u>
- Ⓐ weak
- Ⓑ slippery
- Ⓒ damp
- Ⓓ strong

8 a good <u>pitch</u>
- Ⓐ catch
- Ⓑ throw
- Ⓒ hit
- Ⓓ score

9 <u>brush</u> a horse
- Ⓕ ride
- Ⓖ groom
- Ⓗ catch
- Ⓙ follow

SAMPLE C Find the answer that best fits in the blank.

Hector _____ his shirt on a thorn.
- Ⓐ tore
- Ⓑ folded
- Ⓒ handed
- Ⓓ grabbed

10 Which word means cutting the onions made Casper cry?

Cutting the onions made Casper _____.
- Ⓐ satisfied
- Ⓑ tired
- Ⓒ weep
- Ⓓ blush

Directions: Find the word that correctly completes both sentences.

11 Janna will _____ the table. This _____ of books is rare.
- Ⓕ clear
- Ⓖ group
- Ⓗ move
- Ⓙ set

12 My _____ is broken. Let's _____ a movie.
- Ⓐ watch
- Ⓑ toy
- Ⓒ rent
- Ⓓ radio

Directions: For each blank, look at the words with the same number. Find the word from each list that fits best in the blank.

Jim __(13)__ Michele's bike. His bike had a flat tire. He wouldn't be able to __(14)__ a new tire until next week.

13
- Ⓕ found
- Ⓖ lost
- Ⓗ borrowed
- Ⓙ disliked

14
- Ⓐ inflate
- Ⓑ require
- Ⓒ purchase
- Ⓓ express

GO

Summer Link Super Edition Grade 4   248

Name _____

Directions: For Sample D and number 15, find the part of the sentence that needs a capital letter. Mark "None" if a capital letter is not needed.

SAMPLE D   This street (A) | usually has (B) | heavy traffic. (C) | None (D)

15   Did carla (A) | give you (B) | her phone number? (C) | None (D)

16 Find the punctuation mark that is needed in the sentence.

The mall is just up the road

? (F)   . (G)   , (H)   None (J)

Directions: For numbers 17 and 18, find the sentence that has correct capitalization and punctuation.

17   Ⓐ She and i will study now.
Ⓑ the library is closed.
Ⓒ Let's leave now?
Ⓓ Can Peg borrow your book?

18   Ⓕ Our coats' are wet.
Ⓖ Watch out for that ice!
Ⓗ What did you say.
I didn't hear you.
Ⓙ This desk is yours?
Mine is over there.

Directions: Read the letter. Find the answer that shows the correct capitalization and punctuation for the underlined parts.

(19)   March 2 1998,
Dear Lena,
(20)   Thanks for the football. I can't believe you sent it. I got other birthday presents, but yours was the best. I'll try it out tomorrow.
     Your friend,
     Ronnie

19   Ⓐ March, 2, 1998
Ⓑ March 2 1998
Ⓒ March 2, 1998
Ⓓ Correct as it is

20   Ⓕ cant   Ⓗ ca'nt
Ⓖ cant'   Ⓙ Correct as it is

GO

249   Summer Link Super Edition Grade 4

Name _____

Directions: For Sample E and numbers 21 and 22, find the word that is spelled correctly and best fits in the blank.

 **SAMPLE E** My sister got _____ on that hill.

- Ⓐ maried
- Ⓒ marreed
- Ⓑ married
- Ⓓ marread

21 Jamie's _____ will be next week.

- Ⓐ berthday
- Ⓒ birthday
- Ⓑ burthday
- Ⓓ birthdey

22 At _____, we began our hike.

- Ⓕ daun
- Ⓗ dawn
- Ⓖ dawne
- Ⓙ dawen

Directions: Find the underlined word that is not spelled correctly. If all the words are correct, mark "All correct."

23
- Ⓐ <u>clear</u> day
- Ⓒ famous <u>artist</u>
- Ⓑ gold <u>medal</u>
- Ⓓ All correct

24
- Ⓕ <u>usefull</u> hint
- Ⓗ <u>lock</u> the door
- Ⓖ go <u>swimming</u>
- Ⓙ All correct

STOP

Summer Link Super Edition Grade 4

Name _____

Mathematics

Lesson 1 **Mathematics Skills**

SAMPLE A

How many inches long is the fish?

Ⓐ 5 inches

Ⓑ 6 inches

Ⓒ 8 inches

Ⓓ 12 inches

Read the problem carefully. Look for key words, numbers, and figures. Look carefully at all the answer choices.

If you use scratch paper, transfer the numbers correctly. Work neatly and carefully so you don't make a careless mistake.

Name _____

1. What is the best estimate of the number of beans on the plate?

   Ⓐ 30
   Ⓑ 20
   Ⓒ 12
   Ⓓ 10

2. Look at the number pattern in the box. Find the number that is missing.

   11, 22, ____, 44, 55

   Ⓕ 33
   Ⓖ 23
   Ⓗ 32
   Ⓙ 42

3. Look at the clock. How long will it take the minute hand to reach the 6?

   Ⓐ 3 minutes
   Ⓑ 5 minutes
   Ⓒ 12 minutes
   Ⓓ 15 minutes

4. Marlow noticed that the parking lot at the store had 11 red cars, 6 blue cars, 4 white cars, and 3 cars of other colors. If someone leaves the building and walks to a car, which color car is it most likely to be?

   Ⓕ red
   Ⓖ blue
   Ⓗ white
   Ⓙ another color

5. Sandy had 5

   She read 2  .

   Find the number sentence that tells how many books Sandy has left to read.

   Ⓐ 5 + 2 = 7
   Ⓑ 5 − 2 = 3
   Ⓒ 2 + 3 = 5
   Ⓓ 2 − 1 = 1

Name _____

6 Look at the pattern of fruit. Which of these is the missing piece of fruit?

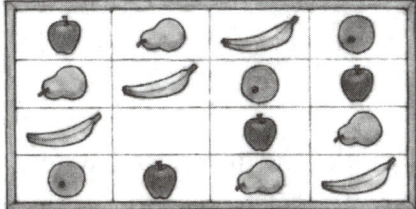

- Ⓕ orange
- Ⓗ pear
- Ⓖ banana
- Ⓙ apple

7 Mr. Lowell paid $0.59 for a bag of chips and $0.39 for a bottle of juice. How much money did he spend all together?

- Ⓐ $0.79
- Ⓑ $0.88
- Ⓒ $0.89
- Ⓓ $0.98

8 Look at the number sentences. Find the number that goes in the boxes to make both number sentences true.

6 + ☐ = 7
7 − ☐ = 6

- Ⓕ 1
- Ⓖ 0
- Ⓗ 13
- Ⓙ 7

9 Look at the picture. What number tells how many blocks are in the picture?

- Ⓐ 100
- Ⓑ 115
- Ⓒ 110
- Ⓓ 15

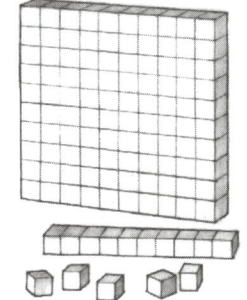

Directions: For numbers 10 and 11, estimate the answer to each problem. You do not have to find an exact answer.

10 Which two things together would cost about $30.00?

- Ⓕ hat and shirt
- Ⓖ belt and socks
- Ⓗ shirt and socks
- Ⓙ hat and belt

11 Use estimation to find which of these is closest to 1000.

- Ⓐ 591 + 573
- Ⓒ 392 + 589
- Ⓑ 499 + 409
- Ⓓ 913 + 183

Name _____

Directions: The third grade students at Millbrook School made a graph about where they wanted to go on vacation. Study the graph, then do numbers 12–14.

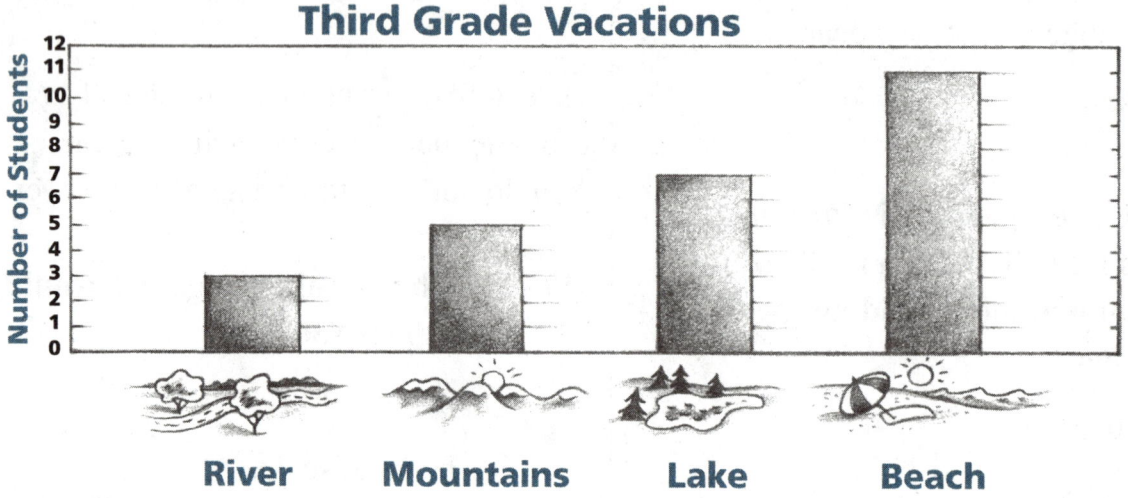

12 Which of these is another way to show how many students went to the beach?

Ⓕ 𝍷𝍷𝍷𝍷𝍷 𝍷𝍷𝍷𝍷𝍷 𝍷

Ⓖ 𝍷𝍷𝍷𝍷𝍷 𝍷

Ⓗ 𝍷𝍷𝍷𝍷𝍷 𝍷𝍷𝍷𝍷𝍷

Ⓙ 𝍷𝍷𝍷𝍷𝍷 𝍷𝍷𝍷𝍷𝍷 𝍷𝍷𝍷𝍷

13 How many students went to a lake for vacation?

Ⓐ 11   Ⓒ 8

Ⓑ 7   Ⓓ 5

14 Two of the students changed their minds and decided to go to a lake instead of the beach. How many students then wanted to go to a lake?

Ⓕ 7   Ⓗ 5

Ⓖ 8   Ⓙ 9

GO

Name _____

15 Look at the paper clip and the pencils. Which pencil is about three inches longer than the paper clip?

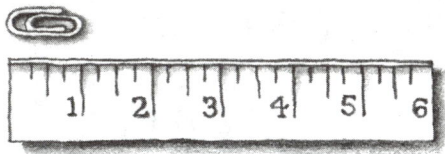

Ⓐ   Ⓑ   Ⓒ   Ⓓ

16 Bonnie folded a piece of paper in half and then folded it in half again. The picture shows how she folded her paper. What will the piece of paper look like when Bonnie unfolds it?

Ⓕ   Ⓖ   Ⓗ   Ⓙ

17 Find the answer that shows 35 peanuts.

Ⓐ   Ⓑ

Ⓒ   Ⓓ

STOP

Name _____

| Lesson 2 | Review |

MAIN STREET FAIR

SAMPLE A Last week, two hundred fifty-three people attended the Main Street Fair. Which of these numbers is two hundred fifty-three?

Ⓐ 235 Ⓑ 20053 Ⓒ 253 Ⓓ 2053

Directions: Study the schedule for the Main Street Fair. Use it to do numbers 1 and 2.

1 Mrs. Barnes arrived 15 minutes early for the softball game. What time did she get there?

Ⓐ 8:15 Ⓒ 7:15
Ⓑ 8:45 Ⓓ 7:45

2 Exactly 60 people brought their pets to the show. Half the people brought dogs and 20 people brought cats. How many people brought other kinds of pets?

Ⓕ 30 Ⓗ 20
Ⓖ 10 Ⓙ 40

Summer Link Super Edition Grade 4

Name _____

3 Pepper's little brother made this castle with toy blocks. Which shape did he use just once?

- Ⓐ circle
- Ⓑ triangle
- Ⓒ rectangle
- Ⓓ square

4 The chart below shows the number of cars parked in a lot. Which of these is the same number as is shown on the chart?

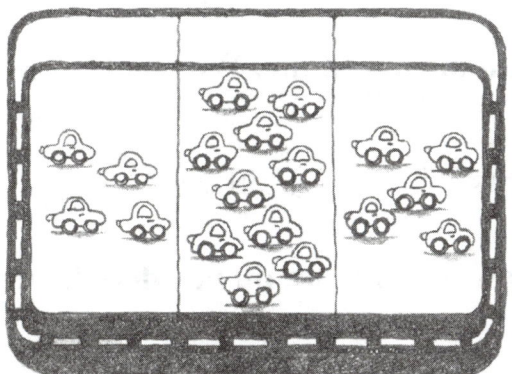

- Ⓕ 100 + 40 + 5
- Ⓖ 1 + 4 + 5
- Ⓗ 400 + 100 + 5
- Ⓙ 4 + 10 + 5

5 Paul and Vesta used a computer to solve a problem. Which of these is the same as the number on the computer screen?

- Ⓐ three thousand one hundred eight
- Ⓑ thirty one thousand eight
- Ⓒ three hundred eight
- Ⓓ three thousand eighteen

6 Sarah just read that her town has the highest population in the county. Where should she mark on the chart below to show her town's population?

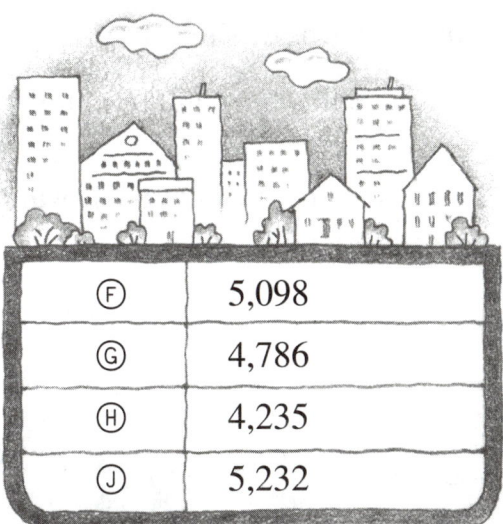

Ⓕ	5,098
Ⓖ	4,786
Ⓗ	4,235
Ⓙ	5,232

GO

Name _____

Going to the Bank

7 What do the numbers on the sign tell you?

- Ⓐ how much money is in the bank
- Ⓑ how many people work in the bank
- Ⓒ what time the bank opens and closes
- Ⓓ the bank's address

8 Jawan's sister has four coins. One is a nickel and one is a dime. Which of these amounts might she have?

Ⓕ 15 cents　　Ⓖ 20 cents　　Ⓗ 24 cents　　Ⓙ 30 cents

9 A sticker costs 20 cents. Jawan has 12 cents. How much more money does he need to buy the sticker?

- Ⓐ 8¢
- Ⓑ 10¢
- Ⓒ 12¢
- Ⓓ 32¢

STOP

Social Studies

Lesson 1

Directions: Study the time line that shows when four U. S. Presidents took office. Then do numbers 1–3.

When U. S. Presidents Took Office

John Adams	Abraham Lincoln	Woodrow Wilson	John F. Kennedy
1797	1861	1913	1961

1 Which person on the time line became President first?

- Ⓐ Woodrow Wilson
- Ⓑ John Adams
- Ⓒ John F. Kennedy
- Ⓓ Abraham Lincoln

2 Which person on the time line became President last?

- Ⓕ John F. Kennedy
- Ⓖ Woodrow Wilson
- Ⓗ Abraham Lincoln
- Ⓙ John Adams

3 Which person on the time line became President in 1861?

- Ⓐ John Adams
- Ⓑ John F. Kennedy
- Ⓒ Woodrow Wilson
- Ⓓ Abraham Lincoln

Name _____

Directions: Study the map of the United States. Then do numbers 4–7.

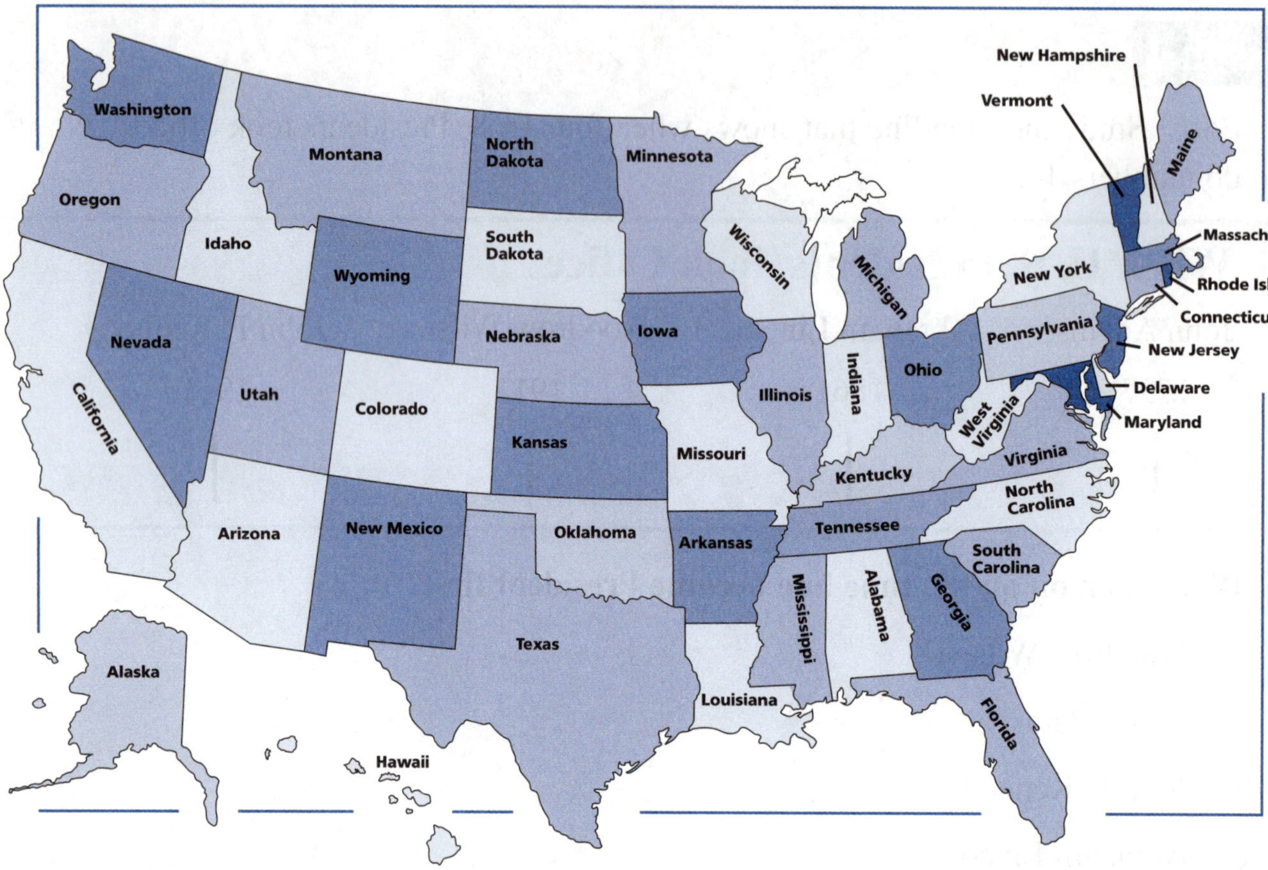

4 Which state is a peninsula?

- Ⓕ Nevada
- Ⓖ Florida
- Ⓗ Washington
- Ⓙ Georgia

5 Which state is farthest north?

- Ⓐ Texas
- Ⓑ Arizona
- Ⓒ New York
- Ⓓ Kansas

6 Which state is on the West Coast?

- Ⓕ California
- Ⓖ North Carolina
- Ⓗ Utah
- Ⓙ Minnesota

7 Which state is east of Nebraska?

- Ⓐ Oregon
- Ⓑ Mississippi
- Ⓒ Idaho
- Ⓓ New Mexico

STOP

Summer Link Super Edition Grade 4

Lesson 2   Review

Name _____

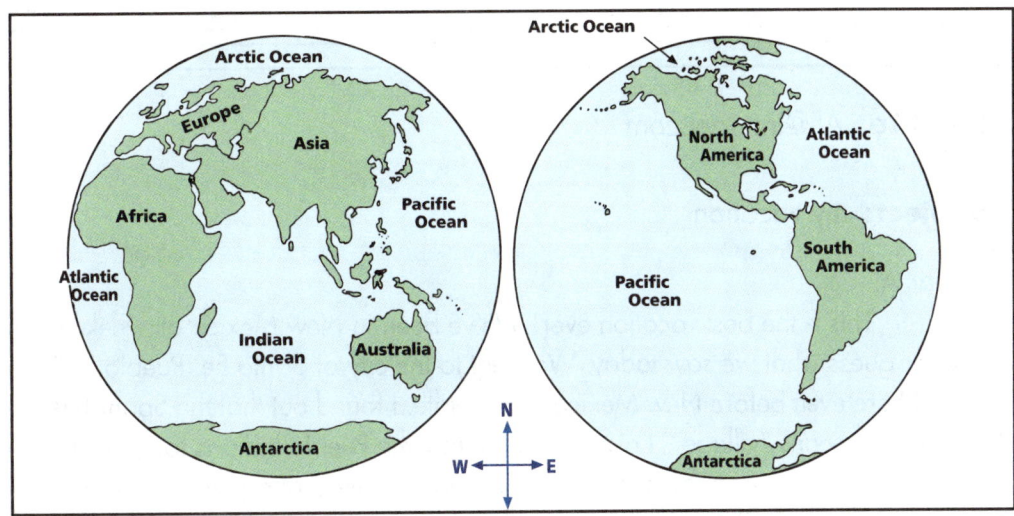

Directions: For numbers 1 and 2, find the answer that best completes each sentence.

1 The United States is a

- Ⓐ continent.
- Ⓑ country.
- Ⓒ hemisphere.
- Ⓓ state.

2 A compass rose is

- Ⓕ a type of flower.
- Ⓖ an imaginary line around Earth.
- Ⓗ a way to tell direction.
- Ⓙ a tool for making math shapes.

Directions: Read numbers 3–5. Decide whether each one is true or false.

3 The land on Earth is divided into seven continents.

- Ⓐ True
- Ⓑ False

4 José and Ling have been studying the southern hemisphere. One of the countries they have likely been studying is France.

- Ⓐ True
- Ⓑ False

5 Muhammad's teacher will travel from the United States to Europe. To reach Europe, he will not have to cross an ocean.

- Ⓐ True
- Ⓑ False

261   Summer Link Super Edition Grade 4

Name _____

Directions: Read the e-mail about a vacation and then do numbers 6–8.

Send To: Ali@internet.com

Subject: my vacation

Dear Ali,
    This is the best vacation ever! We've been in New Mexico all week. You'll never guess what we saw today. We went to the city of Santa Fe. Pueblo Indians lived here even before New Mexico was a state. I found out that the Spanish word "pueblo" means "village." I also found out that the Pueblo Indians found a special way to water crops in the heat. They also made pottery and jewelry and wove beautiful baskets. They're still making these things today. I'm bringing a basket back for you. See you soon!

                                                            Tyree

---

6 Tyree is *most likely* a

  Ⓐ farmer.
  Ⓑ hotel owner in New Mexico.
  Ⓒ Pueblo Indian.
  Ⓓ student.

7 From the passage, you can tell that Pueblo Indians *probably did not*

  Ⓕ work hard.
  Ⓖ grow crops.
  Ⓗ make bracelets.
  Ⓙ live in a cold climate.

8 The word *pueblo* means

  Ⓐ Indian.
  Ⓑ village.
  Ⓒ jewelry.
  Ⓓ baskets.

STOP

Summer Link Super Edition Grade 4   262

Name _____

Science

Lesson 1

Directions: Read the Venn diagram, and then do numbers 1–4.

African Elephant
- ears cover shoulder
- back dips
- two finger-like lobes at the end of trunk
- smooth forehead
- wrinkled skin

Both Elephants
- long tusks
- tail
- eat plants

Indian Elephants
- ears do not cover shoulder
- back arches
- one lobe on trunk
- two lumps on forehead
- less wrinkled skin

1 Which elephants have long tusks?
- Ⓐ Only the African elephants
- Ⓑ Only the Indian elephants
- Ⓒ Both the African and Indian elephants

2 Which elephants have one lobe at the end of their trunks?
- Ⓕ Only the African elephants
- Ⓖ Only the Indian elephants
- Ⓗ Both the African and Indian elephants

3 Which elephants have ears that cover their shoulders?
- Ⓐ Only the African elephants
- Ⓑ Only the Indian elephants
- Ⓒ Both the African and Indian elephants

4 Which elephants eat plants?
- Ⓕ Only the African elephants
- Ⓖ Only the Indian elephants
- Ⓗ Both the African and Indian elephants

Name _____

Directions: For numbers 5–7, find each true statement.

5 Ⓐ Chlorophyll is the process in which plants turn water and air into food.

  Ⓑ Photosynthesis is the process in which plants turn light, water, and air into food.

  Ⓒ Plants need leaves in order to turn water and air into food.

  Ⓓ Light is not necessary for plants to turn water and air into food.

6 Ⓕ The seeds take in light and nutrients from the air.

  Ⓖ The leaves take in water and nutrients from the soil.

  Ⓗ The roots take in water and nutrients from the soil.

  Ⓙ The flowers take in light and water from the soil.

7 Ⓐ Conifers (example: pine trees) lose their leaves in the fall.

  Ⓑ Conifers stay green year round.

  Ⓒ Conifers have broad leaves.

  Ⓓ Conifers' leaves turn gold in the fall.

Directions: Do numbers 8–11.

8 Which is not part of a flower?

  Ⓕ pistil
  Ⓖ stamen
  Ⓗ thorax
  Ⓙ petal

9 Which part of the flower holds the pollen?

  Ⓐ stamen
  Ⓑ pistil
  Ⓒ sepal
  Ⓓ petal

10 Food-making material in leaves is called

  Ⓕ chlorophyll.
  Ⓖ photosynthesis.
  Ⓗ sunlight.
  Ⓙ water.

11 Which does a plant not need to grow?

  Ⓐ light   Ⓒ soil
  Ⓑ water   Ⓓ sand

STOP

Summer Link Super Edition Grade 4

Lesson 2 Review

1 Which is an example of evaporation?

2 A rainstorm is an example of

- Ⓕ precipitation.
- Ⓗ condensation.
- Ⓖ evaporation.
- Ⓙ reformulation.

3 Which of these is not a type of cloud?

- Ⓐ cirrus
- Ⓒ humerus
- Ⓑ cumulus
- Ⓓ stratus

4 What does a meteorologist use to measure air pressure?

- Ⓕ barometer
- Ⓗ odometer
- Ⓖ kilometer
- Ⓙ thermometer

Directions: Study the graph of rainfall in Kansas, and then do numbers 5 and 6.

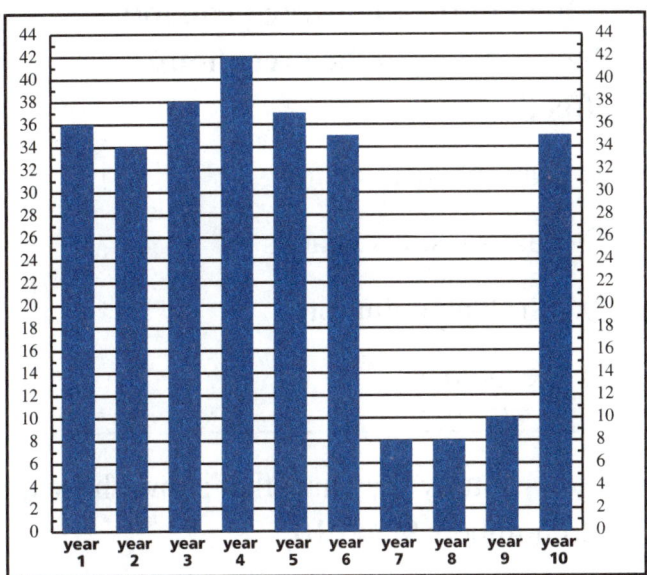

5 What weather condition is suggested by the rainfall data for years 7–9?

- Ⓐ flood
- Ⓒ hurricane
- Ⓑ tornado
- Ⓓ drought

6 Which period of time showed the greatest increase in rainfall?

- Ⓕ from year 2 to year 3
- Ⓖ from year 6 to year 7
- Ⓗ from year 7 to year 8
- Ⓙ from year 9 to year 10

Science

Directions: Do numbers 7 and 8.

7 Which of the following probably does not add to the greenhouse effect?

- Ⓐ car exhaust
- Ⓑ factory smokestacks
- Ⓒ airplane pollution
- Ⓓ pesticides

8 A species of animal that has been completely wiped out is

- Ⓕ endangered.
- Ⓖ extinct.
- Ⓗ hibernating.
- Ⓙ migrating.

Directions: Study the chart that shows how much one school has helped the environment. Then do numbers 9 and 10.

Conservation Efforts at Coe School			
Year	Pounds of Paper Recycled	Pounds of Cans Recycled	Number of Trees Planted
1990	550	475	120
2000	620	469	250
2001	685	390	320

9 Which sentence is true about paper recycling at Coe School?

- Ⓐ Students recycled more paper each year.
- Ⓑ Students recycled less paper each year.
- Ⓒ Students never recycled paper.
- Ⓓ Students recycled the same amount of paper each year.

10 Which conservation project did not show better results each year?

- Ⓕ recycling paper
- Ⓖ recycling cans
- Ⓗ planting trees
- Ⓙ They all showed better results each year.

STOP

Reading and Language Arts

SAMPLE A Find the underlined part of the sentence that is the **simple subject**.

Two <u>planes</u> flew <u>over</u> our <u>house</u> yesterday <u>morning</u>.
     Ⓐ   Ⓑ   Ⓒ   Ⓓ

Directions: Read this story about a woman pilot and then do numbers 1–7.

THE FORGOTTEN FLYER

More than 80 years ago, Jacqueline Cochran was born to a poor family in Pensacola, Florida. Like many girls at the time, she went to work at an early age. When she was just eight years old, Jacqueline Cochran worked in a cotton mill. Jacqueline went on to do many things in her life, but her great dream was to become an aviator.

When Ms. Cochran became a pilot in the 1930s, flying was still in its infancy. Planes were still new inventions, and only the most daring men flew them. Almost no women were flyers, but that didn't stop Jacqueline. She took flying lessons, and was soon good enough to enter famous races. In 1938, she won first prize in a contest to fly across America.

Near the beginning of World War II, Jacqueline trained women in England to become pilots. She later did the same thing for over a thousand American women. In 1945, she was awarded the Distinguished Service Medal, one of America's highest honors.

When the roar of jet planes replaced the clatter of propeller planes, Jacqueline learned to fly them, and soon was the first woman to fly faster than the speed of sound. Jacqueline also set many other records, including flying higher than anyone had before her.

In many ways, Jacqueline Cochran is the forgotten flyer. But she should be remembered, because this aviation pioneer helped establish flying as one of our most important means of transportation.

GO

267   Summer Link Super Edition Grade 4

Name _____

1 What makes Jacqueline Cochran so special?

- Ⓐ working at an early age
- Ⓑ founding a business
- Ⓒ being an early flyer
- Ⓓ being born in Florida

2 This story suggests that

- Ⓕ jets came after propeller planes.
- Ⓖ propeller planes came after jets.
- Ⓗ many people flew in the 1930s.
- Ⓙ Jacqueline Cochran founded an airline.

3 Another way to say "flying faster than the speed of sound" is

- Ⓐ making a loud sound.
- Ⓑ breaking the sound barrier.
- Ⓒ flying a loud plane.
- Ⓓ winning an important race.

4 Look at the picture of Jacqueline Cochran below. The picture shows Jacqueline

- Ⓕ winning an important award.
- Ⓖ working at a mill.
- Ⓗ with her invention.
- Ⓙ getting ready to fly.

Summer Link Super Edition Grade 4

268

GO

Name _____

5 The story says that "flying was still in its infancy" when Jacqueline began. What does this probably mean?

- Ⓐ It was something new.
- Ⓑ She was very young.
- Ⓒ Infants could fly.
- Ⓓ Planes were small.

6 Cotton is a kind of fabric.

Find another thing that is a fabric.

- Ⓕ paper
- Ⓗ silk
- Ⓖ a comb
- Ⓙ shoes

7 *Roar* is a word that sounds like the sound it names. Some other examples are *buzz*, *splash*, and *croak*.

Find another word that sounds like the sound it names.

- Ⓐ catch
- Ⓑ beep
- Ⓒ drive
- Ⓓ loud

GO

Name _____

Directions: For numbers 8 and 9, find the word or words that best complete the sentence.

8 My sister _____ to Space Camp.

- Ⓕ gone
- Ⓗ go
- Ⓖ going
- Ⓙ went

9 She said it was the _____ she had ever had.

- Ⓐ funniest
- Ⓒ most fun
- Ⓑ more fun
- Ⓓ most funner

10 Find the word that fits both sentences below.

We _____ at eight o'clock for the lake.
The house on the _____ is mine.

- Ⓕ left
- Ⓗ side
- Ⓖ went
- Ⓙ right

11 Find the underlined part of the sentence that is the simple subject.

A large tree grew beside the lake.

  Ⓐ Ⓑ   Ⓒ   Ⓓ

STOP

Summer Link Super Edition Grade 4

Name _____

Directions: Read the passage. Then, answer numbers 12–21.

Therapy Dogs

Therapy dogs can help patients **recover** from many illnesses. The dogs' owners or handlers bring them into hospital rooms and encourage patients to **interact** with the animals. Dogs sometimes get right up on patients' beds. People who are sick or recovering from surgery pet the dogs, brush them, talk to them, and even allow the friendly pets to **nuzzle** their faces. Studies have shown that interacting with dogs and other animals is highly **therapeutic**: it can **reduce** stress, lower blood pressure, and even promote healing.

Obviously, not all dogs are **well-suited** for this important job. To be a therapy dog, a dog must have a calm, friendly **disposition**. Some therapy dog owners feel their pets were born to help sick people get well.

12 What is this passage mainly about?

- Ⓕ working dogs
- Ⓖ therapy dogs
- Ⓗ hospital volunteers
- Ⓙ friendly pets

13 Which words help you figure out the meaning of *therapeutic*?

- Ⓐ "well-suited for this important job"
- Ⓑ "interacting with dogs and other animals"
- Ⓒ "reduce stress, lower blood pressure"
- Ⓓ "Studies have shown"

14 Which word is a synonym for *recover*?

- Ⓕ heal
- Ⓖ sleep
- Ⓗ suffer
- Ⓙ avoid

15 *Nuzzling* is like

- Ⓐ rubbing.
- Ⓑ kissing.
- Ⓒ drinking.
- Ⓓ biting.

16 Which word is not a synonym for *reduce*?

- Ⓕ shrink
- Ⓖ lessen
- Ⓗ increase
- Ⓙ decrease

17 When you *interact* with another person, you

- Ⓐ communicate with him or her.
- Ⓑ copy his or her behavior.
- Ⓒ avoid speaking to him or her.
- Ⓓ tell others about him or her.

18 A person who is *well-suited* for a certain job is

- Ⓕ wearing a special uniform.
- Ⓑ able to afford the right clothes for the job.
- Ⓗ someone who can do the job well.
- Ⓙ calm and gentle.

GO

Summer Link Super Edition Grade 4

Name _____

19 *Disposition* means about the same as

- Ⓐ breed.
- Ⓑ personality.
- Ⓒ work experience.
- Ⓓ reputation.

20 The writer of the passage mainly wants to

- Ⓕ persuade readers to volunteer in hospitals.
- Ⓖ entertain readers with some dog stories.
- Ⓗ give information about therapy dogs.
- Ⓙ give information about one special dog.

21 What kind of dog would probably not make a good therapy dog?

- Ⓐ a golden retriever
- Ⓑ an older dog
- Ⓒ a dog that lived with children
- Ⓓ a dog that does not like to be petted

Directions: For numbers 22–25, decide whether each statement is true or false.

22 Therapy dogs are pets that belong to patients.

- Ⓐ true
- Ⓑ false

23 The writer thinks that bringing therapy dogs into hospitals is a good idea.

- Ⓐ true
- Ⓑ false

24 No sick person would turn down a visit from a friendly dog.

- Ⓐ true
- Ⓑ false

25 Interacting with dogs probably makes some patients feel happier and calmer.

- Ⓐ true
- Ⓑ false

STOP

Name _____

Directions: Read the passage. Then, answer numbers 26–34.

MAKING CLAY MOVE

Beginning in the late 1900s, **claymation** became very popular. **Animators** have used clay animation to make several famous movies and TV commercials. However, claymation is not a new **technique**. In 1897 a clay-like **substance** called plasticine was invented. Moviemakers used plasticine to create clay animation films as early as 1908.

Here's how claymation works. First, an artist makes one or more clay models. Moviemakers **pose** each model, take a camera shot, and stop. Next they move the model a tiny bit (into a very slightly different pose), and **shoot** again. They continue to shoot, move the model, shoot, move the model, and so on. It takes many separate shots to make one second of film.

Today's animators usually use clays such as Sculpey™ or Fimo™. Computer techniques have made the claymation process much less **time-consuming**. However, the basics of clay animation have not changed in almost 100 years!

26 What is this passage mainly about?

- Ⓕ plasticine
- Ⓖ types of clay
- Ⓗ claymation techniques and history
- Ⓙ famous movies made with claymation

27 An *animator* is someone who

- Ⓐ creates clay sculptures.
- Ⓑ makes animated films.
- Ⓒ uses claymation only.
- Ⓓ invents clay substances.

28 The word *claymation* comes from the words *clay* and

- Ⓕ movement.
- Ⓖ technician.
- Ⓗ concentration.
- Ⓙ animation.

29 Which word means the same as *technique*?

- Ⓐ technical
- Ⓑ method
- Ⓒ movie
- Ⓓ talent

30 Which word is a synonym for *substance*?

Ⓕ sound

Ⓖ substitute

Ⓗ liquid

Ⓙ material

31 What does it mean to *pose* something?

Ⓐ roll it into a ball

Ⓑ squash it flat

Ⓒ use it to make a model

Ⓓ move it into a certain position

32 In this passage, the word *shoot* means

Ⓕ to fire a gun.

Ⓖ a part of a plant that has just begun to grow.

Ⓗ to take a photograph or make a movie.

Ⓙ to move quickly.

33 Which word means the opposite of *time-consuming*?

Ⓐ speedy

Ⓑ sluggish

Ⓒ frustrating

Ⓓ satisfying

34 The writer of the passage mainly wants to

Ⓕ persuade readers to rent certain videotapes.

Ⓖ entertain readers with some filmmaking stories.

Ⓗ give information about claymation.

Ⓙ give information about plasticine.

Name _____

Directions: Choose the correct answer to each question to complete the analogies.

35 <u>Rose</u> is to <u>flower</u> as <u>oak</u> is to _____.

- Ⓐ leaf
- Ⓑ furniture
- Ⓒ bush
- Ⓓ tree

36 <u>Begin</u> is to <u>cease</u> as <u>confuse</u> is to _____.

- Ⓕ clarify
- Ⓖ annoy
- Ⓗ continue
- Ⓙ stop

37 <u>Supermarket</u> is to <u>groceries</u> as <u>bookstore</u> is to _____.

- Ⓐ food
- Ⓑ paper
- Ⓒ reading materials
- Ⓓ library

38 <u>Fork</u> is to <u>eat</u> as <u>ruler</u> is to _____.

- Ⓕ cut
- Ⓖ measure
- Ⓗ spoon
- Ⓙ inch

Directions: Match words with the same meanings. Mark the letter of your choice.

39 frothy	A	delicious	**39**	Ⓐ Ⓑ Ⓒ Ⓓ
40 tasty	B	raw	**40**	Ⓐ Ⓑ Ⓒ Ⓓ
41 uncooked	C	foamy	**41**	Ⓐ Ⓑ Ⓒ Ⓓ
42 spicy	D	hot	**42**	Ⓐ Ⓑ Ⓒ Ⓓ

Directions: Match words with opposite meanings. Mark the letter of your choice.

43 polite	F	backward	**43**	Ⓕ Ⓖ Ⓗ Ⓙ
44 behind	G	rude	**44**	Ⓕ Ⓖ Ⓗ Ⓙ
45 forward	H	fantastic	**45**	Ⓕ Ⓖ Ⓗ Ⓙ
46 realistic	J	ahead	**46**	Ⓕ Ⓖ Ⓗ Ⓙ

STOP

Name _____

Directions: Read the paragraph that tells how to make a peanut butter and jelly sandwich. Then think of something you like to make or do. Write a paragraph that tells how to make it. Use the words *first*, *next*, *then*, *last*.

These steps tell how to make a peanut butter and jelly sandwich. First get two pieces of bread, peanut butter, jelly, and a knife. Next spread peanut butter on one piece of bread. Then spread jelly on the other piece. Last press the two pieces of bread together.

Directions: Read the letter below. In the letter, a girl explains to her father why she should be allowed to try inline skating. Then think of something you would like to be allowed to do. Write a letter to explain to someone why you should be allowed to do it.

Dear Dad,

I would like to try inline skating. I know that you think it is not safe, but I would be very careful. I would follow every safety rule. I would wear a helmet, elbow pads, and knee pads. I would only skate in safe places. Please give me a chance.

Love,

Bonita

Basic Skills

SAMPLE A Find the word in which the underlined letters have the same sound as the picture name.

   Ⓐ la_st_   Ⓑ _s_leep   Ⓒ _c_lip   Ⓓ _sh_ip

1.    Ⓐ _ch_ase   Ⓑ cri_s_p   Ⓒ _c_lub   Ⓓ _sh_irt

2. Find the word that has the same ending sound as
      Ⓕ ha_nd_   Ⓖ ju_mp_   Ⓗ cha_nce_   Ⓙ char_m_

3. Look at the first word. Find the other word that has the same vowel sound as the underlined part.

   br_ou_ght   Ⓐ l_o_st   Ⓑ p_ou_nd   Ⓒ st_o_ne   Ⓓ cr_ow_d

4. Look at the underlined word. Find a word that can be added to the underlined word to make a compound word.

   air   Ⓕ cut   Ⓖ plane   Ⓗ grass   Ⓙ green

5. Find the word in which just the prefix is underlined.

   Ⓐ _p_review   Ⓑ _de_cide   Ⓒ _a_lert   Ⓓ _mon_ster

6. Find the word in which only the root word is underlined.

   Ⓕ _ol_der   Ⓖ _car_t   Ⓗ _room_y   Ⓙ _full_y

7. Find the word in which only the suffix is underlined.

   Ⓐ bund_le_   Ⓑ most_ly_   Ⓒ run_ner_   Ⓓ jumpi_ng_

279   Summer Link Super Edition Grade 4

Name _____

Directions: For Sample B and numbers 8 and 9, find the answer that means the same or about the same as the underlined word.

SAMPLE B extremely windy

- Ⓐ slightly
- Ⓒ often
- Ⓑ somewhat
- Ⓓ very

8 famous <u>legend</u>

- Ⓐ person
- Ⓒ place
- Ⓑ tale
- Ⓓ painting

9 <u>create</u> a statue

- Ⓕ enjoy
- Ⓗ see
- Ⓖ make
- Ⓙ drop

Directions: Find the word that correctly completes both sentences.

11 Use the _____ to make the hole. The _____ team won a prize.

- Ⓕ drill
- Ⓗ needle
- Ⓖ nail
- Ⓙ marching

12 This _____ of plant is rare. Mr. Westgate is very _____.

- Ⓐ type
- Ⓒ nice
- Ⓑ kind
- Ⓓ happy

Directions: For Sample C and number 10, find the answer that best fits in the blank.

SAMPLE C Did you _____ the address in the phone book?

- Ⓐ lose
- Ⓒ know
- Ⓑ find
- Ⓓ forget

10 Which word means George's project was in the center of the room?

George's project was in the _____ of the room.

- Ⓐ front
- Ⓒ middle
- Ⓑ back
- Ⓓ side

Directions: For each blank, look at the words with the same number. Find the word from each list that fits best in the blank.

The bus was more __(13)__ than normal. It was raining hard, and many people who __(14)__ walked to work took the bus today.

13
- Ⓕ empty
- Ⓗ expensive
- Ⓖ crowded
- Ⓙ practical

14
- Ⓐ never
- Ⓒ usually
- Ⓑ recently
- Ⓓ quickly

GO

Directions: For Sample D and numbers 15 and 16, find the part of the sentence that needs a capital letter. Mark "None" if no capital letter is needed.

SAMPLE D
| a small bird | landed on | the feeder. | None |
| (A) | (B) | (C) | (D) |

15
| We drove | to iowa | last summer. | None |
| (A) | (B) | (C) | (D) |

16 Find the punctuation mark that is needed in the sentence. *How long will you be gone?*

| . | ! | , | None |
| (F) | (G) | (H) | (J) |

Directions: Find the sentence that has correct capitalization and punctuation.

17
(A) This is a great book
(B) Nora gave it to me.
(C) i'm almost done.
(D) You can have it next?

18
(F) We aren't ready yet.
(G) Dont leave without us.
(H) The bags are packed? Let's go.
(J) The ride to the beach will be an hour

Directions: Read the paragraph. Find the answer that shows the correct capitalization and punctuation for the underlined parts.

(19)   A family of <u>rabbit's visits</u> our yard every day. They eat grass and some flowers. Mom doesn't mind. She says there are plenty of flowers for
(20)   <u>everyone.</u> The baby rabbits seem to get bigger every day.

19
(A) rabbit's visit's   (C) rabbits visits
(B) rabbits visit's   (D) Correct as it is

20
(F) everyone,   (H) everyone!
(G) everyone?   (J) Correct as it is

Name _____

Directions: For each question, find the answer choice that shows correct capitalization and punctuation for the underlined words.

21 The soccer match is <u>thursday the</u> baseball game is Friday.

- Ⓐ Thursday: the
- Ⓑ Thursday. The
- Ⓒ Thursday. the
- Ⓓ Correct as it is

22 "What a terrifying ride that <u>was."</u> <u>Cried</u> Jake.

- Ⓕ was." Cried
- Ⓖ was!" cried
- Ⓗ was!" Cried
- Ⓙ Correct as it is

23 You will need the following <u>materials,</u> <u>Yarn,</u> scissors, cardboard, and paste.

- Ⓐ materials; yarn
- Ⓑ materials: Yarn
- Ⓒ materials: yarn
- Ⓓ Correct as it is

24 The traffic reporter <u>announced, all</u> lanes are now closed on Route 22."

- Ⓕ announced, "All
- Ⓖ announced, "all
- Ⓗ announced: "All
- Ⓙ Correct as it is

25 <u>Greensburg pennsylvania</u> is about 35 miles east of Pittsburgh.

- Ⓐ Greensburg, pennsylvania
- Ⓑ Greensburg, Pennsylvania,
- Ⓒ Greensburg, Pennsylvania
- Ⓓ Correct as it is

26 "<u>Yes, Maggie, you</u> can come over now," said Ann.

- Ⓕ "yes, Maggie, you
- Ⓖ "Yes Maggie you
- Ⓗ "Yes Maggie you,
- Ⓙ Correct as it is

27 We washed <u>dried and put</u> away the dishes.

- Ⓐ washed, dried, and put
- Ⓑ washed dried and, put
- Ⓒ washed, dried and put,
- Ⓓ Correct as it is

STOP

Summer Link Super Edition Grade 4

Name _____

Directions: Read the questions. Mark the letter next to the correct answer. Use the sample index to answer numbers 28–30.

O
Oak, 291-292
Obsidian, 175-176
Oceans, 361-375
  density of, 363-364
  life in, 367-370
  waves, 371-372
  temperature of, 365
  resources, 373-375

28 You will find information about what topic on page 365?

Ⓕ ocean temperatures

Ⓖ density of the ocean

Ⓗ waves

Ⓙ the octopus

29 On what pages will you most likely find information about mining the oceans for minerals?

Ⓐ pages 175-176

Ⓑ pages 368-369

Ⓒ pages 373-375

Ⓓ pages 371-372

30 You can read about octopuses on pages 368-369. This information is part of what section under Oceans?

Ⓕ resources

Ⓖ life in

Ⓗ waves

Ⓙ temperature

Directions: Use the web to answer number 31.

31 Which of the following belongs on the web?

Ⓐ traveling with your pet

Ⓑ heat exhaustion

Ⓒ finding a lost pet

Ⓓ cold weather and your pet

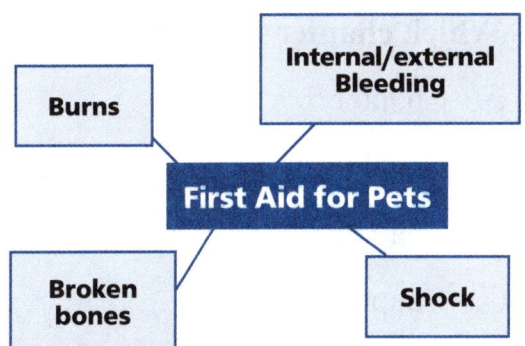

Name _____

Directions: Use the sample table of contents to answer numbers 32–33.

Table of Contents

1 Animals Around the World 11
2 Zoos of the World 42
3 Creatures of the Sea 59
4 Rodents 85
5 Reptiles and Amphibians 101
6 Insects and Spiders 112

32 In which chapter would you most likely read about otters, seals, and walruses?

- Ⓕ Chapter 5
- Ⓖ Chapter 1
- Ⓗ Chapter 4
- Ⓙ Chapter 3

33 Which chapter is the shortest?

- Ⓐ Chapter 5
- Ⓑ Chapter 2
- Ⓒ Chapter 3
- Ⓓ Chapter 1

Directions: Find the choice that rhymes with the underlined word.

34 a <u>tough</u> test

- Ⓕ cough
- Ⓖ rough
- Ⓗ laugh
- Ⓙ thorough

35 <u>chose</u> a new outfit

- Ⓐ lose
- Ⓑ news
- Ⓒ close
- Ⓓ loose

36 <u>Where</u> is the umbrella?

- Ⓕ here
- Ⓖ were
- Ⓗ there
- Ⓙ hear

37 the new <u>roof</u>

- Ⓐ gruff
- Ⓑ truth
- Ⓒ wife
- Ⓓ aloof

GO

Summer Link Super Edition Grade 4

Name _____

Directions: For numbers 38–41, choose the form of the verb that correctly completes each sentence.

38 My parents and I _____ to New York tomorrow.

- Ⓕ flew
- Ⓗ flies
- Ⓖ are flying
- Ⓙ have flown

39 My father _____ to attend a business conference.

- Ⓐ have
- Ⓒ having
- Ⓑ haves
- Ⓓ has

40 While Dad works next week, Mom and I _____ the sights.

- Ⓕ have seen
- Ⓗ will see
- Ⓖ am seeing
- Ⓙ seen

41 This time last year we _____ to San Francisco.

- Ⓐ went
- Ⓒ have gone
- Ⓑ are going
- Ⓓ was going

Directions: For numbers 42–45, choose the answer choice with a usage error. If there are no errors, fill in the last answer choice.

42
- Ⓕ Them cookies we baked are
- Ⓖ really terrible. Even the dog wouldn't
- Ⓗ eat the one I accidentally dropped.
- Ⓙ no errors

43
- Ⓐ The amazed children watched
- Ⓑ as the doe and her fawn
- Ⓒ wandered slow through the yard.
- Ⓓ no errors

44
- Ⓕ I could of done
- Ⓖ that problem
- Ⓗ without your help.
- Ⓙ no errors

45
- Ⓐ I gave the cookies
- Ⓑ to he and she
- Ⓒ because they looked angry.
- Ⓓ no errors

GO

Name _____

Directions: For numbers 46–48, mark the answer choice that best combines the two sentences.

46 **Marla visited the museum today. Her sister visited the museum today.**

- Ⓕ Marla and her sister visited the museum today.
- Ⓖ Marla visited and her sister visited the museum today.
- Ⓗ Marla visited the museum today and her sister visited the museum today.
- Ⓙ Marla visited her sister and the museum today.

47 **Greg attended the concert last night. The concert was in the park.**

- Ⓐ The concert last night was in the park Greg attended.
- Ⓑ Greg attended last night in the park the concert.
- Ⓒ Greg attended the concert last night, and the concert was in the park.
- Ⓓ Greg attended the concert in the park last night.

48 **The campers watched as the bear took their food. The campers watched in horror.**

- Ⓕ The campers watched as the bear took their food in horror.
- Ⓖ The campers in horror watched as the bear took their food.
- Ⓗ The campers watched in horror as the bear took their food.
- Ⓙ The campers watched as the bear took their food, and the campers were in horror.

Directions: For numbers 49–54, mark the letter of the correctly spelled word that completes each sentence.

49 **On Saturday, I work on my _____.**

- Ⓐ hobbies
- Ⓒ hobies
- Ⓑ hobbys
- Ⓓ hobbes

50 **Your sister sings so _____.**

- Ⓕ beautifuly
- Ⓗ beautifully
- Ⓖ beautyfully
- Ⓙ bueatifully

51 **The milk was in a _____.**

- Ⓐ picher
- Ⓒ pitcher
- Ⓑ picture
- Ⓓ pitsher

GO

Summer Link Super Edition Grade 4

52 We are _____ up by 6:30 a.m. every morning.

- Ⓕ alwase
- Ⓗ allways
- Ⓖ always
- Ⓙ alwaze

53 I hope you're not _____ with your gifts.

- Ⓐ unhappy
- Ⓒ unhappie
- Ⓑ unhapy
- Ⓓ unhappe

54 You should always eat a good _____.

- Ⓕ brekfast
- Ⓖ breakfist
- Ⓗ breakfast
- Ⓙ brakefast

Directions: For numbers 55–60, mark the letter of the underlined word that is misspelled in each sentence. Mark the letter for no errors if all the words are spelled correctly.

55 I <u>wouldn't</u> be the <u>least</u> bit <u>suprised</u> if Jack got here late. <u>no errors</u>
       Ⓐ   Ⓑ   Ⓒ   Ⓓ

56 Please <u>print</u> your name, <u>adress</u>, and <u>telephone</u> number. <u>no errors</u>
           Ⓕ   Ⓖ   Ⓗ   Ⓙ

57 The <u>choclate</u> cake you baked is <u>really</u> <u>delicious</u>. <u>no errors</u>
        Ⓐ   Ⓑ   Ⓒ   Ⓓ

58 I <u>received</u> an <u>invitation</u> to Stan's party next <u>Saturday</u>. <u>no errors</u>
      Ⓕ   Ⓖ   Ⓗ   Ⓙ

59 Jody has been my best <u>friend</u> <u>sinse</u> we met in <u>first</u> grade. <u>no errors</u>
                            Ⓐ   Ⓑ   Ⓒ   Ⓓ

60 We're having <u>Thanksgiving</u> dinner with my grandparents <u>tomorow</u>. <u>no errors</u>
      Ⓕ   Ⓖ   Ⓗ   Ⓙ

Name _____

Directions: Find the word that is spelled correctly and best fits in the blank.

61 Let's play _____ it is nice.
- Ⓐ wheil
- Ⓑ wile
- Ⓒ while
- Ⓓ wheil

62 Will you _____ places with me?
- Ⓕ traid
- Ⓖ tread
- Ⓗ traed
- Ⓙ trade

63 An outdoor _____ is near our house.
- Ⓐ market
- Ⓑ markit
- Ⓒ marcket
- Ⓓ marked

Directions: Find the underlined word that is not spelled correctly. If all the words are correct, mark "All correct."

64
- Ⓕ <u>many</u> friends
- Ⓖ funny <u>joke</u>
- Ⓗ feel <u>hungry</u>
- Ⓙ All correct

65
- Ⓐ <u>among</u> us
- Ⓑ <u>common</u> bird
- Ⓒ <u>fortie</u> minutes
- Ⓓ All correct

Directions: Find the answer that is the solution to the problem. If the answer is not given, choose "None of these."

66 $82 - 35 =$
- Ⓕ 53
- Ⓖ 47
- Ⓗ 57
- Ⓙ 117
- Ⓚ None of these

67 $3.40
     +3.60
- Ⓐ $.20
- Ⓑ $3.20
- Ⓒ $6.00
- Ⓓ $8.00
- Ⓔ None of these

68 $9 \times 8 =$
- Ⓕ 17
- Ⓖ 64
- Ⓗ 98
- Ⓙ 72
- Ⓚ None of these

69 305
     × 6
- Ⓐ 311
- Ⓑ 1830
- Ⓒ 3605
- Ⓓ 3065
- Ⓔ None of these

STOP

Mathematics
BUILDING OUR CLUBHOUSE

 **SAMPLE A** Which of these is most likely measured in feet?

- Ⓐ the distance around a room
- Ⓑ the weight of a large box
- Ⓒ the distance to the moon
- Ⓓ the amount of water in a pool

1 Jennie had three bent nails in her pocket. Then she put five straight nails in her pocket. Which answer shows what she had in her pocket?

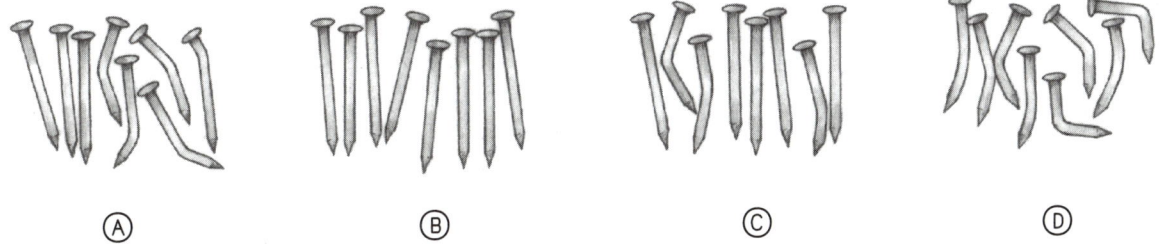

Ⓐ   Ⓑ   Ⓒ   Ⓓ

2 Ricky carried 4 boxes of tiles into the kitchen. Each box held 12 tiles. What would you do to find out how many tiles he carried into the kitchen all together?

add	subtract	divide	multiply
Ⓕ	Ⓖ	Ⓗ	Ⓙ

3 Angela wants to measure a piece of wood. Which of these should she use?

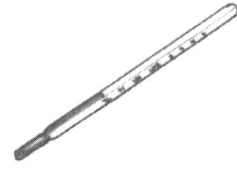 

Ⓐ   Ⓑ   Ⓒ   Ⓓ

GO

289   Summer Link Super Edition Grade 4

4 Mr. and Mrs. Akers are going to build a deck. It will take 2 weeks to finish. They plan to start on April 24. What date will they finish?

- Ⓕ April 10
- Ⓖ May 1
- Ⓗ April 26
- Ⓙ May 8

5 Pam made this pattern of 4 rows of floor tiles. How many gray tiles will she need all together if she adds 1 more row to make 5 rows of tiles?

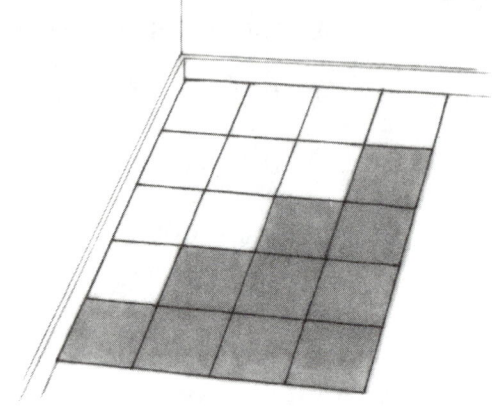

- Ⓐ 5
- Ⓑ 15
- Ⓒ 9
- Ⓓ 20

6 Which pattern of letters could be folded in half on a line of symmetry?

AMOMA	BAGGB	VERDT	UNPOS
Ⓕ	Ⓖ	Ⓗ	Ⓙ

7 The children in the Adams family were stuck inside on a rainy day. They decided to make their own games. They each made a spinner for their game. When Jennie spun her spinner, the color it landed on was gray. Which spinner was probably Jennie's?

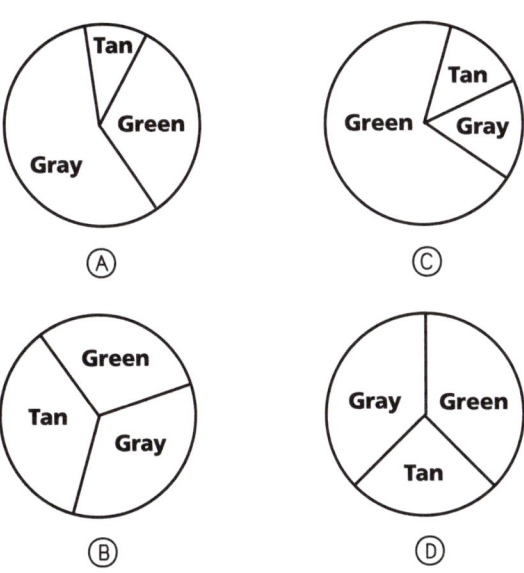

8 This map shows Janelle's yard. She came in through the gate and walked east for 3 yards. Then she went north for 2 yards. What was she closest to?

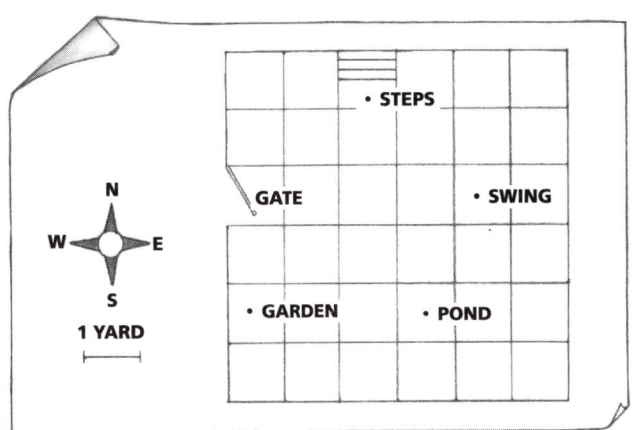

Ⓕ to the swing

Ⓖ to the pond

Ⓗ to the steps

Ⓙ to the garden

9 Rick is carving a pattern in a piece of wood. Which shapes are missing from the pattern?

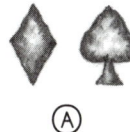
Ⓐ

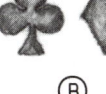
Ⓑ

Ⓒ

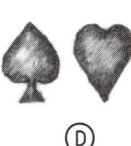
Ⓓ

Name _____

10 Which of these is not the same shape and size as the others?

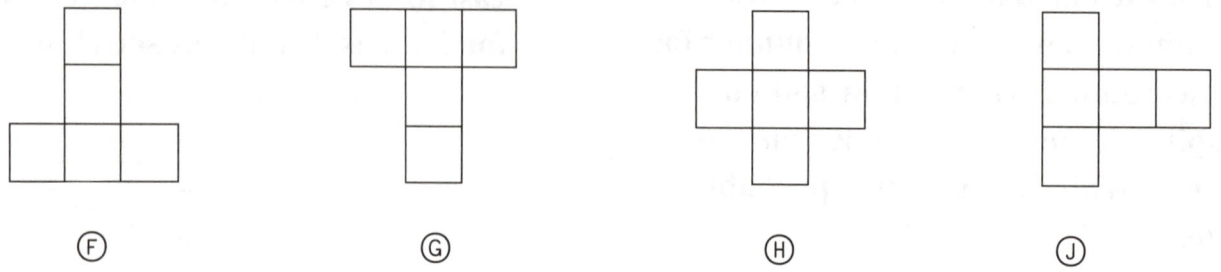

11 Look at the group of socks. What fraction of the socks is black?

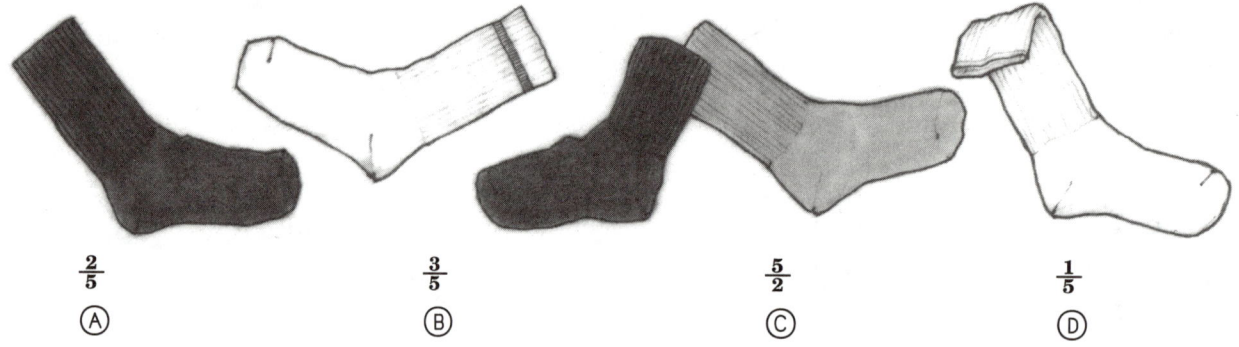

$\frac{2}{5}$ Ⓐ $\frac{3}{5}$ Ⓑ $\frac{5}{2}$ Ⓒ $\frac{1}{5}$ Ⓓ

12 Look at the graph below and the report Willie made about the coins in his change jar. How many dimes did Willie have in the change jar?

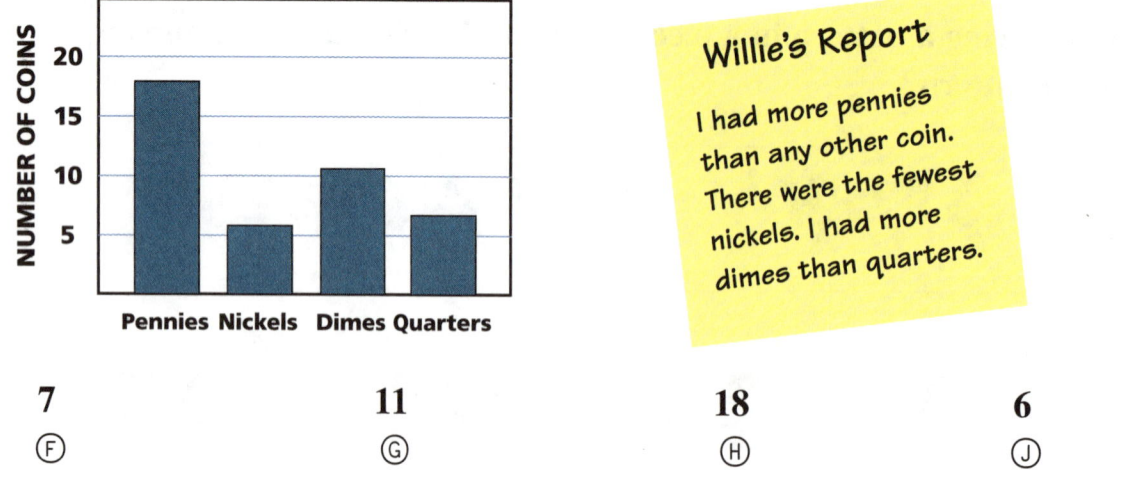

Willie's Report

I had more pennies than any other coin. There were the fewest nickels. I had more dimes than quarters.

7 Ⓕ   11 Ⓖ   18 Ⓗ   6 Ⓙ

STOP

Summer Link Super Edition Grade 4   292

Name _____

Directions: Choose the answer that correctly solves each problem.

13 Which number has a 7 in the ten-thousands place and a 3 in the hundreds place?

Ⓐ 178,234   Ⓒ 498,301

Ⓑ 476,302   Ⓓ 753,092

14 What is the perimeter of the polygon?

Ⓕ 38 inches

Ⓗ 26 inches

Ⓖ 28 inches

Ⓙ not enough information

15 Which decimal is greater than 1.32 but less than 1.41?

Ⓐ 1.42   Ⓒ 1.31

Ⓑ 1.36   Ⓓ 1.30

16 Which decimal is equal to $\frac{1}{4}$?

Ⓕ 0.25   Ⓗ 0.75

Ⓖ 0.025   Ⓙ .033

17 What could be the next number in the pattern? 3, 7, 15, 31, 63, …

Ⓐ 127   Ⓒ 96

Ⓑ 106   Ⓓ 79

18 Which animal is between 15 and 40 feet long?

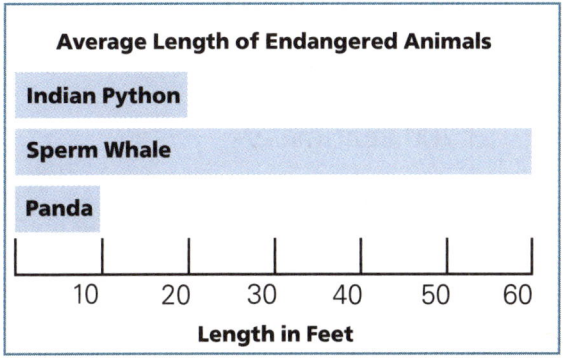

Ⓕ Panda   Ⓗ Indian Python

Ⓖ Sperm Whale   Ⓙ Not here

19 What other equation belongs in the same fact family as 17 × 8 = 136?

Ⓐ 8 × 136 = 1,088

Ⓑ 136 ÷ 2 = 68

Ⓒ 8 × 17 = 136

Ⓓ 17 + 8 = 25

20 Which figure shows parallel lines?

Ⓕ S   Ⓗ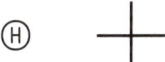

Ⓖ 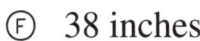   Ⓙ

GO

Name _____

21 A tsunami is a wave created by underwater earthquakes. Tsunamis can reach heights of 37 meters. How many centimeters tall is that?

Ⓐ 37,000 centimeters

Ⓑ 3,700 centimeters

Ⓒ 370 centimeters

Ⓓ 3.70 centimeters

22 What is the temperature shown on the thermometer?

Ⓕ 74° C

Ⓖ 66° C

Ⓗ 64° C

Ⓙ 54° C

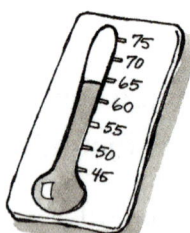

23 How can you write 56,890 in expanded notation?

Ⓐ 5 + 6 + 8 + 9 + 0 =

Ⓑ 50,000 + 6,000 + 800 + 90 =

Ⓒ 56,000 + 8900 =

Ⓓ 0.5 + 0.06 + 0.008 + 0.0009 =

24 Which number is not a multiple of 4?

Ⓕ 86   Ⓗ 40

Ⓖ 68   Ⓙ 32

25 In a pictograph  stands for 5 books. How many books does stand for?

Ⓐ 5 books   Ⓒ 20 books

Ⓑ 8 books   Ⓓ 40 books

26 How long is the paperclip?

Ⓕ 3 inches   Ⓗ 3 centimeters

Ⓖ 5 inches   Ⓙ 2 centimeters

27 How much did the average daily temperature change from February to March?

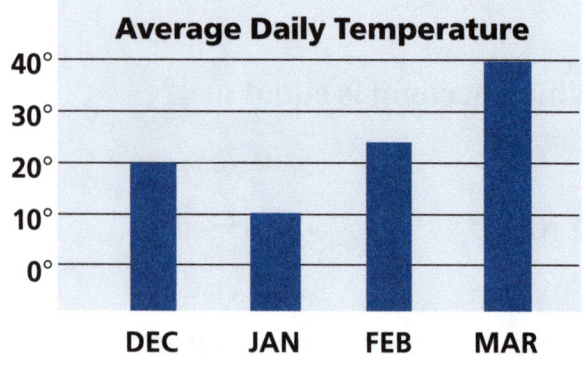

Ⓐ 25° F   Ⓒ 10° F

Ⓑ 15° F   Ⓓ 5° F

Name _____

Directions: Choose the answer that correctly solves each problem.

28 8,906 + 3,897 =

- Ⓕ 11,803
- Ⓗ 12,803
- Ⓖ 12,793
- Ⓙ 3,893

29 467.902 − 56.894 =

- Ⓐ 411.192
- Ⓒ 410.192
- Ⓑ 411.008
- Ⓓ 410.008

30 84 × .65 =

- Ⓕ 44.80
- Ⓗ 53.60
- Ⓖ 52.80
- Ⓙ 54.60

31 $\frac{3}{8} + \frac{1}{8} =$

- Ⓐ 1
- Ⓒ $\frac{4}{8}$
- Ⓑ $\frac{5}{8}$
- Ⓓ $\frac{2}{8}$

32 $\frac{279}{9} =$

- Ⓕ 3
- Ⓗ 31
- Ⓖ 26
- Ⓙ 42

33 $\frac{1}{3} + \frac{2}{3} + 1\frac{1}{3} =$

- Ⓐ $3\frac{2}{3}$
- Ⓒ 2
- Ⓑ $2\frac{1}{3}$
- Ⓓ $1\frac{1}{3}$

34 $\frac{1784}{2} =$

- Ⓕ 876
- Ⓖ 892
- Ⓗ 1,784
- Ⓙ 3,568

35 24.75 + 27.5 + 25.6 =

- Ⓐ 77.85
- Ⓑ 77.4
- Ⓒ 53.10
- Ⓓ 50.35

36 4321 + 2987 =

- Ⓕ 7,308
- Ⓖ 7,208
- Ⓗ 7,108
- Ⓙ 1,334

37 $\frac{15.05}{5} =$

- Ⓐ 3.01
- Ⓑ 3.1
- Ⓒ 31
- Ⓓ 82

Name _____

Directions: Choose the answer that correctly solves each problem.

38 Michael was at a card convention. At the first booth he bought 8 cards. He bought 6 cards at each of the remaining 9 booths. How many cards did Michael buy altogether?

Ⓕ 54 cards
Ⓗ 57 cards
Ⓖ 62 cards
Ⓙ 72 cards

39 There were 85 boxes shipped to the warehouse. In each box there were 22 cartons. In each carton there were 40 water guns. How many water guns are in all 85 boxes?

Ⓐ 880 water guns
Ⓑ 1,870 water guns
Ⓒ 74,800 water guns
Ⓓ Not enough information

40 Mary measured the length of a room at 8 feet. How many inches long is the room?

Ⓕ 12 inches
Ⓖ 24 inches
Ⓗ 96 inches
Ⓙ None of these

41 Mr. Thomas bought 2 adult tickets and 1 child ticket to the amusement park. How much money did he spend altogether?

Ⓐ $44.85
Ⓒ $29.90
Ⓑ $38.85
Ⓓ $23.90

42 Rita left dance class at 3:30 p.m. She arrived home at 4:17 p.m. How long did it take Rita to get home?

Ⓕ 1 hour, 17 minutes
Ⓖ 47 minutes
Ⓗ 37 minutes
Ⓙ 13 minutes

Name _____

Social Studies

Directions: Choose the best answer for numbers 1–6.

1 The Boston Tea Party happened because

- Ⓐ workers didn't like to sail.
- Ⓑ people believed the tax on tea was not fair.
- Ⓒ bosses wanted to take a break and have fun.
- Ⓓ settlers needed to move to a new town.

2 The first President of the United States was

- Ⓕ John Adams
- Ⓖ Thomas Jefferson
- Ⓗ George Washington
- Ⓙ Abraham Lincoln

3 Which *probably* did not happen because of the invention of the steam engine?

- Ⓐ People visited other states more often.
- Ⓑ Children had fewer school days.
- Ⓒ Businesses sent their goods across the country.
- Ⓓ Workers had new jobs.

4 Who *probably* made the first United States flag?

- Ⓕ Betsy Ross
- Ⓖ John Hancock
- Ⓗ Benjamin Franklin
- Ⓙ Dolly Madison

5 What invention helped clean raw cotton?

- Ⓐ sewing machine
- Ⓑ slaves
- Ⓒ cotton gin
- Ⓓ the plow

6 What *probably* helped pioneers decide to go to California?

- Ⓕ There were big cities there.
- Ⓖ There were no Indians.
- Ⓗ Travel was safe and cheap.
- Ⓙ Gold was discovered there.

GO

Name ______________________________

Product Map of Midwestern States

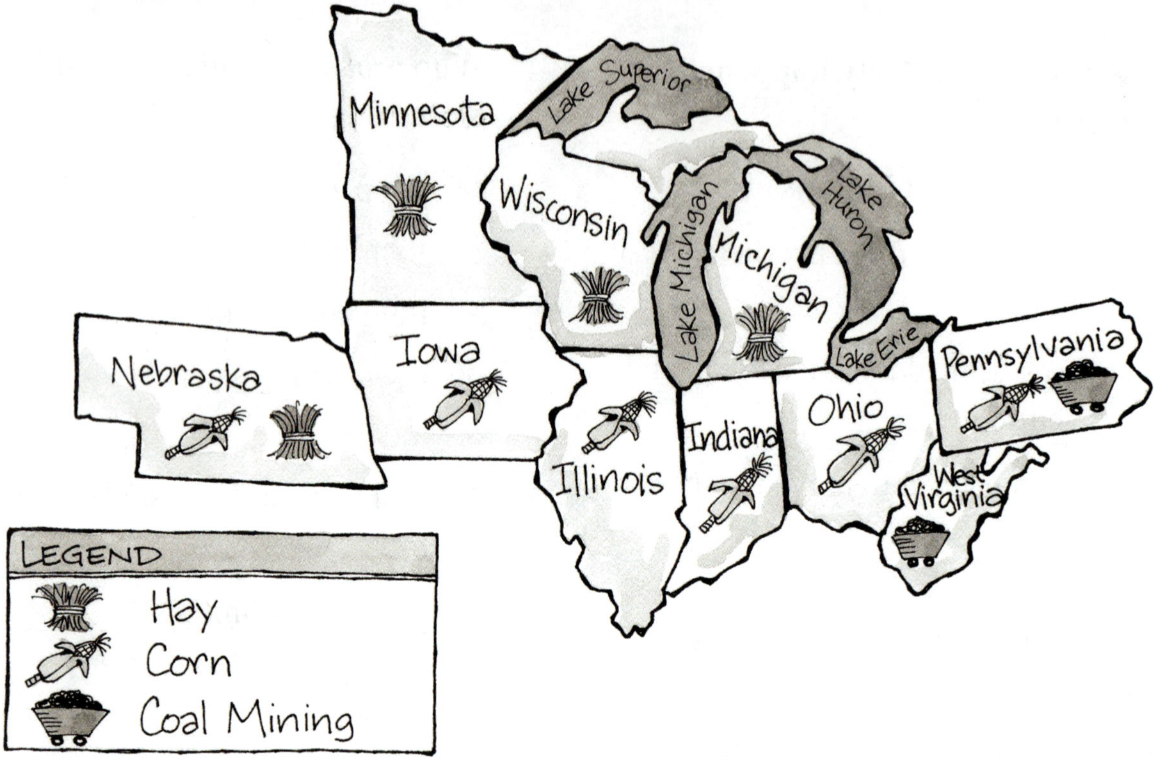

Minnesota
Lake Superior
Wisconsin
Lake Michigan
Michigan
Lake Huron
Nebraska
Iowa
Illinois
Indiana
Ohio
Lake Erie
Pennsylvania
West Virginia
LEGEND
Hay
Corn
Coal Mining

7 **Which state does *not* grow hay?**

Ⓐ Wisconsin

Ⓑ Minnesota

Ⓒ Illinois

Ⓓ Michigan

8 **You would find coal mines in**

Ⓕ Illinois and Pennsylvania.

Ⓖ West Virginia and Indiana.

Ⓗ Iowa and Nebraska.

Ⓙ Pennsylvania and West Virginia.

9 **Which state grows both hay and corn?**

Ⓐ Ohio

Ⓑ Nebraska

Ⓒ Iowa

Ⓓ Wisconsin

STOP

Name _____

Science

Directions: Do numbers 1–6.

1 What kind of scientist studies rocks and minerals?

Ⓐ biologist
Ⓑ botanist
Ⓒ archeologist
Ⓓ geologist

2 A rock that was formed by volcanic activity is called

Ⓕ sedimentary.
Ⓖ igneous.
Ⓗ metamorphic.
Ⓙ mineral.

3 A sedimentary rock is often formed in a

Ⓐ river bed.
Ⓑ volcano.
Ⓒ mesa.
Ⓓ plateau.

4 A scientist scratches a mineral sample with her fingernail, a penny, and then a nail. What property is she testing?

Ⓕ shininess
Ⓖ chemical make-up
Ⓗ weight
Ⓙ hardness

5 The outermost layer of the Earth is called the

Ⓐ outer core.
Ⓑ inner core.
Ⓒ crust.
Ⓓ mantle.

6 A sudden movement of the Earth's crust is known as

Ⓕ a volcano.
Ⓖ an earthquake.
Ⓗ a hurricane.
Ⓙ a tornado.

Name _____

Directions: Read the diagram, and then do numbers 7 and 8.

Before   After

7 Which principle is shown in the diagram?

Ⓐ evaporation

Ⓑ displacement

Ⓒ metamorphosis

Ⓓ isolation

8 What would happen if the rock in Picture 2 were small instead of large?

Ⓕ The water level would be higher.

Ⓖ The water would have evaporated.

Ⓗ The water level would be lower.

Ⓙ The water level would be the same.

Directions: Read the graph, and then do numbers 9 and 10.

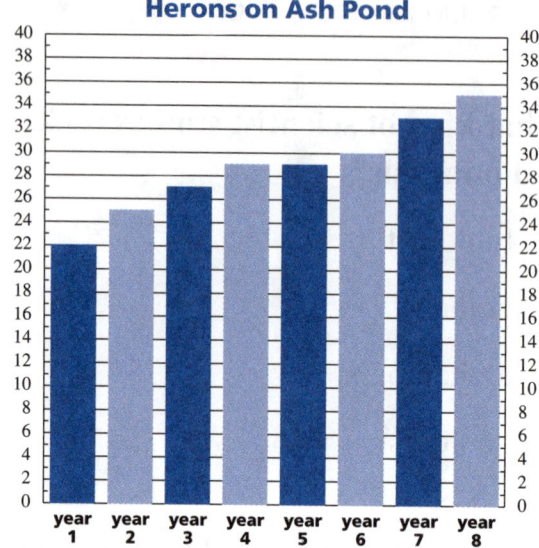

9 In which two years did the number of herons stay the same?

Ⓐ years 1 and 2

Ⓑ years 2 and 3

Ⓒ years 3 and 4

Ⓓ years 4 and 5

10 Based on the data, what could you predict for year 11?

Ⓕ The number of herons will increase.

Ⓖ The number of herons will decrease.

Ⓗ The number of herons will stay the same.

Ⓙ Herons will become endangered.

STOP

Grade 3 Answer Key

Page 220
- **7.** C
- **8.** F

Page 223
- **A.** B
- **B.** F

Page 225
- **1.** C
- **2.** F

Page 226
- **3.** B
- **4.** H
- **5.** C
- **6.** F
- **7.** B

Page 228
- **8.** F
- **9.** C

Page 229
- **10.** J
- **11.** B
- **12.** H

Page 230
- **A.** A
- **1.** A
- **2.** H

Page 231
- **3.** A
- **4.** G
- **5.** C
- **6.** F

Page 232
- **8.** J
- **9.** B
- **10.** F
- **11.** C
- **12.** F
- **13.** D

Page 233
Responses will vary.

Grade 3 Answer Key

Page 234

FIRST QUESTION: Possible response: It is Juan. He is nervous about seeing his friend, because he hasn't seen him in 6 months.

SECOND QUESTION: Possible response: The story doesn't say where the story takes place. It doesn't really matter.

THIRD QUESTION: Possible response: He is afraid that it won't be the same, but the friend puts him at ease.

Page 235
- A. C

Page 236
1. D
2. G
3. A
4. H

Page 237
5. C
6. G
7. A

Page 238
8. H
9. D
10. H
11. A

Page 239
Responses will vary.

Page 240
- A. A
1. A
2. G
3. B
4. J

Page 241
- A. B
- B. F
1. A
2. J
3. C
4. F
5. C

Page 242
- C. B
6. D
7. F
8. A
9. J

Page 243
- A. B
1. A
2. H
- B. C
3. C
4. J

Grade 3 Answer Key

Page 244
5. D
6. H
C. B
7. C
8. J

Page 245
1. A
2. J
3. B
4. G
5. C
A. D
6. B
7. J
8. C

Page 246
A. C
B. K
1. D
2. K
3. A
4. G

Page 247
A. A
1. C
2. H
3. D
4. G
5. D
6. G
7. A

Page 248
B. D
8. B
9. G
C. A
10. C
11. J
12. A
13. H
14. C

Page 249
D. D
15. A
16. G
17. D
18. G
19. C
20. J

Grade 3 Answer Key

Page 250
- **E.** B
- **21.** C
- **22.** H
- **23.** D
- **24.** F

Page 251
- **A.** C

Page 252
- **1.** B
- **2.** F
- **3.** D
- **4.** F
- **5.** B

Page 253
- **6.** F
- **7.** D
- **8.** F
- **9.** B
- **10.** F
- **11.** C

Page 254
- **12.** F
- **13.** B
- **14.** J

Page 255
- **15.** D
- **16.** J
- **17.** A

Page 256
- **A.** C
- **1.** D
- **2.** G

Page 257
- **3.** B
- **4.** J
- **5.** A
- **6.** J

Page 258
- **7.** C
- **8.** J
- **9.** A

Page 259
- **1.** B
- **2.** F
- **3.** D

Page 260
- **4.** G
- **5.** C
- **6.** F
- **7.** B

Grade 3 Answer Key

Page 261
1. B
2. H
3. A
4. B
5. B

Page 262
6. D
7. J
8. B

Page 263
1. C
2. G
3. A
4. H

Page 264
5. B
6. H
7. B
8. H
9. A
10. F
11. D

Page 265
1. B
2. F
3. C
4. F
5. D
6. J

Page 266
7. C
8. G
9. A
10. G

Page 267
A. A

Page 268
1. C
2. F
3. B
4. J

Page 269
5. A
6. H
7. B

Page 270
8. J
9. C
10. F
11. B

Page 271
12. G
13. C

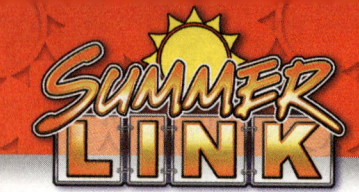

Grade 3 Answer Key

Page 272
14. F
15. A
16. H
17. A
18. H

Page 273
19. B
20. H
21. D
22. B
23. A
24. B
25. A

Page 274
26. H
27. B
28. J
29. B

Page 275
30. J
31. D
32. H
33. A
34. H

Page 276
35. D
36. F
37. C
38. G
39. C
40. A
41. B
42. D
43. G
44. J
45. F
46. H

Page 277
Responses will vary.

Page 278
Responses will vary.

Page 279
A. B
1. A
2. G
3. A
4. G
5. A
6. H
7. D

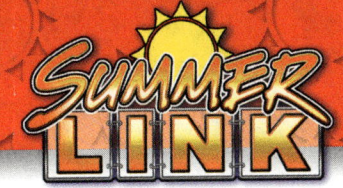

Grade 3 Answer Key

Page 280
- **B.** D
- **8.** B
- **9.** G
- **C.** B
- **10.** C
- **11.** F
- **12.** B
- **13.** G
- **14.** C

Page 281
- **D.** A
- **15.** B
- **16.** J
- **17.** B
- **18.** F
- **19.** C
- **20.** J

Page 282
- **21.** B
- **22.** G
- **23.** C
- **24.** H
- **25.** C
- **26.** J
- **27.** A

Page 283
- **28.** F
- **29.** C
- **30.** G
- **31.** B

Page 284
- **32.** G
- **33.** A
- **34.** G
- **35.** C
- **36.** H
- **37.** D

Page 285
- **38.** G
- **39.** D
- **40.** H
- **41.** A
- **42.** F
- **43.** C
- **44.** F
- **45.** B

Page 286
- **46.** F
- **47.** D
- **48.** H
- **49.** A
- **50.** H
- **51.** C

Grade 3 Answer Key

Page 287
- **52.** G
- **53.** A
- **54.** H
- **55.** C
- **56.** G
- **57.** A
- **58.** J
- **59.** B
- **60.** H

Page 288
- **61.** C
- **62.** J
- **63.** A
- **64.** J
- **65.** C
- **66.** G
- **67.** E
- **68.** J
- **69.** B

Page 289
- **A.** A
- **1.** C
- **2.** J
- **3.** B

Page 290
- **4.** J
- **5.** A
- **6.** F

Page 291
- **7.** A
- **8.** H
- **9.** D

Page 292
- **10.** H
- **11.** A
- **12.** G

Page 293
- **13.** B
- **14.** F
- **15.** B
- **16.** F
- **17.** A
- **18.** H
- **19.** C
- **20.** G

Page 294
- **21.** B
- **22.** H
- **23.** B
- **24.** F
- **25.** D
- **26.** H
- **27.** B

Grade 3 Answer Key

Page 295
28. H
29. B
30. J
31. C
32. H
33. B
34. G
35. A
36. F
37. A

Page 296
38. G
39. C
40. H
41. B
42. G

Page 297
1. B
2. H
3. B
4. F
5. C
6. J

Page 298
7. C
8. J
9. B

Page 299
1. D
2. G
3. A
4. J
5. C
6. G

Page 300
7. B
8. H
9. D
10. F

This page intentionally left blank.

Record Your Scores

After you have completed and checked each test, record your scores below. Do not count your answers for the sample questions or the writing pages.

Practice Test

Unit 1 Reading
Number of Questions: 36   Number Correct _____

Unit 2 Basic Skills
Number of Questions: 57   Number Correct _____

Unit 3 Mathematics
Number of Questions: 26   Number Correct _____

Unit 4 Social Studies
Number of Questions 15   Number Correct _____

Unit 5 Science
Number of Questions: 21   Number Correct _____

Final Test

Unit 1 Reading
Number of Questions: 46   Number Correct _____

Unit 2 Basic Skills
Number of Questions: 69   Number Correct _____

Unit 3 Mathematics
Number of Questions: 42   Number Correct _____

Unit 4 Social Studies
Number of Questions: 9   Number Correct _____

Unit 5 Science
Number of Questions: 10   Number Correct _____

This page intentionally left blank.

Test Practice Worksheet

Test Practice Worksheet

Test Practice Worksheet

Test Practice Worksheet

Test Practice Worksheet

Test Practice Worksheet

Test Practice Worksheet

Test Practice Worksheet